ISABELLA BIRD

and

'A WOMAN'S RIGHT
TO DO WHAT SHE CAN DO WELL'

For Isabella
another time,
another place

ISABELLA BIRD

and

'A WOMAN'S RIGHT
TO DO WHAT SHE CAN DO WELL'

by

Olive Checkland

SCOTTISH CULTURAL PRESS

First published 1996
Scottish Cultural Press
PO Box 106
Aberdeen AB11 7ZE
Tel: 01224 583777 • Fax: 01224 575337

© 1996 Olive Checkland

British Library Cataloguing in Publication Data
A catalogue record for this book is available
from the British Library

ISBN: 1 898218 33 1

Japanese language edition also available:

Nihon Keizai Hyoronsha, Tokyo
ISBN: 4-8188-0796-6

Printed and bound in Great Britain by
Cromwell Press, Melksham, Wiltshire

CONTENTS

LIST OF MAPS

ILLUSTRATIONS

ISABELLA LUCY BIRD BISHOP

A CHRONOLOGY

15 October 1831 – 7 October 1904

1831 15 October, Isabella Lucy Bird (hereafter ILB) born at Boroughbridge Hall, Yorkshire

8 October, Reform Bill defeated, civil unrest in the country

1832 Rev. Edward Bird (hereafter EB) appointed Vicar, Maidenhead, Berkshire

June, Reform Act, extended male franchise

1834 EB called to Tattenhall, Cheshire

1840

Five Chinese coastal ports opened to foreign trade

1842 EB appointed to St. Thomas', Birmingham, where his campaign of Sunday Observance caused great unpopularity

1847 EB suffered ill-health, resigned

1848 EB appointed St. Margaret's, Wyton, Huntingdonshire, in semi-retirement

1849 ILB operation? for fibrous tumour

1850 Summers spent in Scotland (from 1850)

1852? ILB suffering from unrequited love

1854 June, ILB sent on recuperative journey – Canada and Eastern USA, **7 months abroad**

1856 January. *The English Woman in America* published, John Murray

1857 ILB a further 2,000 mile journey alone in USA, **11 months abroad**

1858 3 April, ILB returned to Wyton
14 May, EB died

1859 Summer, *Aspects of Religion in America* published

Treaty ports opened in Japan
Charles Darwin published *The Origin of the Species*

1860	ILB, mother and sister settled Edinburgh ILB contributing articles to *The Leisure Hour*, *The Family Treasury*, *Good Words* and *Sunday at Home*. ILB and HAB involved with charity work in Edinburgh	
1866	ILB to Canada to visit emigrants from Scotland settled there. **2 months absence**.	
1867	14 August, mother died Edinburgh	Reform Act extended male franchise. John Stuart Mill tried to extend franchise to include women
1869	*Notes of Old Edinburgh* published, an indictment of living conditions in the old town	J S Mill published *The Subjection of Women*
1872	Spring, ILB and HAB gave up house at 3 Castle Terrace, Edinburgh, thereafter ILB had no settled home, HAB lived mostly at Tobermory, Mull. ILB in health crisis, 11 July sailed for Australia, miserable there.	Girton College for Women, Cambridge, founded
1873	1 January, breakthrough, ILB left New Zealand, excited by dangerous but exhilerating journey, arrived euphoric in Hawaii, spent six months, left eventually arriving USA in August, to the Rocky Mountains, near love affair with Jim Nugent, lingered on, but finally left in December	
1874	Returned to Edinburgh, **over 18 months abroad** ILB now knowing that travel is her salvation. Summer, in Switzerland. Jim Nugent died (after shoot out) 'appeared' to ILB.	
1875	February, *Six months in the Sandwich Islands* published	
1877	July 'conditionally engaged to be married' to Dr. John Bishop (hereafter JB), Edinburgh December, Medical Mission, Grand Bazaar	
1878	February, left for Japan, Far East and Malaya	
1879	May, returned to Scotland October, *Lady's Life in the Rocky Mountains* published. **15 months abroad**	Somerville College, Oxford, for women founded

1880	June, HAB died, *Unbeaten Tracks in Japan* published. December, engagement to Dr John Bishop announced	
1881	8 March, ILB married JB	
1882	JB ill but apparently recovered, illness recurred	Married Womens' Property Act
1883	April, *The Golden Chersonese* published	
1884	Continental travel in S. Europe, looking for 'pure air' to cure JB	Reform Act extended adult male franchise Queen Margaret College for women established in Glasgow
1886	3 January, Sir Joseph Lister gave JB a blood transfusion 6 March JB died of pernicious anaemia	
1887	ILB began public lecturing, ILB undertook course of nursing in London.	
1889	March, en route for India, Memorial hospitals set up for HAB and JB, travelled in Tibet	
1890	'The awful journey' across Persia, Armenia, Turkey, From Persian Gulf to Black Sea, **2 years abroad**	Scottish universities required to accept women students
1891	18 June, 'the Armenian Question'. Mrs Bishop answered questions for MPs, Committee Room 15, House of Commons. Christmas, *Journeys in Persia and Kurdestan* published.	
1892	2 April, JM III died, JM IV became her publisher. Fellow Royal Geographical Society, London. Fellow Royal Scottish Geographical Society, Edinburgh	
1893		Row in RGS over election of women as Fellows
1894	11 January, left for Far East, via Halifax, Vancouver, Yokohama, Kobe, Korea, Manchuria, Vladivostok	
1895	Korea, China, Japan (to rest over summer) Korea again, China	
1896	January, left Shanghai for journey up Yangtse, returned Shanghai, to Japan for summer, Seoul, Korea until end of year	

1897	31 January, left Shanghai for home, 19 March reached London. **3 years 2 months abroad**	
1898	20 January, *Korea and her Neighbours* published	Hawaii (formerly Sandwich Islands) annexed by USA
1899	November, *The Yangtze Valley and Beyond* published	
1900		Boxer Rebellion in China against foreign influence
1901	1 January to Tangier, camped in Morocco **6 months abroad**	
1903	August, ill, returned to Edinburgh	
1904	7 October died in lodgings, Edinburgh	

LIST OF ABBREVIATIONS

AS	Anna Stoddart, *The Life of Isabella Bird (Mrs Bishop),* 1906
BEM	*Blackwood's Edinburgh Magazine*
CIM	China Inland Mission
CUL	Cambridge University Library
DB	Mrs Dora (Lawson) Bird
DNB	*Dictionary of National Biography*
EB	Rev Edward Bird
Eliza B	Mrs Elizabeth Blackie, wife of Professor John Stuart Blackie
EMMS	Edinburgh Medical Missionary Society
EMJ	*Edinburgh Medical Journal*
FRS	Fellow of the Royal Society
HAB	Henrietta Amelia Bird
ILB	Isabella Lucy Bird, from March 1881, Isabella Lucy Bishop
JB	Dr John Bishop
JM	John Murray Papers, John Murray, Publishers, Albermarle Street, London
JM III	John Murray III, 1808-1892
JM IV	John Murray IV, 1851-1928
JMBRAS	*Journal of the Malayan Branch of the Royal Asiatic Society*
JSB	John Stuart Blackie Papers, National Library of Scotland, Edinburgh
KCB	Knight Commander of the Bath
MP	Member of Parliament
n.d.	no date, on letter quoted
NLS	National Library of Scotland, Edinburgh
PB	Pat Barr, *A Curious Life for a Lady,* 1969
RGS	Royal Geographical Society
SGM	*The Scottish Geographical Magazine*
SRO	Scottish Record Office, Edinburgh
TASJ	*Transactions of the Asiatic Society of Japan*

PREFACE

Isabella Lucy Bird (1831–1904)) was a passionate and intelligent woman, who, by insisting on 'a woman's right to do what she can do well', succeeded in carving out for herself a career as a world-wide traveller and writer. That she, an amateur, became a successful professional was a tribute to her determination to break out of the Victorian strait-jacket that usually immobilised women of her class. Finding her way was not easy and until the age of 40 she was baffled and frustrated as she searched for a meaningful role. Escape came unexpectedly, triggered by a Pacific hurricane in which the ill-founded paddle steamer *Nevada* struggled to keep afloat, then, in imminent danger, Isabella came to life. 'At last I am in love', she exulted, 'and the old sea God has so stolen my heart and penetrated my soul that I seriously feel that hereafter though I must be elsewhere in body I shall be with him in spirit'.

She and others like her were the feminists of their generation who could not tolerate the limited role in society then accorded to women. They escaped with immeasurable relief and joy to locations abroad where they could enter without argument into the masculine world of daring and adventure. Isabella Bird herself suffered from chronic ill-health at home, used this as a reason for going abroad, and only attained bounding good health when committed to one of her long, arduous and perilous journeys.

Between the ages of 23 and 70 Isabella made seven major journeys and was away from home for over nine years. She had started modestly enough as a girl who, recovering from unrequited love, made a journey along known paths in North America. She ended with an absence of three years and two months and a remarkable series of challenging journeys in China and Korea. In between she visited Australia and New Zealand, explored Hawaii (then the Sandwich Islands) had a love affair with Mountain Jim in the Rocky Mountains, broke new ground in Japan, where she lived briefly with the indigenous people, the 'hairy Ainu', and undertook an amazing winter journey full of hardship and danger from India through Persia, Turkestan and Armenia to Turkey.

It was her father, the Rev Edward Bird, who must be given the credit for encouraging independence in his older daughter. It seems clear that Edward Bird, himself not altogether happy in the Church of England, treated Isabella as a son rather than a daughter, encouraging her from earliest days to go her own way. The two North American journeys, made as a young woman during her father's life-time, and at his instigation, taught her to travel light and to travel alone.

In later years on much more taxing journeys part of her success was due to her simple retinue, not for her the paraphernalia and problems of a large expedition, for she needed few servants and minimum equipment. By using local men and transport and so living 'off the land' she herself bent to local habits and customs. It was by any standards a remarkable performance and in marked contrast to the behaviour of some famous contemporary male travellers. Only in Muslim countries was Isabella forced to forfeit her independence, submit to the indignity of covering herself like any Muslim woman and travel camouflaged, as they, in a larger caravanserai organised and controlled by others.

Although she carried basic food supplies with her, she could if necessary bake and cook for herself and survive on unaccustomed local food. Dr Bishop, her husband, noted that 'Isabella has the appetite of a tiger and the digestion of an ostrich.' Nor did she take fright at the legion of fleas and bed bugs which were a necessary adjunct of remote travel. Her ability to emerge unscathed from weeks and months of hardship and hazardous travel (without any of the protection provided by modern medicine) were much admired by her Victorian contemporaries and remain remarkable today.

There are several features which distinguish Miss Bird from other male or female travellers. She always wanted to know more of the habits and customs of those among whom she travelled and her patient and sustained enquiries – 'persistent pumping' she called it – was always gentle and courteous. In the Far East with an attendant as servant interpreter she quickly intervened when she was introduced as a grand lady. Her firmness and friendliness commended her to the women, her self-confidence and her foreignness to their men. When, alone with her horse and minimum supplies, she asked for shelter, she usually received a ready welcome.

One of her strengths while travelling was her insistence on writing her diary at the end of every day. However disastrous the day had been, however, hungry, cold or wet, she was, sleep was denied until the day's events had been recorded. Once home she retrieved her letter diaries from relatives and friends and settled down to transform them into the text of a book. Because it had been written 'in the field', her writing had a zest and immediacy which few could match.

The combination of writing and travelling made for Isabella Bird an enviable life. As a young woman she had determined on a writing career but did not know what she should write about. Under her father's influence and after his death she prepared pieces on various church subjects including hymns and revivalism. But religious writing hardly reflected her own interests; she wanted to undertake daring travel journeys and then recount her adventures in popular books. It was a fortunate circumstance that this adventuring lady should be introduced to John Murray, a well-regarded publisher much involved with travel books.

The popularity of her books, which were a sell-out bringing good profits to both author and publisher, encouraged her to become a lecturer who could attract audiences of hundreds and sometimes thousands. By the end of the century, meetings of the British Association and the Royal Geographical Society were hardly complete without her presence. In 1891 her rare first hand knowledge of Armenia, brought her, at a time of continuing crisis in the Near East, to Committee Room No. 15 in the House of Commons where she enthralled the members, including Mr Gladstone, with her careful and detailed answers to their questions.

Isabella must be classed with other strong-minded female contemporaries whose unbending determination succeeded in moulding the stultifying world of polite society to suit their own predilections. For them, although they would have denied it, female docility and conformity was a cover masking suppressed energy and the urge for a meaningful role. In the switch back life which Isabella coveted and indeed achieved she swept from constraining conventional days at home to rollicking remote travel abroad.

Throughout her career as a traveller she needed to know that she had support at home. After her parents' death her letter diaries were addressed to her sister Henrietta, who lived quietly in Scotland at Tobermory on the Isle of Mull. After Henrietta's death she fulfilled an earlier promise and accepted the long proffered hand of the 40 year old Dr John Bishop; her marriage, at the age of 50, lasted a brief five years, as Dr Bishop faded and died after a long lingering illness. During these married years Isabella, a devoted nurse and companion, travelled with him in Europe seeking health. After 1886 and often alone, close female friends gave her security at home.

Wherever she went she sought out and enjoyed the company of her fellow countrymen from whom, whether merchants, traders, consuls or missionaries, she could learn of local conditions and problems and arm herself with special knowledge of the area through which she would be travelling. Although her own skills as negotiator and her success in managing men – she caused amazement by her genuine concern for their comfort and well-being – as well as her determination, carried her through every potential crisis, she did have behind her, however notional and remote, the might and power of the British Empire. She also recognised that her success depended on British supremacy at the time commenting 'people joined my caravan ... for the sake of the protection implied by the presence of a British subject'. She was also a good emissary for the British, being firm and determined but not aggressive.

She was herself more of an anthropologist than a missionary as her sensitivity to local people and customs made her nervous of the intrusions of the Christian mission. Yet increasingly as she herself got older she felt the power of the evangelical legacy left by her family, and found herself drawn more closely to the Christian cause. Her husband, Dr Bishop's, involvement with

the medical mission field, her father's pre-occupation with Sabbath observance, and her mother and sister's interest in Christian charity, all left their
mark. In her later journeys, rather than avoiding them, she was glad to stay
with missionaries while at home she used her considerable reputation as a
traveller to lecture on missionary affairs.

For all her achievements abroad she remained a chronic invalid and accounts of the years she spent in Britain are a sorry catalogue of constant pain
and suffering. As a sick gentlewoman she evolved a foolproof *modus
operandi* which allowed her to have the travel alternative available when
required. Acting through her attentive medical advisers she so arranged
matters that they, once her health had deteriorated sufficiently, readily
recommended that she seek a 'change of air'. She then rose from her sick
bed, made her preparations and set off, not for the staid delights of Worthing,
Torquay or even Cannes but for far off, distant and exotic places.

The two main sources of her own original letters are those held by John
Murray of Albermarle Street, London, and those contained in the John Stuart
Blackie papers held in the National Library of Scotland, Edinburgh. The gen-
erous support given by Virginia Murray at John Murray's and by Elspeth
Yeo at the National Library of Scotland has made the research a pleasure.
Isabella's letters to her publishers are long and detailed and cover the years
from 1858 to the beginning of the twentieth century. Indeed John Murray III,
twenty-three years her senior, took a close fatherly interest in her which went
far beyond the usual relationship between author and publisher. The letters in
Edinburgh are equally important being to Eliza Blackie, an exceptionally
close friend to whom Isabella wrote frequently and in effusive terms.

A friend of Isabella's from 1859 – and her personal choice as biographer –
Anna Stoddart, wrote an important *Life of Isabella Bird*, published in 1906.
Although consistently admiring it is possible to search out the real Isabella
behind the public face. Pat Barr in *A Curious Life for a Lady* is a perceptive
interpreter of Isabella Bird through her travel writings.

Stanley Alstead and Margaret Lamb have considered in some depth the
problems of Isabella's health while Christopher Smout and Ann-Marie
Smout have made constructive comments on the whole work. I am indebted
to them all for the diligence, care and kindness with which they have pursued
these difficult interpretational problems. It is to another contemporary
Isabella that thanks are due for never failing secretarial help.

Olive Checkland,
Cellardyke, Scotland
& Cambridge, England
1995

PART I

1831–1858
APPRENTICESHIP

Rev Edward Bird, whose own ministry in the church had been dogged by his obsession with Sabbath Observance, encouraged his older daughter, Isabella, to do religious research for him in America, and so incidentally, but importantly, embark on a life of travel.

1 *To the Rev & Mrs Bird, Isabella Lucy, a son*

In 1854, at the age of 22, Isabella Lucy Bird,[1] recovering from an unhappy love affair,[2] was advised by her doctor to take a sea-voyage. Her parents, finding that young cousins were travelling to Canada, agreed that Isabella should be of their party.[3] After spending some time with relatives and friends she was later to journey alone to see something of Canada and the United States. Her father passed to her the substantial sum of £100 and told her she could stay away for as long as it lasted. It was a generous but unusual gesture in an age when women of her class, including her younger sister Henrietta, were usually held closely to the routine of petty social and domestic duties. It proved, for Isabella, a passport to freedom.

What possessed the Birds to release their older daughter in this way? In entrusting Isabella with her own freedom and the means to exploit it, they were actively encouraging her independence. Thus the Rev Mr Bird went against the usual pattern of contemporary paternal behaviour, for other fathers of gifted girls strongly resisted their daughters' pleas. Most of the women of the period whose names were known to the outside world, had made their way in spite of the opposition of their fathers. Edward Bird was different; far from creating obstacles he actively encouraged his elder daughter as a young woman to embark upon an independent life. Having put ambition aside, he was prepared to live out his last years through the eyes of his daughter.

The Rev Edward Bird had had a varied career, being educated at Magdalene College, Cambridge,[4] before serving as a barrister in Calcutta. At the age of 38 he decided to return home and take Holy Orders. His first curacy was in Boroughbridge, North Yorkshire, where he met and married Dora Lawson. Isabella Lucy Bird was born at Boroughbridge Hall on 15 October 1831.[5] A baby boy, who did not survive, was born three years later, then came Henrietta Amelia, known generally as Hennie.

As a young husband, earlier in India, Edward Bird had lost to fever his first wife and, at the age of three, an infant son. It sometimes happens that a daughter becomes a surrogate for a longed for son and is given opportunities normally reserved for a boy. This was the case of Isabella Lucy Bird, who from a tender age became for her father a son and his companion as he made his way around his parish. With the keen perception of childhood she recognised that her father was the source of power, whether in the home, the church, the village or the world outside; accordingly she became from child-hood his acolyte. She resolved to emulate him.

The Rev Mr Bird travelled around on horseback and his daughter, as a small girl, rode before him, but soon graduated to a pony and then to a horse of her own. Later she based her career as a traveller on her remarkable skills as a fearless horsewoman. In October 1873 in the Rocky Mountains, when she was 42, the hard-bitten cowboys could not believe that it was a lady 'leaping over the timber and driving with the others'.[6]

Isabella, in responding to her father's early encouragement, soon devel-oped as a precocious child. The story is told of her pert intervention at the age of six, 'electrifying' her unhappy parents by confronting a visiting pro-spective parliamentary candidate, asking, 'Sir Malpas de Grey Tatton Egerton, did you tell my father my sister was so pretty because you wanted his vote?'[7] Did the candidate's tactless fussing over the younger child make the older girl feel that she herself was unattractive? Did this remain in her mind, and reinforce her own determination to make her mark in the world? When Isabella was seven years old she was found, at lunch-time, in the man-ger of the stables reading Archibald Alison's *History of Europe during the French Revolution*.[8] It comes as no surprise that Lady Grainger Stewart, the widow of Isabella's doctor, who wrote the obituary for *Blackwood's Edinburgh Magazine*, commented, 'that although she had not met anyone who knew Mrs Bishop as a child' she knew that Isabella often played the role of *enfant terrible* flashing out pithy sarcasm and she had been told that 'her Sumner cousins found her rather trying'.[9]

Edward Bird also encouraged his daughter, over the years of her girlhood, to use her mind. Had she noticed this? What did she think of that? As she herself wrote, 'As we rode he made me tell him about the crops in such and such a field – whether a water wheel was under-shot or over-shot, how each gate we passed through was hung, about animals seen and parishioners met'.[10] Summer holidays were 'a driving tour and they were taught geogra-phy and history as they went'.[11] Isabella's success as a traveller and as a writer depended not only on her explorations into little known territory but also upon her unusually lively and vivid descriptions of what she had seen. In this way her father's training helped secure her a future as a writer, which was based on her ability to be an intelligent and acute observer.

Mrs Bird was also an important influence for behind her self-effacing ex-terior there was a determination to give her daughters all the opportunities then available. Well-educated by the standards of the day, she came of good family, (the male members of which were active in academic and parliamen-tary life) taught her daughters herself and was regarded by them as a fine teacher. Isabella noted that 'no one can teach now as my mother taught; it was all so wonderfully interesting that we sat spellbound when she

Mrs Dora Bird: despite her image as a self-effacing wife and mother, she herself educated
to high standards her two daughters – Isabella and Henrietta – at home.

explained things to us. We should never have liked an ordinary teacher'.[12] Had the Bird girls – both academically inclined – been born a generation later would they have been in attendance at one of the Colleges set up at Oxford or Cambridge for the higher education of women?

Although the Rev Mr Bird had been slow to find his calling as rector of a parish, he became an enthusiastic Sabbatarian as he contemplated the iniquities of Sunday labour. He made 'fearless protests' against work being done on the Sabbath; this unyielding stance was to bedevil his ministry. From Maidenhead in Berkshire, to Tattenhall, Cheshire, (where he was presented with the living by his cousin, Dr Bird Sumner, then Bishop of Chester), and on to Birmingham where as rector of St Thomas' he was 'pelted with stones, mud and insults'[13] the Rev Edward Bird moved creating antagonism within the church community and distress for himself and his family. Under these adversities his health failed, he resigned his living and later, a venerable family friend, Lady Olivia Sparrow,[14] in 1848 appointed him to a quiet living in Huntingdonshire.

It was a bitter blow, for Edward Bird was strongly influenced by his second cousin William Wilberforce,[15] the great evangelical hero, who had succeeded in 1807 in making British involvement in the slave trade illegal and who had died just prior to the passing of the Emancipation Bill in 1833 which would free the slaves throughout the British Empire. Did Rev Bird hope for a similar successful campaign to encourage strict Sabbath Observance? As would become clear, whereas the freeing of the slaves was an idea whose time had come, the attempt to resurrect repressive standards of Sunday behaviour was an idea whose time had passed.

The failure of Edward Bird's ministerial career was particularly hard to bear in view of the careers of two of his cousins, his contemporaries – Charles Richard Sumner[16] had been since 1827 Bishop of Winchester, while John Bird Sumner[17] (Charles' older brother), who was made Bishop of Chester by Sir Robert Peel (1828), became Archbishop of Canterbury in 1848, the very year that the Rev Edward Bird went into semi-retirement at Wyton.

It is argued here that Isabella at this time, a perceptive girl in her teens, was deeply affected by her father's trials and that, learning from his unhappy experiences, in his failure were the seeds of her success. Did her deep-rooted reserve about the value of missions and missionaries stem from the traumatic years at St Thomas's in Birmingham?

At Wyton, near St Ives, the rectory was a charming, long, low, picturesque house directly across the lane from the tiny church (now abandoned) of St Margaret's; but the parish consisted of barely three hundred souls and the family had ample time for riding and driving around the pleasant neighbourhood, and for spending halcyon days rowing on the nearby river Ouse. Outdoors, Isabella and Henrietta were involved by their patroness and their father in charitable duties, while indoors Isabella pursued her interests of writing, chemical studies and needlework. The Birds, as a well-connected family with many clerical and aristocratic friends, often paid social visits away from home and Isabella became a close friend of Lady Jane Hay,[18] (later Lady Jane Taylor) a daughter of the Marquis of Tweeddale and a niece of Lady Olivia Sparrow.

Much emphasis was put on Isabella's health, for as a girl she was believed 'not strong'. This is hard to interpret. Clearly any family which believes one child to be 'delicate' can soon affect the attitudes of family and friends. Children are easily persuaded to take care of themselves especially if such acceptance means an escape from unwanted and onerous duties. Isabella Bird was in later years very strong indeed. Her determination and persistence in the face of great hardship, her ability not only to endure, survive but to enjoy gruelling journeys must raise questions about her childhood ill-health. And yet she did suffer a pathological condition of the spine which caused 'spinal prostration' and so, at the age of eighteen, she is reported to have undergone a spinal operation – presumably under anaesthetic – for the removal of a 'fibrous tumour'. These growths were often encapsulated and so, once the incision was made, could be readily removed. Nevertheless such early surgical procedures were fraught with danger and the outcome, without antiseptic surgery which was not available until the 1870s, problematic.[19] At this time it was believed that she was suffering from scoliosis or curvature of the spine but photographs taken during her later years reveal no such deformity. Until 1892, she had her dresses made with a 'Watteau plait' or pleat at the back to disguise her spinal condition.[20]

From 1850 in common with others, including Queen Victoria and Prince Albert, who were then developing their Scottish estate at Balmoral, the Birds moved every summer to holiday in North Britain. Each summer they settled in the Scottish Highlands, in Inverness, or Ross-shire or the island of Skye; or Raasay, Harris or Mull where the Rev Mr Bird found the kind of sabbatarianism of which he approved. The affection for Scotland thus engendered caused the girls and their mother, after their father's death, to make their home there.

The Bird family seems to have been a small harmonious unit. Although both girls were accustomed to the demands of running a household, it was Henrietta and her mother who were primarily responsible for the domestic arrangements, creating a support system for father and older daughter. Isabella, as became the acting son, was intent upon developing her career and, when she was 16, it was a bookseller in the nearby town of Huntingdon who published her first work, 'a pamphlet descriptive of a trial between Free Trade and Protectionism, the latter being the Conqueror'.[21] From now on she was embarked – but not as yet with any firm sense of direction – upon a writing career.

St Margaret's Church, Wyton, Huntingdon, which became Rev Mr Bird's charge after his semi-retirement.

St Margaret's Rectory, Wyton, across the lane from St Margaret's Church, on the banks of the River Ouse, which became the Bird's home until 1858.

Shortly after her return from America to England in 1854 she made a most fortunate contact. While staying in Winchester she met Mr John Milford who had written travel books on Spain and Norway. As Milford wrote to his publisher John Murray,[22] of 50 Albermarle Street, London, 'I have the pleasure of introducing you to Miss Bird. I have but a slight acquaintance with her myself but I met her at the Bishop of Winchester's, with whom she is distantly connected. She has recently returned from a tour of a few months in Canada and other parts of America ... I have according to her request given her a letter to you ... She appears to me to be clever and energetic and I understand has written in several respectable periodicals'.[23]

Isabella and John Murray corresponded. In one letter she wrote,

Dear Mr Murray,

It really is very kind of you to wish to assist me in my literary efforts – a wish sufficiently evidenced by your taking the trouble to write me at such length in the midst of your very numerous avocations.

I still think that I should like to write for one of the magazines. There is a pleasant feeling of irresponsibility in so doing. I almost hesitate to trouble you again yet I should be very glad if at your leisure you would lead me the way of obtaining an introduction to the editor of *Blackwood's* or *Fraser's*. With respect to your suggestion as to the *Quarterly Review* my ambition never soared so high. Within the last year I have been a contributor to the *North American* but it is reasonable to suppose that the Editor of the *Quarterly* would be more particular in his selection also my articles for the former were more exclusively critiques than the one you suggest.

However even if my article be rejected the sacrifice of time would not be so great as I shall attempt an article on the subject you name for the October number. I have now written for nine years with (to me) very satisfactory success and the rejection of one article would not make me inconsolable.[24]

No doubt John Murray III (1808-1892) recognised in the offhand tone of this letter the nervousness and inexperience of the young writer rather than any lack of ambition. Murray became her publisher and a friend who also educated her in the intricacies of the book trade and welcomed her into the circle of his family and friends.

She did however have one initial setback when she wrote persuasively to Murray[25] asking him to publish as a book her nine articles on the state of religion in America. As she had already been paid 'liberally' for these articles (earlier published in *The Patriot* newspaper) she suggested that Murray 'should take the risk and the profit', but he, being more interested in travel books – the first of the famous Murray *Handbooks* had been published in 1836 – declined. It was a fortunate circumstance that her publisher should reinforce her own preference for travel, for had she remained committed to religious writing she would never have made good her escape from conventional life and she would have remained unknown today, part of a world of petty religious affairs long forgotten. When she died *The Times*[26] noted her gift for choosing to travel in places which were of interest to contemporaries, was it due to John Murray or to her own predilections that she moved into travel at all?

Murray did agree to publish *The Englishwoman in America* and subsequently almost all her other books. Miss Bird, as author, was always very business-like and professional, 'Would the book be published in America?' she asked; later Murray queried the 25 presentation copies she had claimed.[27] In reviewing this book *The Globe* in Canada noted that it was introduced to the British public by Mr Murray 'the aristocratical publisher of Albermarle Street'.[28] The care with which she cultivated Mr Murray and ensured that he guided and assisted her to become known in the intellectual and literary world, of which he was a part and to which she aspired, is an object lesson to anyone seeking to promote themselves, however delicately, in literary circles. One cannot but wonder at the tact and persistence of this, as yet unknown, young author.

During the Wyton years Isabella and her father became working partners, an apprenticeship for the daughter and a consolation for the father, as they considered and wrote on religious matters. They worked happily together until 1854 when the Rev Mr Bird found his erstwhile cheerful companion sinking beneath the worry of her broken love affair. One must admire his determination, at whatever cost to himself, to send his elder daughter on her first North American journey.

When she returned home early in 1855, after travelling in Canada and the United States (see map, p.17), she aroused her father's curiosity by speaking of religious revivalism, and he felt that if he were to write about the upsurge of religious feeling in America he would need yet more first hand information. Isabella therefore left for a second tour of North America in 1857 concentrating particularly on the southern states and the new western states.

The working partnership which Edward and Isabella Bird had evolved was of importance to them both. For the father it was a life-line giving him occupation and interest to engage him during his semi-retirement at Wyton, while for the daughter the collaboration with her father was even more significant, granting her the freedom of a non-domestic role. She was to travel and enquire, to note down her findings; he was to stay at home to write and complete the work. To be allocated the active travelling role was balm for her restless spirit.

Isabella was welcomed home from her second overseas adventure on 3 April 1858 on what should have been a joyous family reunion.[29] Sadly Edward Bird fell ill 'of influenza' the day his daughter returned and died on 14 May 1858. He was 66. One must pay tribute to Edward Bird, whose generosity of spirit enabled him to see beyond convention and recognise the unusual characteristics of his elder daughter. He died content believing that he had set her feet along the path that she should go. So ended a beneficent partnership: the surrogate son was on her own.

For her part the death of her father – 'the mainspring and object of her life'[30] as she wrote at the time – came as a great blow. She had lost that parent, her sponsor, who had given her the key to contentment in life through travel. Without his encouragement she found herself trapped in the narrow domestic role then the lot of unmarried daughters, and she was to search for the next fourteen years with increasing desperation for an excuse to break out.

By 1870 as she struggled to free herself from the mental depression which haunted her, she wrote a poem, ostensibly about the loss of childhood faith but also revealing about her inner feelings. Three verses are particularly moving in view of her plight.

> Verse 1   Fevered by long unrest, of conflict weary,
>   Sickened by doubt, writing with inward pain,
>   My spirit cries from out the midnight dreary
>   For the old long-lost days of peace again.
>
> Verse 4   No light! no life! no truth! now from my soul for ever
>   The last dim star withdraws its glimmering ray;
>   Lonely and hopeless, never on me, oh never
>   Shall break the dawn of the long-looked for day.
>
> Verse 5   Rudder and anchor gone, on through the darkness lonely,
>   I drift o'er shoreless seas to deeper night,
>   Drifting still drifting – oh, for one glimmer only,
>   One blessed ray of Truth's unerring light.[31]

The image which emerges is that of a lost soul, drifting lonely and abandoned with no hope for the future, while the use of emotive words like 'fevered' and 'sickened' are redolent of the Victorian invalid. Until 1858 she had had a satisfying role as enquirer and traveller, a partner to her father sharing his various pursuits and interests. After his death she felt that she was forever trapped.

Notes

1. Isabella Lucy Bird is here referred to variously as Isabella, Miss Bird or Mrs Bishop. Although she became Mrs Bishop in 1881, and published under that name, her books, subsequently, also carried the name (Isabella L. Bird).
2. 'for I have never alas been in love but once'. JSB, ILB to Eliza B., 23 November 1879, Ms 2633, f.143, AS, p.28.
3. AS, p.28 and PB, Chapter 5, pp.163-180.
4. AS, p.6.

5. AS, p.8.
6. *A Lady's Life in the Rocky Mountains* (reprint 1960), p.129.
7. AS, p.12, A. Grainger Stewart, Obituary, *BEM*, November 1904, p.699.
8. AS, p.13, Alison's book was published in Edinburgh in 1833.
9. Agnes Grainger Stewart, Obituary, *BEM*, November, 1904, p.699.
10. AS, p.10
11. A. Grainger Stewart, Obituary, *BEM*, November 1904, p.699.
12. AS, p.12.
13. AS, p.21.
14. Lady Olivia Sparrow, daughter of the 1st Earl of Gosford, married 1797, Brigadier General Bernard Sparrow, *Peerage, Baronetage and Knightage of Great Britain and Ireland*, (1858), p.684.
15. William Wilberforce (1759-1833) reformer and philanthropist, who entered Parliament, was a friend of William Pitt, campaigned for abolition of Slave Trade (1807) and of Slavery in British possessions (1833).
16. Charles Richard Sumner (1790-1874), *Concise DNB to 1900*, p.1265.
17. John Bird Sumner, (1780-1862), *Concise DNB to 1900*, pp.1265-1266.
18. Lady Jane Hay, daughter 8th Marquis of Tweeddale, born 1830, married 1863, Col. Richard Taylor, *Peerage, Baronetage and Knightage of Great Britain and Ireland*, 1876, p.820.
19. Cases of this operation were being undertaken, see J. Syme, 'Fatty tumour of an unusual form; removal, recovery', *Edinburgh, Medical and Surgical Journal*, (1838), Vol.1, p.385. Nevertheless doubts remain. Was the operation done at home? with chloroform? which had just been introduced in 1846, amid much controversy. Or was it possible that ILB was a sufferer from acute anterior poliomyelitis which caused inflammation of the motor nerve cells of the spine? See Chapter 15, Note 4.
20. JSB, ILB to Eliza B., Tobermory, 27 December 1891, Ms 2638, f.294.
21. AS, p.21-22, *The Times*, Obituary, 10 October 1904.
22. John Murray, publishers of 50 Albermarle Street, London, originally had made fame and fortune by publishing Byron's works. John Murray III (1808-1892) became Isabella's publisher and mentor. He suggested that ILB might write one of the famous Murray *Handbooks* on Scotland (JM, ILB to JM, Wyton Rectory, January 1857) but this idea came to nought.
23. JM, John Milford to JM, 26 June 1955.
24. JM, ILB to JM, Wyton Rectory? 1856?
25. JM, ILB to JM, 14 February 1859.
26. *The Times*, Obituary, 10 October 1904.
27. JM, ILB to JM, 16 November 1956.
28. JM, ILB to JM, n.d. but January or February 1856.
29. AS, p.45.
30. AS, p.44, PB, p.173.
31. AS, pp.74-75.

2   *North American Journeys – a precedent is set*

The first time Isabella needed to get away was in 1854. Did her father recognise in this twenty-two year old any parallel with the aspirations of his own youth? Whatever he felt he organised, financed and approved her first solo adventure abroad.

On a Saturday morning in June 1854, Isabella Bird sailed from Liverpool bound for Halifax, Nova Scotia, in the 1850 ton Royal Mail paddle wheeler *Canada*, owned by Cunard whose steamers she regarded as 'powerful, punctual and safe'.[1] As they steamed down the Mersey they passed the troop-ship *Himalaya* and she noted the Scots Greys embarking for the Crimea.[2] Isabella was not pleased to be sharing a cabin with an Englishwoman[3] who, frequently intoxicated, was endlessly voluble. Isabella proved to be a good sailor, enjoyed her meals and observed her fellow travellers of many nationalities.

At the time of her first visit, Canada consisted of two sections, Upper Canada around Toronto, and Lower Canada centred on Montreal and Quebec. She found Lord Elgin,[4] the retiring Governor General, to whom she had an introduction, on the point of departure for home. Elgin had been in Canada since 1848 and in 1849, determined to force a modicum of democracy onto the reluctant Anglo-Scots ruling clique, had provoked, by his even-handed treatment of the French Canadians, riots in Montreal during which the Canadian Parliament building had been burnt down. As a result Montreal lost its capital status which then alternated between Toronto in the West, and Quebec in the east. In 1858 Queen Victoria was to choose Ottawa as Canada's capital, nearly equidistant between the then rival settlements of Upper and Lower Canada. Canada was at this time flourishing following the Reciprocity Treaty which Lord Elgin had succeeded in making with the United States, although there had been difficult times earlier as thousands of sick, starved, Irish had arrived following the famine.

In her first travel book *An Englishwoman in America*, written from the diaries she kept during this journey, her comments were frank and forthright. As a young woman of twenty-two she wrote for her friends and compatriots at home, frankly noting shortcomings as she saw them, and she was not overly sensitive about the reaction of Canadian or American readers. As she grew older her writing softened, partly because she concentrated more on the positive things she saw and partly because she always told good stories, relishing those which were against herself. Her comments on Halifax, her first landfall in Canada, were harsh for the streets were 'Dirty ... though the weather was very dry, for oystershells, fish-heads and bones, potato-skins and cabbage stalks littered the road; but *dirty* was a word which does not give the faintest description of the almost impassable state in which I found them when I waded through them ankle-deep in mud some months later'.[5] She was equally biting about Nova Scotians generally who 'appeared to have expunged the word progress from their dictionaries'.

The Bird cousins travelled by coach up country via Truro and Pictou county towards Prince Edward Island where she was to stay, as a guest of her second cousin, Captain Swabey in Charlottetown, Prince Edward Island. The vehicle which consisted of a large coach body 'slung upon two leather straps, sides open, screened by heavy curtains of tarnished moose deer hide',[6] was not comfortable but did complete 120 miles in twenty hours. Six horses drew the coach which carried twelve persons on four cross-seats over shocking roads made of planks, corduroy or sand. The corduroy roads, which consisted of tree trunks in parallel formation often across swampy ground, gave a bumpy ride and were a particular strain.[7]

Isabella was especially interested in two groups of people, the Indians and the Scots, the latter re-settled in Canada, especially in Pictou County. She was delighted at one place to speak in Gaelic (a little of which she had learned while on holiday in Scotland) to someone from Snizort on the Isle of Skye.[8] For the local Indian tribe, the Mic-Mac people, she had much sympathy, calling them a fierce and war-like people who had 'melted away before the poisonous firewater'.[9]

She and her cousins were welcomed by Captain Swabey, and the six weeks with them in an 'old English-looking red brick mansion'[10] passed quickly. She was pleased with what she saw and enjoyed the relative freedom of local expeditions with a Mr and Miss Kenjins. She called it 'roughing in the bush' and wrote that they 'sang and roared and fished and laughed and made others laugh and were perfectly happy never knowing and scarcely caring where we could obtain shelter for the night'.[11] To her amazement her clothes were admired too: 'I was requested to take off my cloak to display the pattern of my dress and the performance of a very inefficient country *modiste* passed off as the latest Parisian fashion'.[12]

One of her most interesting conversations concerned the slow development of railways in Canada. As one Canadian complained, 'Well the fact is old father Jackey Bull ought to help us, or let us go off on our own hook right entirely' to which she riposted 'You have responsible government and ... you are on "your own hook' in all but name'.[13] There could be various interpretations of Canada's 'independence' *vis à vis* Britain at this time. At the end of her stay in Prince Edward Island she left her cousins and moved south alone; and was impressed by her first glimpse of the United States writing, 'Fair was the country we passed through; in the States of Maine, New Hampshire and Massachusetts. Oh! very fair, smiling cultivated and green, like England, but far happier; for slavery which disgraces the New World and poverty which desolates the Old are nowhere to be seen'.

She stayed in the American House at Boston[14] which she found 'luxurious and handsome' but she was dismayed at having to remove her antiquated goose-quill and rusty looking ink-stand from the Ladies Parlour where writing was not allowed. She booked to leave Boston on the Lightning Express which promised to take her '1,000 miles in 40 hours'[15] via Rochester, Buffalo, Erie and Cleveland and five different railway lines to Cincinnati 'the Queen City of the West'.[16] As a young lady travelling alone she was indebted to various gentlemen who with 'hearty unostentatious good nature' helped her across the tracks to link up the separately constructed sections of the railway. She was relieved to arrive at Clifton, Cincinnati, the home of Dr McIlvaine, the Bishop of Ohio, where she was able to remove the accumulation of 'soot, dust and cinders' from her person and her clothes.

Cincinnati, 'a second Glasgow in appearance'[17] startled her with its contrasts. At one and the same time the city boasted fine public libraries and reading rooms and yet could be called 'Porkopolis' for swine, 'lean, gaunt and vicious looking, riot through her streets'. She understood the good sense of the *pig system* fattening the animals, not only after the harvest on the cornfields, but also on the beech-mast and acorns of their gigantic forests; nevertheless, the presence of hogs in the streets was unnerving.[18]

While resident in Cincinnati she was eager to cross over into Kentucky at Covington to see a slave state for herself, commenting that despite 'the same soil, same climate, same natural advantages' the absence of progress and decay, loungers in the streets as well as the peculiar appearance of the slaves showed her that she was in a slave state. In the course of her enquiries she was informed that property valued at £300 in Kentucky would be worth £3,000 in Ohio.[19] Anti-slavery was to be one of her themes when in 1859 she published *The Aspects of Religion in the United States of America*.

As Cincinnati was to be the extent of her 'western' travel, on this occasion she said farewell to this land of 'adventure and romance' and entered 'the car' for Chicago. It was on this leg of the journey that she was 'robbed' by a new passenger with a low forehead and 'deep set and restless eyes significant of cunning' who sat himself beside her. With great presence of mind she removed her purse, leaving only her baggage checks in her pocket. These were taken by the thief but when the checks were required by the conductor she turned to her neighbour and said 'this gentleman has the checks for my baggage'. The thief produced them and no more was said. Whether this story improved with the telling, her friends in America were impressed, as one of them remarked, 'you English ladies must be cute customers if you can outwit Yankee pickpockets'.[20]

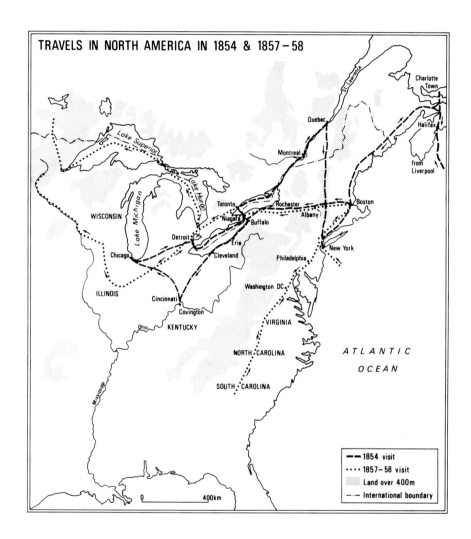

TRAVELS IN NORTH AMERICA IN 1854 & 1857-58

Legend:
- — — 1854 visit
- ····· 1857–58 visit
- Land over 400m
- —·—· International boundary

Chicago was, she felt, a wonderful place, for whereas there had been no railways in 1850 by 1854 there were fourteen lines radiating from it. It illustrated for her 'the astonishing energy and progress of the Americans'[21] better than anything she had seen elsewhere. From Chicago she booked a ticket, which only cost $8.50 for a journey of 700 miles, by rail and steamer for Detroit.[22] She noted the method of running the railway along the edge of the lake supported only on wooden piles and remarked, 'these insecure railways are not uncommon in the States'.

The journey onward from Detroit was eventful, as the steamship *Mayflower* battled with the 'raging furious billows of Lake Erie', while fellow passengers in the ladies' quarters were distraught, Isabella sought to calm them saying there is 'no danger, the engines work regularly, the ship obeys her helm'.[23] In the course of this storm she who had, 'never taken a baby in my arms before and so I held it in an awkward manner', nursed a baby for its sick and distracted mother. She also noted the good behaviour of the baby reporting 'poor little black thing, it lay very passively turning its monkey face up to mine'.[24]

At the Niagara Falls 'dressed in a suit of oiled calico' and looking like a 'tatterdemalion'[25] she gained a certificate saying she had travelled '230 feet behind the Great Horseshoe Fall' although one of her fellow-travellers complained that this was 'an almighty, all-fired flim flam'. No doubt remembering the riots in Montreal earlier she regarded Toronto as 'the stronghold of Canadian learning and loyalty'. She nearly drowned in Lake Ontario on a voyage to Hamilton, being thrown into the water as the steamer toppled over. By great good fortune a great wave washed her back into the state room and seconds later the ship righted itself. It was as she reported, 'the first and only time during my American travels I was really petrified with fear'.

She found much pleasure, while staying with some friends in the 'backwoods' of Ontario, in the long rides through the woods as well as in wonderful gallops along the shores of Lake Ontario. On Sundays at the local church she became conscious of the strong Scottish connection as one old Scotchwoman asked 'Are ye frae the braes o' Gleneffer? Were ye at oor kirk o' Sabbath last, ye wadna' ken the differ.'[26]

She left Toronto on the *Arabian* and steamed on to the Thousand Islands where the rapids required a land trip around the falls before re-embarking on the *New Era*. After cruising among the islands they anchored at La Chine and then shot the rapids before arriving at Montreal. The Bishop of Montreal welcomed her but Montreal was, she noted, 'a very turbulent place'. This comment no doubt related to the serious riots of May 1849 during which there had been much damage and the life of the Governor General threatened. Lord Elgin, the retiring Governor General, was at his headquarters at Spencer Wood outside Quebec. At this stage she succumbed to fever although, despite the fact that cholera had been in the area, Lord Elgin reported that she had had an attack of ague.

Her other introduction was to the Honourable Mr Ross, then President of the Legislative Council. The Rosses not only took her in and cared for her but also answered her questions, furnishing her with information 'in most favourable circumstances'. She visited New York and Boston before departing from Halifax in the *America*.

She arrived home after seven months absence, bearing £10 of her original £100, 'better in health and full of animation'. As a girl of 23, despite the support which she had received from friends in North America, she had established her independence and taken responsibility for herself travelling alone for hundreds of miles. This first journey, although accomplished by public transport along known ways, was an achievement which was to give her valuable experience.

On 1 October 1855 Isabella submitted her work on her travels in North America under the title of *The Car and the Steamboat* to John Murray. Murray liked the text but not the title. He accepted the book on condition that it be called *The English Woman in America*. It was published in January 1856; an immediate success. The journey followed by a period of writing – to transform her letters and diaries into a book – was to be her programme over many years. It was a neat device, to write *en route* long entertaining travel letters conveying immediacy – including her miseries as well as her triumphs – post them off to family and friends and then once returned to base to retrieve them and work on them at leisure.

Perhaps her parents hoped that restored to her family and friends and with a successful book behind her she might now settle down. But this was not to be as 'her health declined with the spring of 1857' and her doctor obligingly recommended further travel.

The Rev Mr Bird had been much interested in all that Isabella had told him regarding life in America although she had not always been able to answer all his questions about religious experience in America. As he himself planned to write about this, they resolved that she would return to America and Canada and gather material on religious observance, Sabbatarianism and Revivalism, as well as slavery, in an American context.

This second journey to North America saw Isabella travelling as her father's collaborator and it was he who wrote in 1857 to John Murray outlining her travel route explaining that 'She landed at New York and travelled as far south as Savannah thence to New York and East to Boston – making a visit to Cambridge and to Southampton, Massachusetts, thence to Albany and into Canada. From London, Ontario via Chicago, La Prairie du Chien [sic] to St Paul, Minnesota to Detroit, thence up the Great Lakes to Superior City and return to Saulte St Marie ... I hope on her way to Lake Huron and Michigan. I do not expect her return until end February'.[27]

In fact the six months planned away extended almost to a year as she followed up various invitations and introductions. On her return she explained to John Murray where she had actually been, writing, 'I remained a fortnight in New York, which I had visited before – from which point my route was new – and three weeks in Philadelphia; two months in the slave states, Virginia, South Carolina, and Georgia; a fortnight in Washington during the session of Congress; a month in the neighbourhood of Boston; a week at Longfellow's; two months in a beautiful village in Western Massachusetts; two weeks in Albany; a week in Niagara; two weeks in Toronto; one month in the bush; two weeks at Detroit; six weeks in making a tour in the far, far west – over the prairies of Illinois and Wisconsin, forty miles beyond railroads, up the Upper Mississippi, into the Minnesota country, to the Falls of Minnehaha, up Lake Huron and to the extreme end of Lake Superior, and into the Hudson's Bay Territory among the Wild Indians – a journey altogether of 2,000 miles, during which I did not remain stationary for four weeks, as it was considered that frequent change was the most likely to benefit my health.'[28]

Anna Stoddart remembered one or two anecdotes, retold by Isabella herself, during the week at Longfellow's enjoying the company of 'a memorable evening around the great fireplace of the "Wayside Inn" with Longfellow, Dana, Lowell, Emerson and other members of the fraternity'.[29] There is also an account of the tall Red Indian who leapt into the water and saved her life when, waiting for a boat on Lake Huron, she was hustled and fell into the water between pier and steamer.[30]

Her main concern was with the religious life of the Americans and she is reported to have listened to some 130 sermons in all areas and of all denominations. One service, held in the African Baptist Church, Richmond, Virginia, was particularly notable for there 'an aged negro, called upon to pray, did so in such a manner, reverent, apt and eloquent, with such perfect diction and accent and with such a fulness of thoughtfull petition, that she burst into tears....'[31]

Later the task of converting her own notes into text reverted to her. Towards the end of 1858 Isabella produced nine papers on 'Aspects of Religion in the United States'. These, published in *The Patriot*, were well received and so were (in 1859) issued in bound form by Samson Low in London. The book, clearly and attractively written, was useful in informing church people in Britain of religious matters in the USA.

Despite the fact that John Murray had declined to publish *Aspects of Religion*, he and Isabella, both with strong views on the United States, continued to correspond at some length. Miss Bird felt she could speak with some authority, writing:

I am inclined to think that you take rather a disastrous view of both the present and the future of the US. I have seen a great deal of American politicians, both at Washington and elsewhere from the President down to the western stump orator and by preserving a non-committal form of discretion have heard a great deal more than perhaps an Englishman would hear. I have no hesitation in saying that taken altogether with astonishingly few exceptions they are a set of office seeking, unprincipled rogues. They have no studied views, no definite aims or purpose – the aggrandisement of self is thus one object for which they are ready to trail any higher principles which at any time they have felt or professed – through the mire.[32]

In her book *Aspects of Religion* she wrote of the size of the country: 'America cannot in any sense be viewed as a whole ... more tongues are spoken within her borders than Rome ever compelled to subjection. More races are congregated under her fiat than ever met under the same equal government'.[33] She reserved her strongest words for slavery in the Southern States explaining 'In English minds the "South" is less associated with its varied beauties, its forests of almost tropical vegetation, the fragrance of its orange groves, and the rich scent of its blossoming magnolias, its many tinted flowers and scarlet-winged flamingoes and all the rich productions of its sunny climate than with the one great curse of slavery with which all things are interwoven. It is the existence of this blot on Christianity ...'[34]

Isabella did not return to the family home until 3 April 1858. The collaboration so eagerly anticipated by both father and daughter on the subject of religious life in America was never to take place, for Edward Bird was taken ill the very evening Isabella returned. He preached his last sermon on 18 April and died in mid-May 1858.

It was a sad parting – just when father and daughter felt that they had achieved a fruitful accommodation each with the other. The memories of the pleasures of adventurous travel, and of her father's support for them, were to remain in her mind – although in the summer of 1858 the first priority for this older daughter, and acting son, was to take over the family and draw up plans to leave Wyton, the parsonage of which could no longer remain their home.

Notes

1. *Englishwoman in America* (hereafter *America*), p.14, (this copy CUL, Class mark, 8660, d.132).
2. *America*, p.7.
3. *America*, p.10.
4. S. Checkland, *The Elgins, A Tale of Aristocrats, proconsuls and their wives*, (1988), Chapter 12, Encounter with Canada, pp.118-138.
5. *America*, p.16.
6. *America*, p.23.
7. *America*, p.26.

8. *America*, p.57.
9. *America*, p.20.
10. *America*, p.35.
11. *America*, p.51.
12. *America*, p.66.
13. *America*, p.80.
14. *America*, p.99.
15. *America*, p.106.
16. *America*, p.99.
17. *America*, p.117.
18. *America*, pp.124-5.
19. *America*, pp.126-132.
20. *America*, p.147.
21. *America*, p.154.
22. *America*, p.156.
23. *America*, p.173.
24. *America*, p.175.
25. *America*, p.231.
26. *America*, p.212.
27. JM, EB to JM, Wyton Rectory, October 1857.
28. JM, ILB to JM, Wyton Rectory, 26 June 1858.
29. AS, p.43, Henry Wadsworth Longfellow (1807-1882) poet, 'Dana', probably Richard Henry (1787-1879), poet and critic, James Russell Lowell (1819-1891), poet, essayist and diplomat, and Ralph Waldo Emerson (1803-1882), lecturer, essayist and poet. These famous American literary figures were much involved with the *North American Review* and other critical literary journals. It was a remarkable privilege for Miss Bird, at the age of 26, to have the opportunity to be in the company of these men.
30. AS, p.44.
31. AS, p.45.
32. JM, ILB to JM, n.d.
33. ILB, *Aspects of Religion in the United States of America*, (hereafter *Aspects of Religion)*, p.5.
34. ILB, *Aspects of Religion*, p.93.

PART II

1858–1881
ACHIEVEMENT

Henrietta Bird's Cottage at Tobermory, Isle of Mull, to which she retreated after her mother's death, and where she died in 1880.

Henrietta Amelia Bird had studied Greek, but was perhaps overwhelmed by Isabella, her older sister. She died in her mid-forties.

3   *Mrs Bird's daughter and Henrietta's sister*

The Bird ladies could not remain at Wyton rectory after the death of the Rev Mr Bird. What were they to do? Where were they to go? They were in residence and apparently settled at Hurst Cottage, Hadley Common near Barnet, Middlesex, in May 1860[1] but as the summer advanced it became clear to them all that they would prefer a Scottish base. As a country woman, brought up in Yorkshire mid-way between Edinburgh and London, Mrs Bird was content to move north. Edinburgh was at the centre of Scottish life – for Scots Law, the Church of Scotland and the Free Church of Scotland as well as the University were based there.[2] Would Edinburgh's bracing climate be good for Isabella's health? Less happily Robert Louis Stevenson – growing up in Edinburgh at this time – expressed sentiments which Isabella was later to echo, concerning the stultifying atmosphere in many middle class homes in the Scottish capital.

On arrival they established themselves in a flat at 3 Castle Terrace, where they were neighbours of Dr Hanna, of the Free Church of Scotland – and Dr Thomas Chalmers' son-in-law. Other Church leaders, mostly from the Free Church, including Dr Guthrie, Dr John Brown and the Rev George D Cullen[3] welcomed them. Some families had unmarried daughters, of the same generation as the Bird girls, who became dear friends. They also became part of the academic and medical circle which included Professor John Stuart Blackie[4] the idiosyncratic professor of Greek of the University of Edinburgh. Perhaps because the Blackies had no children, and 'the Pro' was away a lot, Mrs Eliza Blackie became a close friend of Isabella's. The first letter, which survives, was to 'Dearest Mrs Blackie' but soon it was, in effusive style 'My Dearest one'.[5]

The usual outlet for the energies of all these unmarried women of the middle classes – whether in the village of Wyton or in the city of Edinburgh – was charitable work.[6] Because social problems were acute and ameliorative measures rare, the Bird girls were soon drawn by their friends into philanthropic endeavour working in the Highlands and Islands as well as in Edinburgh itself.

The nineteenth century was a sad and troubled period for the remote north west of Scotland, where people lived on uneasily in a pre-industrial mode which had long vanished elsewhere. With the temptation of other potentially profitable land uses, land-owners sought to rid themselves of unwanted tenants. Although at the bitter end those remaining were to be protected, during most of the century efforts were being made to divest the poor land of its poor people.

Isabella with her knowledge of the Highlands and of Canada, determined to launch an emigration scheme for those Hebrideans who felt that the only course open to them was to leave. As a young woman in the early 1850s, on her first journey overseas, she had enjoyed practicing her Gaelic on the *emigrés*, the Highland Scots both in Pictou county and again in Western Ontario. By marshalling her influential friends on both sides of the Atlantic she succeeded in arranging, between 1862 and 1866, for a handful of Hebridean people to emigrate. Isabella was also keen to find alternative forms of employment at home for Highland people and she is credited with being involved with the early manufacture and marketing of Harris tweed.[7]

There was nothing careless or slap-dash about her arrangements, with help from her friends plans were made for the journeys and the safe reception and settlement of the peoples. She spent much time in Glasgow arranging passages and negotiating with ship-owners; while Edinburgh ladies organised sewing bees and made up gowns, coats, kilts, as well as under clothes so that all the emigrants could receive new garments for their journey. Other necessaries such as brushes, combs, shawls, bags and hold-alls were provided. Much has been written about the sufferings of those who, having bravely taken the decision to leave, were exploited at every turn by those eager to squeeze a profit from their going. This can hardly have happened to those under Isabella's wing, as she explained, 'I went down to Greenock on July 2 with the Skye emigrants and remained with them on board the *St Andrew* until the evening of July 4 when they sailed all in excellent spirits. They were delighted with your hoods, the scarlet braid attracted them and they acted like savages dancing and screaming with pleasure'.[8] Early in 1866 she visited them in Canada to make sure they were well-settled.

This emigration scheme appears to have been a private initiative; no trace has been found of any organisation to which she was attached. In her obituary article in *Blackwood's Magazine* Agnes Grainger Stewart remarks that, 'There is a letter from Miss Catherine Sinclair in which she thanks Miss Bird for so much trouble taken for two *protegés* of hers. I enclose what will perhaps be sufficient to embark the two emigrants, but if more be absolutely necessary I must not, to use a vulgar phrase, choke upon the tail'.[9]

In 1861 Isabella had written an article for the *Leisure Hour* on Dr Thomas Guthrie's initiative in organising Ragged Schools in Edinburgh. These schools received boys, often from the police, who had previously been living rough, and subjected them to a rigorous residential programme of education and training. Some boys reformed: others did not. This drew her attention to the shocking conditions of life in the Old Town of Edinburgh and so she set off to examine the 'misery and moral degradation' to be found 'under the shadow of St Giles' crown and within sight of Knox's house'; that is along the wynds and closes off and adjacent to the High Street of Edinburgh. The results of her survey – an unusual task for a woman to undertake – were published as *Notes on Old Edinburgh* in Edinburgh in 1869.[10]

She notes that the Edinburgh slums, although they were in her view the worst, were not the first such that she had visited as she had already seen 'the worst slums of the Thames district of London, of Birmingham, and other English and foreign cities, the "water-side" of Quebec, and the Five Points and mud huts of New York'. Her explorations in Edinburgh, covering closes in the High Street, Cowgate and the West Port convinced her that this was indeed a *Via Dolorosa*. There were as she explained, 'dirty little children as usual rolling in the gutter or sitting stolidly on the kerb-stone; as usual haggard, wrinkled vicious faces were looking out of the dusty windows above and an air of joylessness, weariness and struggle hung over all'.[11]

Miss Bird also invokes God but in a way rather different from the usual exhortations delivered to the poor by male contemporaries. Her admonitions are to the better off, 'those who sit at ease at communion-tables, content to leave those to the outer darkness for whom that same body and blood were broken and shed'. She agreed that the masses had 'lapsed' and 'gone under' but she condemned 'a condition of things which is a disgrace to Scottish Christianity'. Although much along the lines of what Dr Guthrie was saying, it was an extraordinary tirade to come from a female observer.

Throughout her exposition she juxtaposed living conditions of the comfortably off with those poor she visited in the Old Town. The tenements, entered by one long dark stone stair provided neither gas, water-pipes, water-closet, sink or temporary receptacle for fire ashes. There could be as many as 240-290 persons living within one house and someone was making a profit of from 45 per cent to 60 per cent from these miserable rooms. She quotes from a *Report on the Condition of the Poorer Classes in Edinburgh*[12] instancing windowless houses, cellars and 'shelters' all accommodating people herded together with less space than would be allocated to animals. She claimed that some 66,000 persons, more than one third of the population, lived in these dens.

Part of her argument was that no-one could maintain standards of decency in the circumstances in which these families found themselves in Edinburgh. One woman told her that her husband took the 'wee drap'. 'So,' cried Isabella, 'would the President of the Temperance League himself if he were hidden away in such a hole'.[13] She also quoted Dr Guthrie, who of his Ragged School Boys, wrote, 'I believe if I was as poor as they I should be as deceitful ... There is not a wretched child in this town but if my children had been born and bred up in its unhappy circumstances they might have been as bad'.[14]

In some senses this is a feminist pamphlet, as the impossible burdens facing working women living in such conditions are stressed. A prime complaint was that of the non availability of water and she noted that from 6 a.m. to midnight a crowd of women and children jostled at the single tap – the only water available for hundreds of people. As the bedraggled crowd waited from one to five hours for the water 'to wash the faces, cook the food and quench the thirst of the family for the day' ... 'It is impossible', she thundered, 'for these people to be clean in their dwellings, clothes or persons under present circumstances'.

Nor did she draw the veil over the immorality which flourished in these dens. One respectable working man reminded her of problems other than those of water which assailed those attempting to bring up children decently in these circumstances. Looking out of his window they saw, 'not a pistol shot off, three debased women sitting in the broad daylight, absolutely nude as far as we could see'.[15] On another occasion they found a young girl 'very poorly dressed' and two others, 'very much undressed' – part of a group of five (with only two gowns between them) who lived with an old woman. This house of ill-repute was clearly noisy and unpleasant to live near but this writer was no social reformer and she did not go on to examine a system whereby women were always paid low wages.

Isabella Bird's *Notes on Old Edinburgh* is a powerful indictment of conditions in the Old Town in the 1860s. As an ameliorative measure she argued strongly for the renovation and upgrading of houses in and around the High Street. She knew it was considered a poor investment to re-model houses in this way, but she claimed investors could expect a return of from 8 to 10 per cent[16] and, as she pointed out, the risks involved in improving houses for the poor were no greater than those cheerfully undertaken year after year by those investing in railroads, mines and cotton whether at home or overseas. Nothing came of these ideas.

Those who read *Notes on Old Edinburgh* by the author of *The Englishwoman in America* must have found it a hard-hitting pamphlet. It was prefaced by remarks by one of their neighbours, Rev Dr Hanna, one of the Free Church luminaries, who commended the *Notes* to readers and explained that it had been written and published to aid the cause of the newly organised Association for Improving the Condition of the Poor. No doubt doctors involved in public health, including Dr Littlejohn and Dr Alexander Wood, would applaud her efforts, although *Notes on Old Edinburgh* was dismissed by one commentator as 'a wicked book'.[17]

Following her *Notes on Old Edinburgh* Isabella was drawn into charitable work in the city. Edinburgh was still served by inadequate private local water companies – unlike Glasgow which had tapped the water from Loch Katrine in 1858 – so she tried to raise money to provide more stand-pipes for water, believing that if a regular water supply were available, money could be raised to provide wash-houses.

Isabella's outlook was similar to that of many others, as she wrote, 'The other plan ... is to open a wash-house with the necessary appliances for taking in washing for the poor at sixpence a dozen. This furnishes a labour test also, as no women who are not industrious as well as poor *will* wash such clothes at 1s. and 3s. [15p] a day ... Does your aunt know of ladies of devotion and administrative ability, who would learn to organise and work such odious details'? 'If I can get £100 I shall lose no time in trying to start a wash-house in the Grass market'.[18] Little came of any of these plans. Although as she wrote 'several taps or spigots have been placed in closes' no one came forward to organise the wash-houses and the tenements remained dirty and unredeemed. Was Isabella's commitment half-hearted? She did not herself offer her services.

In addition at this time Isabella was also using her wide contacts in the remoter areas of Scotland to inspect Highland schools which she found, perhaps to her surprise, 'efficient'.[19] Her next enthusiasm was for a 'Cabman's Shelter and Refreshment Room', a popular small charity in many parts of the country at this time, to be erected in central Edinburgh. Elegant ladies using cabs for their many journeys were distressed at the long hours and awful weather which cabmen had to endure in order to make a living. Edinburgh Town Council eventually provided a site near the Scott Memorial in Princes Street and, after further argument, an attendant 'to clean, cook meals and keep it in order'.[20] To her satisfaction the shelter promised to be self-supporting. These worthy but petti-fogging concerns were unlikely to absorb all the energy of this particular lady.

Dora Bird died in Edinburgh in August 1866, when her daughters were aged 34 and 29 years; as an exemplary wife and mother she had submerged her interests in those of her husband and daughters. Plots were bought in Dean Cemetery, Edinburgh, for the whole family; and there Mrs Bird was buried and Mr Bird's remains were brought from Houghton to lie by her side.

The two girls were 'sole executrices' of Mrs Bird's Will;[21] her personal estate, amounting in cash terms to the substantial sum of over £3,346, was to be divided equally between her 'two dear daughters'. Mrs Bird had held Debenture Bonds, totalling £1,500, (issued by the Governments of Canada and that of Nova Scotia); two 500 dollar bonds on the United States Illinois Central Railway Company, as well as other sums held in bank accounts.

This modest inheritance was sufficient to give each girl a sufficient competence to live independently if she wished. With their mother's passing the girls went their separate ways and within a few years the Castle Terrace house was given up.

During her mother's life Isabella had retained her responsibilities, bequeathed to her by her father, as head of the household. She took her duties seriously, writing in 1863, 'We are proposing to return to Edinburgh on 29th and I precede the others on the 26th to get a few of *the worries over* before Mama arrives'.[22] However this scheme fell through and departure was delayed as, 'I have not been at all well and Mama thinks that sailing about would be a panacea and as we have the loan of the *Pioneer* for a while, we are going to remain until the 29th. Then I sleep a night at Glasgow....'[23] It was the years between 1866, when her mother died, and 1873 when she finally broke away from convention which were the most difficult of her life.

The Bird sisters were remarked on by contemporaries for their closeness, but did they recognise that harmony was the more easily maintained because they led separate lives? After the death of their mother they parted, leaving Edinburgh for nearly six months; Henrietta removed herself to Mull where she settled in a cottage at Tobermory, while Isabella visited London, Tunbridge Wells and Farnham. There was apparently no question of their remaining together to comfort each other following the loss of their mother. Was it a relief for each sister to be able to go her own way, meeting up to live together as sisters only occasionally?

Henrietta, it was claimed by Mrs Brown, a neighbour at Wyton who knew both girls well – 'was timid except where her sense of duty bade her be courageous, very simple in her tastes and very fond of study and scholarly pursuits. Above everything she loved nature ... Henrietta looked up to Isabella with reverence as well as love, delighting in her strength, energy of purpose and power of mind, and finding in her spiritual understanding and true sympathy'.[24] Hennie's own intellectual interests were in Greek and other ancient languages, for she believed that this study would assist her in understanding the scriptures. Despite the fact that Hennie studied Greek in Edinburgh during the winter, attending Professor Blackie's class for ladies and coming second in the examination, she remains a shadowy figure as public attention was lavished on Isabella. Was she envious of Isabella's ability to become the centre of attraction, whether sick or well, in any society?

Once they had reached the happy arrangement of living apart they were, during the periods they spent together, on intimate terms, as Isabella explained early in 1878 before she left for Japan, 'We slept together for a fortnight'.[25] The Bird sisters' modest private means gave them the freedom to live apart, although when Isabella was far away on one of her adventures it was important to her to know that Hennie, 'My own darling' and 'My dearest pet', was waiting at home to receive the long intimate letters.

They did not share the same doctor, for when Dr Moir retired he brought in his stead Dr Grainger Stewart[26] and he – later Professor Sir Thomas Grainger Stewart – remained Isabella's doctor and friend until his death in 1900. It was Dr John Bishop who stepped in as Henrietta's medical attendant after the retirement of her earlier doctor.

Ill-health remained the dominating feature of their lives. Isabella, always considered in the family to be 'not strong', suffered various unspecified ill-nesses in addition to her back trouble. Following a visit to a London specialist she was advised 'to stay in bed as if she had a fever'. At various times 'the old insomnia returned and her nervous system was affected'. She suffered from 'spinal prostration' and so spent the mornings in bed, propped up by pillows. So established, she was equipped with a 'flat writing board' on which she wrote her letters and her articles for journals such as *The Leisure Hour*, *The Family Treasury*, *Good Words* and *Sunday at Home*.

If the summer of 1869 is taken as an example the all-pervading nature of her ill-health can be judged. Dr Moir had advised that she 'should go to the sea, sleep on the ground floor, and be out in a boat most of the day'. The sisters complied and settled themselves near Oban. As Isabella seemed better, Henrietta travelled south to see friends, upon which her sister at once developed inflammation of the throat and was 'as ill as could be with choking, aching, leeches, poultices, doctors twice a day'.[27] Was it this never-ending cycle, this profusion of illness which had caused Henrietta to remove herself to Mull where she could for most of the time avoid serving as hand-maiden to her sister's ill-health?

The following year she was advised to wear 'a steel net to support her head at the back when she required to sit up', her suffering being caused by 'the weight of her head on a diseased spine'. Later the same year a London doctor advised her to stay in bed and keep quiet. This resulted in a complete collapse for as she lay in bed 'resting' for the most of the twenty-four hours, 'the old insomnia returned and a constant distress assailed her spirits and kept her in mental as well as physical anguish'. Her life, centred at this time on her health did not please her for she appreciated that she was 'in great danger of becoming perfectly encrusted with selfishness'. During these years she was, according to her friend and biographer Anna Stoddart, 'frail, dependent, timid...'

But how much dosing did she receive and what of the drugs to which she refers? Did she suffer from doctor-induced illness? The medicines which were used by Isabella herself included bromides[28] and chlorodyne. Bromide – especially potassium bromide – was frequently prescribed in the late nineteenth century as a mild sedative. Such preparations were highly unsatisfactory because they became concentrated and accumulated in the body tissues – producing a toxic state known as 'bromism' or 'bromidism' – resulting in drowsiness and producing various psychological derangements. In addition, there could be a 'bromide rash' bringing its own disabling complications. But bromides did not produce a state of euphoria and were not addictive. Medical journals in the 1880s and 1890s were full of articles on treating illnesses with bromides; the principle references are to 'toxilogical action of' and 'risks attending use of'. Chlorodyne, advertised in the *Medical Directory* of the 1890s as a 'superior hypnotic' did contain both opium and cannabis. Official doses of chlorodyne might not become addictive but an overdose could result in effects on the alimentary canal, including nausea, loss of appetite and constipation. Could they have influenced Isabella's behaviour? She certainly knew of and carried chlorodyne although no direct reference has been found to her using it herself.

But in Australia, in late 1872, she was 'taking bromide three times a day'. She was deeply depressed and 'unable to get any sleep. I am more nervous than I have ever been and cannot remember anything or read a book. These last two days I have felt shaking all over and oppressed with undefined terror. The loneliness of a long voyage and these uninteresting regions is killing'.[29]

Was the bromide habit itself creating all this misery?[30]

The years since her father's death in 1858 had certainly been difficult, although as acting head of a household which contained her mother and sister she had been reasonably content in Edinburgh until 1866. After her mother's death with her sister Henrietta eager to live permanently on Mull, she felt greatly frustrated. On 15 October 1871 she was 40 years of age.

Notes

1. Mrs Dorothy Louisa Bird drew up and signed her Last Will and Testament at Hurst Cottage, Hadley Common, Middlesex on 31 May 1860.

2. See T.C. Smout, *A Century of the Scottish People*, (1988), and for a study of the efforts to Anglicise Scottish intellectual life see G.E. Davie, *The Democratic Intellect*, (1961).

3. It may have been Rev George Cullen in Edinburgh who first made contact with Rev and Miss Bird, see AS, pp.76-77.

4. John Stuart Blackie (1809-1895), born Glasgow, educated Marischal College, Aberdeen, Edinburgh University, and in Germany. Professor 1st Latin at Aberdeen, then Greek at Edinburgh (from 1852-1882), prominent educational reformer and Scottish Nationalist, influential in founding Chair of Celtic at University of Edinburgh and in supporting the crofters' cause in the Highlands. See A. Stoddart, *John Stuart Blackie*, 1895, and J.S. Blackie, *Notes of a Life*, edited by A.Stodart Walker, (Edinburgh, 1910).

5. The letters from ILB to Mrs Blackie are in the John Stuart Blackie papers (hereafter JSB) held in the National Library of Scotland, Edinburgh, (hereafter NLS). The letter addressed to 'Dearest Mrs Blackie' is dated 18 July 1863. Elizabeth Helen (Eliza) Blackie was the daughter of James Wyld of Gilston, Fife.

6. O. Checkland, *Philanthropy in Victorian Scotland*, (1980).

7. See F. Thompson, *Harris Tweed, the Story of a Hebridean Industry* (1969). It would appear that ILB was probably associated with Lady Gordon Cathcart who is credited with acting as an agent for the tweed which her tenants produced in the Uists and in Barra. She sent the tweed to Messrs Parfitt in London for sale. My thanks to Alan Cunningham, Chief Librarian, Western Isles Island Council, Stornoway.

8. JSB, ILB to Eliza B., 18 July 1863, Ms 2626, f.29.

9. A. Grainger Stewart, Obituary of ILB, *BEM*, November 1904, p.699.

10. ILB, *Notes on Old Edinburgh* (hereafter *Old Edinburgh*), (Edinburgh 1869), (Copy in NLS, No.B1.9/3.3(8)).

11. *Old Edinburgh*, p.14.

12. This was probably Henry D. Littlejohn (1st Medical Officer of Health, Edinburgh), *Report on the Sanitary Condition of the City of Edinburgh*, (Edinburgh 1866).

13. *Old Edinburgh*, p.11.

14. *Old Edinburgh*, p.14.

15. *Old Edinburgh*, p.20.

16. *Old Edinburgh*, p.25.

17. AS, p.71.

18. AS, p.72.

19. AS, p.74.

20. AS, p.90.

21. Mrs Dorothy Louisa Bird, Testament, SRO, reference SRO SC 70/1/131, pp.470-8; SC 70/4/105, pp.1055-6.

22. JSB, ILB to Eliza B., 23 September 1863, Ms 2626, f.40.

23. JSB, ILB to Eliza B., 23 September 1863, Ms 2626, f.41, 42.

24. AS, p.123, but note ILB's comment, 'How different my Hennie who studied Astronomy, Botany and Thematics' (JSB, ILB to Eliza B., 28 November 1899, Ms 2640, f.243),
    see also JSB's poem to HAB called 'A Ballad of Mull'. There are 13 verses in all, AS, Appendix, pp.394-397. Verse 1 is:

> In a tiny bay
>> Where ships lie sure and steady,
> In a quite way
>> Lives a tiny lady
> In a tiny house
>> Dwells my little fairy
> Gentle as a mouse
>> Blithe as a canary

25. JSB, ILB to Eliza B., 1 May 1878, Ms 2633, f.16.

26. Sir Thomas Grainger Stewart (1837-1900) physician, M.D., Edinburgh 1858, Studied Berlin, Prague and Vienna, FRSE 1866, Professor of practice of physics at Edinburgh University, 1876, physician in Ordinary to Queen Victoria in Scotland, 1882; Knighted 1894. *DNB* Supplement 3, (London 1901), pp.360-361).

27. AS, p.68.

28. The effect of using bromides is cumulative as such substances are not excreted rapidly from the body and so concentrate in the tissues. Bromides were not addictive.

29. JM, ILB to HAB, 13 October 1872 (a handful of ILB's letters to Henrietta are to be found in the John Murray Collection).

30. See Richard Asher, *Talking Sense*, (1972), Chapter 14, 'Diseases caused by doctors', which discusses iatrogenic (doctor induced) disease and bromidism (p.158).

4 'The Summer Isles of Eden'

In 1872 matters came to a head, Isabella's illness became acute and her doctors, unable to effect any improvement, advised a sea voyage. She sailed for the Antipodes in the autumn of 1872 in time to start her letter diary to her sister Hennie – 'my own darling' – from Chalmers' Manse, Melbourne on 13 October 1872, two days before her 41st birthday.[1]

When she arrived in Melbourne it was Spring in Victoria and as it became ever hotter, Isabella wilted and soon was writing bitter and uncomplimentary things about 'the country which is too hideous'. The trouble was that in substituting Chalmers' Manse in Melbourne for home in Edinburgh she had moved from one conventional environment to another. Even when she was provided with a horse, the heat and the dust and the flies only added to her misery and as a result her precarious health deteriorated even further. She appeared to be suffering from 'neuralgia, pain in my bones, pricking like pins and needles in my limbs, excruciating nervousness, exhaustion, inflamed eyes, sore throat, swelling of the glands behind the ear, stupidity'.[2] She moved on to New Zealand and was equally miserable there under what she called 'A white unwinking scintillating sun'.[3] In desperation she boarded the *Nevada* bound for San Francisco and home.

The *Nevada* had been 'patched-up' for this trip. She was 'a huge paddle-steamer, of the old-fashioned American type, deck above deck, balconies, a pilot-house aloft the foremast, two monstrous walking beams and two masts which ... might serve as Jury masts'. Eight passengers had committed themselves to journey on her; as they assembled rumours flew – was she seaworthy? There are graphic details of some of the more technical faults which were assigned to the *Nevada*, noting that even the caulking on the deck was so poor, that 'during heavy rain above, it was a smart shower in the saloon, keeping four stewards employed with buckets and swabs, and compelling us to dine in waterproofs and rubber shoes'.[4]

Two days out from Auckland the *Nevada* encountered 'a revolving South Seas hurricane'. At first the passengers lay terrified in their cabins, foodless and neglected, while the captain and crew struggled to keep the ship afloat, later they assembled in the deck-house and 'sat there for five hours'. With a paddle wheeler the wild tossing of the sea determined whether the rotating paddles provided propulsion, if in water, or not, if revolving uselessly in the air above the waves. Isabella describes vividly 'the one loud awful undying shriek, mingled with a prolonged relentless hiss' with which the noise of the hurricane overwhelmed 'the strainings, sunderings and groanings' of the ship itself.[5]

On the Pacific Ocean in peril of her life in January 1873 Isabella Bird, distracted by the danger, had no time or thought to dose herself with medicines. To her amazement she found herself naturally excited and exhilerated by the struggle to keep the *Nevada* afloat. It was the breakthrough which changed her life.

To the intense relief of passengers and crew the engines continued to function. There was, she writes, 'a sublime repose in the spectacle of the huge-walking beams, alternately rising and falling slowly, calmly, regularly as if the *Nevada* were on a holiday trip within the Golden Gate'. She much commended Captain Blethen's 'quiet and masterly handling of this dilapidated old ship beyond all praise'. The following day when the storm was over, the engines did fail for an hour; had this happened during the hurricane some sixty lives would have been lost.[6]

After the storms subsided the passengers became more conscious of other horrors, for everything about the old ship was worn out. As she noted, 'the mattresses bulge and burst, and cockroaches creep in and out ... the bread swarms with minute ants, and we have to pick every piece over because of weevils. Existence at night is an unequal fight with rats and cockroaches ....'[7]

Isabella's health stabilised and then improved. She felt wonderful. It was, she declared, 'like living in a new world, so free, so fresh, so vital, so careless, so unfettered, so full of interest that one grudges being asleep'.[8] It was this exposure to danger on board the creaking *Nevada* in the South Pacific which was to be the turning point. Thereafter she was never at a loss for she knew she needed the spice of danger to keep her well and happy.

In the course of the voyage, protracted because of the storms, one passenger, 'young Mr Dexter', 'ruptured a blood vessel' in the lungs and lay in a critical condition. Miss Bird as the only woman passenger, other than his mother, at once offered her services as nurse. The young man survived, although it was decided that the Dexters would disembark at the Sandwich Islands where 'young Mr Dexter' could recuperate.

When the new, euphoric Isabella Bird landed on the Sandwich Islands, (now the American State of Hawaii) they were indeed 'The Summer Isles of Eden'. Politically they were under American protection and were later to be annexed (1898) by the United States.[9] Mark Twain had described them (in 1866) as the 'peacefullest, restfullest, sunniest, balmiest, dreamiest haven of refuge for the worn and weary spirit the surface of the earth can offer'.[10] On these as yet undeveloped islands Isabella was to find salvation and in this Pacific paradise she was to stay for nearly seven months.

As they approached the island of Oahu she noted 'lofty peaks, truly – grey and red, sun-scorched and wind-bleached, glowing here and there with traces of their fiery origin; but they were cleft by deep chasms and ravines of cool shadow and entrancing green, and falling water streaked their sides'.[11] When they came nearer they could see the coral reef, and then Honolulu. The existence of the capital of the Islands had to be taken on trust, she remarked, because apart from 'the lovely wooden and grass huts, with deep verandahs, which nestled under palms and bananas on soft green sward ... only two church spires and a few grey roofs appeared above the trees'.[12] One can sense her mounting excitement as they approached the 'environing coral reef' and passed through 'a narrow intricate passage of the deepest indigo' into the calm lagoon. It was a busy scene which met them as the *Nevada* manoeuvred into the wharf. The American iron-clad *California* was there as was the *Benicia*. The Royal Navy was represented by the corvette *Scout*. Two 'coasting schooners' were just leaving, as was the inter-island ferry, *Kilauea*, packed with people, while in between scurried countless native canoes.

By the time they docked she was able to 'look down from the towering deck' on the extraordinary range of races represented. Apart from native islanders there were Chinese, half-whites, negroes, and a few dark skinned Polynesians, as well as some white foreigners. As she wrote in admiration, 'Such rich brown men and women they were, with wavy shining black hair, large brown lustrous eyes and rows of perfect teeth like ivory. Everyone was smiling'. She noted that some of the women wore black dresses, but many of those worn by the younger women were of pure white, crimson, yellow, scarlet, blue or light green. 'The men displayed their lithe, graceful figures to the best advantage in white trousers and gay Garibaldi shirts ... Without an exception the men and women wore wreaths and garlands of flowers, carmine, orange, or pure white, twined around their hats, or thrown carelessly around their necks ....'[13] What surprised her most was the apparent carefree happiness of the crowds. In her euphoric mood she wondered 'where were the hard, angular, care worn, sallow, passionate faces' of men and women who form the majority of every crowd 'at home as well as in America or Australia?'[14]

She also noted as she waited to disembark, 'about 200 saddled horses standing'; although the horses themselves were 'sorry, lean, undersized beasts, looking in general as if the emergencies of life left them little time for eating and sleeping', she was interested in their accoutrements for each horse stood bearing 'the Mexican saddle, with its lassooing horn in front, high peak behind, immense wooden stirrups, with great leather guards, silver or brass bosses and coloured saddle-cloths'.[15] She did not then know that the Mexican saddle was to revolutionise her own potential for travel.

The passengers who were leaving the *Nevada* settled themselves in the recently-opened Hawaiian hotel in Honolulu. An expedition was made with

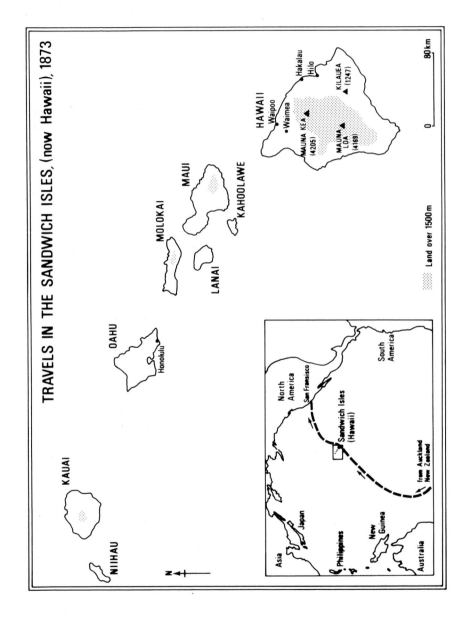

TRAVELS IN THE SANDWICH ISLES, (now Hawaii), 1873

other visitors to 'the Pali' – the now famous Palissades – the great rock face outside of Honolulu. She enjoyed a Christian Sunday going to the English Cathedral, the islands having been proselytised by clerics from a variety of Christian denominations.

Her carefree days in the Hawaiian hotel came to an abrupt end when she was persuaded by friends to leave – 'young Mr Dexter' was progressing favourably – and accompany an American lady who was going on an expedition to climb the volcano on the largest island of Hawaii. She left on the steamer *Kilauea* named for the active volcano Kilauea which she was now intending to climb.

The voyage was its own adventure. Initially she declined to have a mattress and sleep on deck with hundreds of others, but having sampled the cockroaches below deck which seemed 'tremendous creatures, dark red, with eyes like lobsters, and antennae two inches long'[16] she changed her mind and for the second night she was glad to accept 'a mattress on the sky light'. Eventually they arrived at Hilo, 'the paradise of Hawaii' where the crescent-shaped bay was said to be 'the most beautiful in the Pacific'. Hilo had 'rich soil, rain, heat, sunshine which stimulate nature to supreme efforts, and there is a prodigality of vegetation which leaves nothing uncovered but the golden margin of the sea'.

They were greeted by hundreds of people; swimmers, 'like the bronzes of Naples museum, rode the waves on surf-boards, brilliantly dressed riders',[17] boats being rowed and canoes being paddled, all escorted the *Kilauea* to dock. As there were no hotels at Hilo, Isabella and Miss Karpe (her climbing companion) were welcomed into his home by Luther Severance, the Sheriff of Hawaii. Miss Karpe was, wrote Isabella tartly, 'the typical American travelling lady, who is encountered everywhere from the Andes to the Pyramids, tireless, of indomitable energy, Spartan endurance and a genius for attaining everything'. Isabella on the other hand despite her exuberant spirits had her own problems. The short expedition organised by Miss Karpe before the journey to the volcano was a near disaster for Isabella, as 'the ride was spoiled by my insecure seat in my saddle and the increased pain in my spine which riding produced'. In crossing a stream the horses had 'to make a sort of downward jump from a rock and I slipped round my horse's neck'.[18]

On her return from this miserable outing it was her host Luther Severance who urged her to ride astride the horse using a Mexican saddle. Previously, according to strict Victorian convention, she had always ridden side-saddle, her body awkwardly twisted with both legs on one side of the horse making it difficult for her to keep her balance over difficult terrain and exacerbating her spinal condition. Isabella was, as she acknowledged, strongly prejudiced against ladies riding astride but gossips from home were far away and she knew that many foreign ladies had adopted the Mexican saddle, 'for greater security to themselves and ease to their horses'. She recognised that they maintained full decorum by wearing 'full Turkish trousers and jauntily made dresses reaching to the ankles'.[19] She accepted the loan of a Mexican saddle, and borrowed a lady's costume.

The adoption of the Mexican saddle and the wearing of trousers were for her a revolution, sharpening the pleasures of her travel journeys and enabling her to gain an independence otherwise denied. It was this which made the subsequent years of Isabella's travels so exciting and her so memorable a traveller. Wherever she went thereafter, her Mexican saddle was in her luggage.

When the expedition to Kilauea left, the guide, Upa, 'supplied the picturesque element' while the ladies, according to Isabella, looked 'grotesque'. Miss Karpe, whose efficient arrangements drew barbed comments from her travelling companion, 'mounted her horse on her own side-saddle, dressed in a short grey waterproof and a broad-brimmed Leghorn hat tied so tightly over her ears with a green veil as to give it the look of a double spout'. Miss Bird had on her 'coarse Australian hat' which acted as sunshade and umbrella, a lady's riding costume and her 'great rusty New Zealand boots'. She had borrowed a 'very gaily ornamented brass-bossed *demi-pique* Mexican saddle'.[20] Miss Karpe would have been well-advised to have followed Isabella's lead and used the Mexican saddle for she never recovered from the exertions of climbing Kilauea and as Isabella remarked later 'seemed quite ill'.[21]

They set off, travelling occasionally over green sward, then through the densest of 'true tropical jungle', across immense plains of lava called 'satin rock', a 'cooled and arrested torrent of lava' which lay, across the land. Halfway through this long exhausting day their guide insisted upon buckling a heavy Mexican spur onto Miss Bird's foot believing that the horse needed such persuasion to travel more quickly. It was with a great sense of relief that they arrived at the hospitable, if lonely, 'Crater House' where travellers were welcomed for the night before the final ascent.

The next morning the horses were left at 'Crater House' and the two ladies set off with 'stout staffs' and three guides, two men and a woman, who did not attempt to disguise the amusement occasioned by the ladies' appearance. To climb to the crater of Kilauea involved first scrambling down an outside wall before crossing 'a new Plutonic region of blackness and awful desolation, the accustomed sights and sounds of nature all gone. Terraces, cliffs, lakes, ridges, rivers, mountain sides, whirlpools, chasms of lava surrounded us, solid, black and shining, as if vitrified, or an ashen grey, stained yellow with sulphur here and there, or white with alum. The lava was fissured and upheaved everywhere by earthquakes, hot underneath and emitting a hot breath'.[22]   They continued over what sounds like very dangerous shifting ground for thirty miles over the lava flow to the crater's edge.

As she noted, 'there was no smoke or sign of fire, and I felt sure that the volcano had died out ... for our especial disappointment'. Then suddenly as she recounted, 'gory drops were tossed in the air, and springing forward we stood on the brink of Hale-mau-mau which was about 35ft below us. I think we all screamed, I know we all wept, but we were speechless, for a new glory and terror had been added to the earth'.[23] As she explained, 'On our arrival, eleven fire mountains were playing joyously around the lakes and sometimes the six of the nearer lake ran together in the centre to go wallowing down in one vortex, from which they re-appeared bulging upwards, till they formed a huge cone 30 feet high, which plunged downwards in a whirlpool only to re-appear in exactly the previous number of fountains in different parts of the lake, high leaping, raging, flinging themselves upward'.[24]

The return journey seemed 'a dull trudge over the black and awful crater' yet in leaving the volcanic crater she was as she wrote 'exchanging "the place of hell" for the bright upper earth with its endless summer, and its perennial foliage, blossom and fruitage'.[25] It was a time of deep emotion for Miss Bird had stood on the edge of Mount Kilauea, of a real biblical hell, of a 'bottomless pit' where lay 'the fire which is not quenched', and 'the molten lake of Hale-mau-mau which burneth with fire and brimstone'.[26] When she returned to the Crater House with 'stiff and painful limbs' she described the beautiful grass and bamboo house, and how the cooking was done 'in a steam apparatus of nature's own work' although she 'peeled'[27] her hand dipping it into the steam bath, which was built over a sulphur steam crack.

She was back in Hilo on 3 February and considered returning to Honolulu and her nursing duties with Mrs Dexter but somehow she missed the infrequent steamer and was glad to settle down in Hilo where she was so wonderfully well and happy. She was invited to visit at the family of Judge Austin at Onomea and rode there enjoying an extremely beautiful ride – along the coast– which required the party to ride across narrow deep ravines or gorges, which cross the track as rivers in the form of cascades.[28] These gulches were severe tests of horsemanship as the descents were very steep requiring the rider to stand on the stirrups as the horse moved carefully like a goat finding each foothold with care. The Mexican saddle proved to have great advantages although Miss Bird did not as yet regard herself as an expert. She successfully 'kept her seat' although not without occasional fears of an ignominious downfall. But she was in good spirits, writing 'I am gaining health daily, and almost live in the open air. I have hired a native policeman's horse and saddle and with a Macgregor flannel riding costume, which my kind friends have made for me, and a pair of jingling Mexican spurs am quite Hawaiianised. I ride alone once or twice a day exploring the neighbourhood, finding some new fern or flower daily and abandon myself wholly to the fascination of this new existence.'[29]

From Onomea she went for a further adventure north along the coast to Waipo some 60 miles from Hilo. Her escort was a beautiful Hawaiian girl of seventeen who had recently married a white man. Deborah, who looked very *piquante* in a bloomer dress of dark blue, with masses of shining hair in natural ringlets mixing with her *lei* of red rose buds, was keen to visit her home at Waipo and agreed that Miss Bird should accompany her.

The journey was somewhat marred by their guide Kaluna's furious and constant beating of his horse; but Kaluna did know his way, along a track which was frequently cut across by the gulches which usually brought small torrents of water dashing down to the ocean. She marvelled that horses and mules should be expected to climb down and then up on these precipitous ledges. The first day one dizzying descent landed them at the house of a native called Bola Bola where they dismounted 'from wet saddles in which we had sat for ten hours, and stiffly hobbled up to the littered verandah, the water dripping from our clothes and squeezing out of our boots at every step'.[30] The simple facilities of the house prevented any attempt at dry clothes, so she put on a wrapper over her wet clothes. They ate a mess of *poi* served communally in a calabash. When it got dark 'a deeply hollowed stone was produced, containing beef fat and a piece of rag for a wick', this 'burned with a strong flaring light'. They all lay down in rows on the floor to sleep and as Miss Bird observed it seemed 'so new, so odd to be the only white person among eleven natives in a lonely house, and yet to be as secure from danger and annoyance as in your own home'.[31]

She saw a great waterfall to which access was so difficult that she travelled 'without stockings'. She was told she could go no further 'in her clothes' but regardless she plunged into the river in her riding dress which she thought of as 'not unlike a fashionable Newport bathing suit' – it was, she remarked, 'a thoroughly rough tramp wading ten times through the river, which was sometimes up to our knees, and sometimes up to our waists'. Eventually, after an hour's struggle, she was able to stand up to her throat in the still water of a pool as the water cascaded and dropped for a height of some 1800ft. As she stood alone – her native companions 'regaling themselves on papaya and on live fresh-water shrimps' – 'a ray of sunshine turned the upper part of the spray into a rainbow, and never to my eyes had the bow of promise looked so heavenly as when it spanned the black solemn, tree-shadowed abyss'.[32]

The days, the weeks, the months sped by. She returned briefly to Honolulu in April to discover that the Dexters had no further need of her assistance. But in Honolulu she at once felt her good health draining away and so left for further adventures on the smaller islands of the group, staying on Kauai, Maui and Lauai. On the islands she did more riding and knew she was – with the blessing of her Mexican saddle – as good a rider as any. On the island of Kauai some girls showed her how to make the Mexican knot 'with the thong which secures the cinch, which will make me independent henceforward'.[33]

By the end of May she was back on the island of Hawaii in her own camp – alone – on her own horse Kahele, with her luggage in her saddlebags, aiming for the volcano at Kilauea and planning a journey of some 350 miles. Shortly after she returned to Hilo in early June, a Mr Green appeared and suggested that she accompany him on an attempted climb of Mauna Loa, which at nearly 14,000 ft was a serious challenge. Previously when asked if she had plans to climb this mountain she had always replied, 'Oh dear no! I should never dream of it' or 'Nothing would persuade me to think of it';[34] so she accepted Mr Green's invitation joyfully and they set about their preparations. Mr Green obtained tent, horses, a baggage mule and a servant. Isabella borrowed 'a stout flannel shirt' and 'venerable worsted stockings, much darned, knitted in Fifeshire a quarter of a century ago'. There was much talk and some worry about mountain sickness at such an altitude.

The party set off from Hilo on the morning of 4 June 1873 stopping first at Crater House, Kilauea, then crossing the crater area 'the crust becoming more brittle and the footing hotter at each step'. Mr Green, enthusiastic for new knowledge, with Miss Bird in close attendance, pushed on further across the unsettled lava where from this 'perilous standpoint' they could gaze upon 'the horrors below'. To keep any sort of footing as they were 'burned, singed, stifled and blinded' they stood on one foot at a time. It seemed a foolhardy position in which to remain for three hours. After this adventure they separated, she taking the high road and he the low road as they searched for a guide for the mountain. Neither local employers nor their employees could be persuaded to help. She stayed overnight in very rough circumstances with some farm people, and there eventually Mr Green joined her. He had found a guide 'a young goat hunter who had not been to the top of Mauna Loa but knew the slopes well'.[35]

They collected wood for their camp fire on the edge of the timber line and then set off upwards over the uneven old lava, the *pahoehoe*. It was gruelling work and very hard on the soft hooves of the animals. They bathed their heads with snow and added even more clothing as Isabella noted that she looked like 'a puffin or Esquimaux' wrapped up as she was. Their difficulties in crossing and climbing the lava were exacerbated by the *a - a*, slow streams of hardening lava over which they had to force their animals. In this way they finally reached the edge of the crater and knew although they were still three-quarters of a mile away they could go no further. As it became dark they saw the myriad lights of that 'glorious, far-off fire-fountain'.

The tent was pitched 'as near to the crater as was safe with one pole in a crack and the other in a great fissure'. Because they could not boil water for tea at such an altitude they made 'a great tin of brandy toddy' and this together with tinned salmon and doughnuts constituted their meal. They watched the extraordinary display for some hours before retiring to rest. Mr Green and the two servants took one side of the tent while Miss Bird slept on the other. Although they were very weary and exhausted by the altitude she did not sleep well on the rough lava and spent more night hours gazing over the volcano, fascinated by the constantly changing scene which reinforced the strong impression that she was in some way observing the awful gates of a biblical Hell.[36] They were all feeling the effects of the height as they descended the following day; again the animals suffered badly. Returning to the lower slopes was a long gruelling ride but it was with some triumph that they returned from 'the most successful ascent of Mauna Loa ever made'. At Crater House on 9 June she parted with Mr Green who rode off to the west while she, alone, rode down to Hilo.

This final solo ride would have proved daunting to anyone for she had to travel across the *pahoehoe* and the *a - a* streams where the different types of lava produced 'jugged spikes' which were the height of her horse. She had difficulty finding any vestige of a trail and was often reduced to dismounting and feeling for marks of abrasion caused by shod horses with her hand. She eventually emerged after some seven hours of travelling on what she was later told was a track disused because of the unsettled lava.[37]

A few days later (12 June) she moved to the West coast at Kona, where she landed at Kealakakua Bay, where a century earlier Captain Cook had been killed. From Kona she made two ascents of the mountain Hualailai, the second one alone, but later settled at a sheep station – remote at 6,000 feet above sea level – where the idyllic life continued and she was exhilerated to be part of a cattle lassooing party.

Some time in July she received a letter from home; Henrietta had been astonished and mystified at the flood of good cheer which poured from Isabella's Hawaiian letters. Hennie had written to Mrs Blackie about Isabella, 'She is evidently better, for she views everything cheerfully, delights in my letters, approves of all I do, worries about nothing. She has continued to enjoy herself wonderfully'.[38] When Henrietta wrote she asked, should she come out and join Isabella in the 'Summer Isles of Eden?'

Isabella was brought abruptly to her senses. The Sandwich Islands would always remain in her mind as the place where she had found that danger and adventure were for her a necessary ingredient for good health. It was no part of her plan to have her sister share the magic. Within days she was back in Honolulu, her passage booked on the *Costa Rica* for San Francisco. The brisk no-nonsense Miss Bird had replaced the romantic sybaritic Isabella. 'I shall be in the Rocky Mountains' she wrote, 'before you receive my hastily-written reply to your proposal to come out here for a year'.

On 7 August she sailed from Honolulu, 'Farewell for ever, my bright tropic dream! *Aloha nui* to Hawaii-nei'.

Notes

1. JM, ILB to HAB, 13 October 1872 (one of a small group of letters from ILB to HAB in JM's care).

2. JM, ILB to HAB, 13 October 1872.

3. ILB, *Six Months in the Sandwich Islands*, but references here are taken from the facsimile reprint, *Six Months in Hawaii* (hereafter *Hawaii*), published by Kegan Paul Incorporated Limited (Pacific Basin Books, 1986), p 6

4. *Hawaii*, p 8.

5. *Hawaii*, p.8-9.

6. *Hawaii*, p.11.

7. *Hawaii*, p.13.

8. ILB to Eliza B. quoted in AS, p.79.

9. R.S. Kuykendall, *The Hawaiian Kingdom*, Vol.II, *Twenty Critical Years 1854-1874*, (1953), A.L. Korn, *Victorian Visitors* (1958).

10. Mark Twain, *Letters from Hawaii* (1866), PB, p.23.

11. *Hawaii*, p.18.

12. *Hawaii*, p.19.

13. *Hawaii*, pp.20-21.

14. *Hawaii*, p.22.

15. *Hawaii*, p.22.

16. *Hawaii*, p.45.

17. *Hawaii*, p.55.

18. *Hawaii*, p.66.

19. *Hawaii*, p.67.

20. *Hawaii*, pp.69-70.

21. *Hawaii*, p.174.

22. *Hawaii*, p.81.

23. *Hawaii*, p.83.

24. *Hawaii*, p.85.

25. *Hawaii*, p.88.

26. *Hawaii*, p.84.

27. *Hawaii*, p.91.

28. *Hawaii*, p.110.

29. *Hawaii*, p.109.

30. *Hawaii*, p.140.

31. *Hawaii*, pp.142-3.

32. *Hawaii*, p.151.

33. *Hawaii*, p.297.

34. *Hawaii*, p.378.

35. *Hawaii*, p.398.

36. *Hawaii*, pp.399-416.

37. *Hawaii*, pp.418-21.

38. JSB, HAB to Eliza B., 10 September 1873, Ms 2641, f.19.

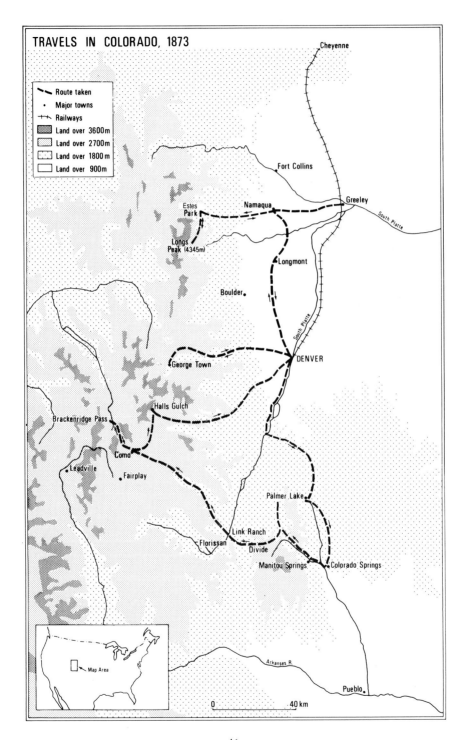

TRAVELS IN COLORADO, 1873

Route taken
Major towns
Railways
Land over 3600m
Land over 2700m
Land over 1800m
Land over 900m

Cheyenne

Fort Collins

Namaqua
Greeley

Estes
Park
Longs
Peak (4345m)

Longmont

Boulder

South Platte

George Town

DENVER

Halls Gulch

Brackenridge Pass

Como

Leadville
Fairplay

Palmer Lake

Link Ranch

Florissan
Divide

Manitou Springs
Colorado Springs

Map Area

Arkanses R.

Pueblo

0 .... 40 km

5 'My poor dear erring Jim'

To land in 'the clang'[1] – as Isabella called the noise and bustle of San Francisco in August 1873 – was a great shock. She quickly made her arrangements to leave by train and by 2 September she was at Lake Tahoe on the California/Nevada border en route for Colorado where she hoped to stay in the Rocky Mountains.

At Colfax (at a height of 2,400 ft) she took a walk along the length of the train noting the 'two great gaudy engines, the Grizzly Bear and the White Fox'[2] both with their respective tenders loaded with logs and great solitary reflecting lamps in front above the cow guards. She resolved to disembark at Truckee where the train, some 700 metres long, drew up right there, in the street, in front of a crowded and noisy 'rough Western hotel'. She slept soundly in a bed which looked 'quite tumbled-looking',[3] as the bedrooms were used more or less continuously over the 24 hours.

The next morning Truckee was quiet and she proceeded to the livery stables, where she was dismayed to find that local ladies did not necessarily ride 'cavalier fashion' astride the Mexican saddle, but the quick-thinking liveryman insisted that riding cowboy-style was proper for a lady and her Mexican saddle was put on a 'large grey horse'. She was assured that no one would molest her, although she did on this trip temporarily lose her horse when a bear came lumbering across the trail causing the horse to rear and its rider to fall. The scenery was 'truly magnificent and bright with life'.

She moved on to Cheyenne, Wyoming, via the Great Salt Lake, then to Ogden and on to the plains at Canyon where she stayed with the Hughes family who had recently arrived from England. Dr Hughes was ill with 'threatened pulmonary disease' and he and his wife, thoroughly unaccustomed to the farming and pioneering life, were vainly struggling to make a living.[4] Isabella enjoyed being with them and appreciated Dr Hughes' poetry reading during the long evenings while the ladies sewed. As Isabella remarked, as she harvested tomatoes, squash and pumpkin and pulled a quarter of an acre of maize, 'I much prefer field work to the scouring of greasy pans and to the wash tub'.

From Canyon she moved to Longmount intending to go up to the cool high valleys in the mountains. But she was shaken by her earlier fall from her horse, 'ill with the smothering heat' of the plains and had almost decided to continue by train to Denver and New York when her landlord told her two young men were 'going up to Estes Park tomorrow'. Thus fortunately, on 28 September 1873, she, with her companions, 'just dropped into the very place I have been seeking but in everything it exceeds all my dreams'.[5] In 1873 the Rocky Mountain area in Colorado was undeveloped, but was increasingly regarded as a good place for people suffering from lung diseases. Isabella had undoubtedly landed on her feet with Mr and Mrs Griff Evans – from Llanberis in North Wales – who rented her her own, very rough, log cabin 'raised on six posts, all to myself ... and a small lake close to it'. She relished 'a clean hay bed with six blankets, and there are neither bugs nor fleas'.

Although she appreciated her privacy in her own hut, the first night she spent there was one she would never forget. She went, accompanied by Griff Evans to her 'solitary hut' at 9 o'clock, hearing wolves howling and owls hooting. Evans lit a candle and left her, and as she was very tired she quickly fell asleep only to be wakened, 'by a heavy breathing, a noise something like sawing under the floor, and a pushing and upheaving, all very loud. My candle was all burned and in truth, I dare not stir. The noise went on for an hour fully, when, just as I thought the floor had been made sufficiently thin for all purposes of ingress, the sounds abruptly ceased, and I fell asleep again. My hair was not, as it ought to have been, white in the morning'.[6]

Next morning, in the main log cabin, Evans and the others laughed uproariously, explaining to her that a skunk's lair lay beneath her cabin but that because of the possibility of making the hut uninhabitable because of the protective odour which he would give off, they could not touch him. Miss Bird found that for $8 a week she was provided with her hut, all meals, and a horse to ride. She was enchanted, for the main cabin itself, 'a good-sized log room, unchinked, with windows of infamous glass, looking two ways' was serviced by Mrs Evans who 'baked bread every day and provided fresh meat, milk, cream, excellent potatoes and tea and coffee'.

It was in this wonderful place that she had her most notable romantic adventure. When she first called at 'Mountain Jim's' cabin she was looking for water but she was not put off by the scatter of hunter's rubbish lying around. He was she thought a man of about 45 years who had been strikingly handsome but who had lost one eye (in a tussle with a bear) but who otherwise had 'large grey-blue eyes, deeply set, well-marked eyebrows, a handsome aquiline nose and a very handsome mouth'. Rocky Mountain Jim had previously been a Scout but he and his like were being pushed mountainwards as development and railroads dissected the Plains. Being originally a man of culture and education he relished Miss Bird's company for with her he could turn his back on the drink and violence by which he had lived.[7]

Isabella celebrated her 42nd birthday on 15 October in Estes Park finding the sweeping of snow, which blew in through the chinks of the logs into the cabin, both 'fun and exercise'.[8] She had murmured to her host as to the possibility of climbing Long's Peak, 'the American Matterhorn' nearby, but he had been discouraging, saying it was too late in the year and that the winds would be too strong. When Evans left for an expedition to Denver, Mountain Jim appeared and offered to act as guide to her and to two young men.

It seems clear that Mountain Jim was from the first much taken by Miss Isabella Bird. He first invited her and Mr and Mrs Dexter, other visitors to Estes Park, 'to take a ride' and after 'they were fatigued' Isabella rode Jim's 'beautiful mare, while Jim rode her heavy wagon horse, as they galloped and raced in the beautiful twilight'.[9] This small middle-aged lady intrigued him and brought to him echoes of a respectable and cultured past. With her own brand of formality – she always addressed him as Mr Nugent – she treated him as a trustworthy gentleman. It was a sure way of breaking down the defences of a proud and unhappy man, whose notoriety as a rough and violent character coloured the responses of all others who encountered him.

They set off for their expedition with their supplies and equipment limited by what their horses could carry. 'Jim' as Isabella described 'was a shocking figure, for he had on an old pair of high boots, with a baggy pair of old trousers made of deer hide, held on by an old scarf tucked into them; a leather shirt, with three or four ragged unbuttoned waistcoats over it, an old smashed wideawake, from under which his tawny neglected ringlets hung; and with his one eye, his one long spur, his knife in his belt, his revolver in his waistcoat pocket, his saddle covered with an old beaver skin, from which the paws hang down; his camping blankets behind him, his rifle laid across the saddle in front of him, and his axe, canteen, and other gear hanging to the horn, he was as awful looking a ruffian as one could see'.[10]

He set off over the first half mile 'at a hard gallop' but subsequently settled down 'with such a grace of manner' to ride beside her that she forgot his awful appearance during a conversation which lasted three hours as they carefully traversed some difficult territory. They passed some beautiful country, notably the hollow which contained 'The Lake of the Lilies', and then climbed up through the great primeval pine forests which rose to a height of 11,000 ft. She was awed by 'the gloom of the dense ancient silent forest' but then found the trees becoming smaller and more sparse as they climbed higher past the timber line.

They camped for the night in view of the 'bold white crest' of Long's Peak some 3,000 ft further up. In the light of 'a big half moon which hung out of the heavens' they saw snow above them which never melted. She thought it was fairyland. They made a big fire, picketed the horses securely and made beds of pine shoots. After they had eaten, the young men sang student songs and Negro melodies while Jim sang 'one of Moore's melodies in a singular falsetto' and recited poems of his own. At bed-time she retired, with Jim's dog 'Ring' to lie at her back to keep her warm, to a small bower of small silver spruces. The night was bitterly cold and they were up early to see the sunrise. The perfect beauty of the scene moved them deeply.

After breakfast they started up on foot over the 'lava beds', which was irregular ground of boulders encased in snow and ice. It was very cold and treacherous underfoot but she was, until they reached 'the Notch', able to remain independent. From this point she was dragged up as she said 'like a bale of goods, by sheer force of muscle'. The young men, irritated by her incompetence, would have left her but Jim would have none of this. They squeezed themselves up small spaces between the rocks by a passage called the 'Dog's Lift'. She proceeded by climbing on the shoulders of one man and then being hauled up by another. When they eventually struggled to the 'well-defined mountain top' she felt amazed to be on one of the mightiest of the vertebrae of the backbone of the Rocky Mountains from which she could see the waters start for both oceans. She, only the second woman to make the ascent, felt 'uplifted above love and hate and storms of passion'.

At over 14,000 ft they were all suffering from the altitude and were glad to begin the hazardous descent. The young men took a more direct route leaving Isabella and Jim to follow by a longer but less demanding route. It was an unprecedented journey as she explained 'I had various falls and once hung by my frock, which caught on a rock', 'Jim severed it with his hunting knife upon which I fell into a crevice full of snow'. It was a gruelling ordeal for her, sometimes drawing herself 'up on hands and knees, sometimes crawled, sometimes "Jim" pulled me up by my arms or a lariat, and sometimes I stood on his shoulders, or he made steps for me of his feet or his hands'.[11]

It was an extraordinarily intimate journey which must have affected them both. Once the young men had left them Jim abandoned his *'brusquerie'* and was 'gentle and considerate beyond anything'. They stayed overnight in the same place and she again slept in her bower of small trees but during the bitterly cold night she came by the fire with Ring the dog. Jim told stories 'of his early youth and of a great sorrow which had led him to embark on a lawless and desperate life. His voice trembled and tears rolled down his cheek'. She felt humiliated at being so helpless in these conditions and she believed Jim 'must be grievously disappointed' with both her 'courage and her strength'. Jim doubtless was enjoying the pleasure of assisting this gallant lady who made him feel worthy of respect.

The attraction was mutual. She found Mr Nugent to have 'pathos, poetry and humour, an intense love of nature, strong vanity ... an obvious desire to act and speak in character, and sustain his reputation as a desperado, a considerable acquaintance with literature, a wonderful verbal memory, opinions on every person and subject, a chivalrous respect for women ... a great power of fascination and a singular love of children'.

Although Isabella found Jim Nugent so engaging, others viewed him less charitably. George Henry Kingsley, brother of Charles and father of Mary, the African explorer, arrived in Estes Park shortly after Isabella had left, serving as doctor and companion to Lord Dunraven. Kingsley regarded Nugent as a 'humbug and a scoundrel' who astonished everyone with the 'extraordinary altitude of his lies'. As Kingsley commented, Jim was 'a great ruffian but he was certainly an educated man. Some said that he was a de-frocked Canadian priest, others that he was an expelled Canadian School-master. Others that he was both'.[12]

The weather closed in. By 18 October Miss Bird was snow-bound in her hut until the men came to see 'if she was alive' and dig her out.[13] She had gone to sleep under six blankets but awoke in the dark, with the sheet frozen to her lips, feeling the flimsy cabin being lifted by the snow-driving wind. Everything including the bed was covered with fine snow which drifted in through cracks in the walls, door and window. As soon as the storm abated she set off on a solitary expedition via Longmount and Denver, where she stayed with Mrs Evans, already established with her children for the winter. From Denver she and Birdie made a 'very cheerful ride' ending that day at Plum Creek. Later she travelled happily to Colorado Springs, 'riding for a week, seeing wonders and greatly enjoying the singular adventurousness' of her tour, although her days of some ten hours in the saddle predisposed her to sleep rather than letter writing in the evenings.

She stayed overnight in fine houses and simple huts, wherever she could find settlers to take her in. She learnt of the Colorado economy, of Texas or Spanish cattle roaming huge areas of land, of attempts to use the land for sheep farming. Birdie, by refusing to set foot on a poor make-shift bridge, may have saved her mistress from a serious fall. Horse and rider moved on – via the Great Gorge of the Manitou, Bergens Park, Twin Rock, Hall's Gulch, through superb country and occasional snowstorms – enjoying most of all the long solitary rides with Birdie until she returned to Denver; then after seeing some good friends – and quickly tiring of 'city' life – via Boulder back to Longmount and back into Estes Park. As she made the 'beautiful and incomparable ride up to the Park, snow was threatening and as it grew dark it was Ring, Mountain Jim's dog, who first acknowledged her. Mountain Jim then appeared and because both horse and rider were very tired 'they walked the remaining three miles' to the Evans house. Only two young men were left 'baching' it on their own but they greeted her warmly, and for the next month the three of them ran the household together. When the young men went elk hunting she cleaned out the cabin, working steadily from 9.30 until 2 p.m. and ending by making 'a batch of rolls and four pounds of sweet biscuits'.[14]

She had long excursions with Mr Nugent, who confided in her shocking tales of his life as a desperado, and reminded her how much he hated himself after one of his wild outings to Denver. She hurried to his aid when he was ill, suffering 'from an old arrow wound in the lung'.[15]

They were running short of food and with worsening weather she decided to try to get through alone to the plains. Mountain Jim found her lost in the snow storm and he 'stormed and scolded her' for trying to travel in such weather although in the end she insisted upon continuing. It was perilous travelling but she did pass Mr Evans going back up to Estes Park bearing funds for her and the necessary supplies. She returned to Estes Park once more.

Although Mr Evans had, in October, offered her $6 a week to remain at the ranch as cook throughout the winter, she knew how hard Mrs Evans had worked during the summer baking bread every day for the men, and so she said she would prefer to herd the cattle. Each time she left 'the Island Valley of Avillon' on a short excursion with her horse she knew she would go back. How could she tear herself away from its 'freedom and enchantments?'

By 13 December 1873 she had hardened her heart and resolved to leave. As an ernest of her determination she wrote a long letter to John Murray advising him of her intention to return and to write a book. She told him of her adventures in Hawaii and then explained her journeys in the Rockies. 'I have been travelling on horse-back', she wrote, 'through the interior ranges of these mountains for three months. It is a very wild and a most fascinating life. Sights and sounds are peculiar and the scenery in its monotonous grandeur is unique. In all my travels the only accident I have met with was being thrown from my horse in the Sierra Nevada owing to his being frightened by a grizzly bear and plunging violently. The air here is elixir – Colorado seems to be on its way to being one of the great health resorts of the world. I have succeeded in keeping in advance of its imperfect civilization confining myself to the regions which have not yet passed the log-cabin phase of existance. I shall carry this note home with me.'[16]

When she left, Mr Nugent escorted her to Namaqua. 'I shall see you again', he begged, 'I must see you again'. They made a pact agreeing that whichever of them died first would appear to the other. She made her way to New York and then returned home to Scotland.

Within six months Mountain Jim was dead, shot in a fight. Isabella wrote from Switzerland to Eliza Blackie as follows, 'My dearest one, I know you will be shocked to hear that Mr Nugent was killed five weeks ago – shot in a pass in the mountains in a fray – by Evans at whose house I boarded for three months. He lived I believe for some hours and I fancy that Henry Kingsley was with him in his late hours. I await the fuller particulars which will come.... I would have given anything to have been with him. "My poor dear erring Jim!" I often feel "would to God I had died for him". It is conceivably horrible, I heard the news the night before I left England and have not been able to sleep since. He never got my last letter, and perhaps even, no tender image of me, in dying, soothed his last hours. May He who for our sakes consented to be numbered with the transgressors have mercy on this sinful man's soul. I do not feel able to write on any other subject'.[17]

Isabella was right; it was Henry Kingsley who had attended the fatally injured Jim, although Kingsley's account of the wounding – and of the death three months later – differs markedly from that retold to Mrs Blackie. Kingsley wrote that, when he examined Jim after the shooting incident during which Griff Evans had shot him with his scatter gun loaded with 'Blue whistler' bullets, he found that there were 'five small bullet wounds about the head and face and one of the bullets had most certainly penetrated the cerebellum. He was prostrate of course and I must say as calm and plucky as any man I ever saw in trouble'. Dr Kingsley's employer Lord Dunraven insisted upon Jim being taken down to Denver Hospital, as there was a possibility of recovery 'where he lived on for three months with a split bullet in the brain', then one day 'Jim tumbled head over heels – there was a Post Mortem and there was the bullet'.[18]

Isabella believed that Jim Nugent had kept his promise to appear before her. She was in her room in the hotel at Interlaken when Jim, in his trappers' dress, stood there in the middle of her room. He bowed slowly to her twice and disappeared. Others had been told that 'she had been sitting at her window in an Interlaken Hotel reading' when Mountain Jim, again appeared, silently; he 'waved his hands twice' before disappearing.[19]

She related this incident, which she found deeply disturbing, to Dr Bishop, (her future husband), to Sir Thomas (her medical attendant) and Lady Grainger Stewart, to Dr Horton, to Mr Murray (her publisher) and his wife and to Anna Stoddart, her first biographer.

John Murray IV (1851–1928), in writing to Anna Stoddart in 1905, had his own interpretation of the Jim Nugent story, writing, 'The variations in the story of Mountain Jim interest me intensely – not so much on account of the story itself, but as throwing a light on Mrs Bishop's character. She was intentionally the most truthful of people, but she had that endowment which I have come across in several people, of seeing incidents in the superlative degree – if I may coin the expression. This involves a high colouring of the mental picture and the colouring used to vary in varying recitals. I have very often noticed this, and it is a quality which must be borne in mind, tho' not perhaps expressed, in describing her character'.[20]

The year 1873 was the emotional high point of Isabella Bird's life. Nothing – not even her relationship with her husband – was to affect her in quite the same way as the Jim Nugent affair. On Christmas Eve 1873, when she reached New York, on her way home from the Rockies, she wrote – for the first time in a whole year – to her closest woman friend Eliza Blackie. She excused her long silence saying that she had written 'in spirit every week for a year'; she then explained herself, 'I have been utterly unintellectual, absorbed in making bread, washing and riding. I was very audacious and without one atom of shyness – but I have cast off my swagger with my spurs and I am afraid you will see me very much like my old dull self'.[21] In this way Isabella abandoned her romantic persona and forced herself back onto the procrustean bed of convention.

But one problem remained, for she had promised John Murray a book on the 1873 adventures. He insisted on two books, one on Hawaii (published February 1875) and another on the Rocky Mountains. How was she to recount the months with Jim Nugent? The British reading public would swiftly sniff out 'impropriety' and yet Jim Nugent was so much the focus of much of the excitement in the Rockies that she could not in all honesty exclude him. There is little doubt that she agonised about this for some years. *A Lady's Life in the Rocky Mountains* was not published until October 1879 some six years after the romantic events of 1873 had taken place. By contrast *Unbeaten Tracks in Japan*, which resulted from her travels of 1878, appeared in late summer 1880.

She was extremely nervous when *A Lady's Life ...* appeared, writing to Mrs Blackie, 'The Critics have not scented out impropriety in the letters. Dr J. Brown [one of the reviewers] was prudish. Travellers are privileged to do the most improper things with perfect propriety – that is one charm of travelling'. The same letter continued, 'Don't let anybody think that I was in love with Mountain Jim, for I have never alas been in love but once, but the pity and yearning to save him that I felt have brought me a little of what I think may be an immeasurable distance the pity and yearning of the Father'.[22] That she was more than half in love with Jim Nugent seems abundantly clear. To play the evangelical card may have allowed a tactical retreat but it would hardly convince today.

The book was a roaring success 'the first edition went in a week'. *The Times* reviewer quickly fastened on Mountain Jim, 'the staunchest friend she made, a notorious villain who terrorised the country around his cabin and drank himself into fits of insanity from time to time to drown the memory of innumerable atrocities'. He also admired 'the unpretending way she treats us to a narrative of most thrilling adventure ... for Miss Bird armed only by her sex and helplessness lived among squatters, miners and desperadoes'.[23] Dean Stanley commented to John Murray that 'everybody asked everybody, have you read the *Rocky Mountains*?'[24]

Isabella Bird had in the *Rocky Mountains* allowed her romantic self to carry her along, once the book was safely out and her public excited, but not scandalised, she had again scored a notable triumph.

Notes

1. ILB, *A Lady's Life in the Rocky Mountains* (hereafter *Rocky Mountains*), introduction by Daniel J. Boorstin, University of Oklahoma Press, (Reprint 1969), p.3.
2. *Rocky Mountains*, p.5.
3. *Rocky Mountains*, p.8.
4. *Rocky Mountains*, pp.65-67.
5. *Rocky Mountains*, p.72.
6. *Rocky Mountains*, pp.114-115.
7. *Rocky Mountains*, p.85.
8. *Rocky Mountains*, p.110.
9. *Rocky Mountains*, pp.124-125.
10. *Rocky Mountains*, p.85.
11. *Rocky Mountains*, p.99.
12. G.H. Kingsley, *Sport and Travel*, p.179.
13. *Rocky Mountains*, p.133.
14. *Rocky Mountains*, p.208.
15. *Rocky Mountains*, p.215.
16. JM, ILB to JM, 13 December 1873.
17. JSB, ILB to Eliza B., 4 August 1874, Ms 2631, f.167.
18. G.H. Kingsley, *Sport and Travel*, pp.171-178.
19. AS, p.84.
20. JM, JM IV to Anna Stoddart, 10 August 1905, (my thanks to Virginia Murray for finding this).
21. JSB, ILB to Eliza B., New York, 24 December 1873, Ms 2631, f.83.
22. JSB, ILB to Eliza B., 23 November 1879, Ms 2633, f.143.
23. *The Times*, 21 November 1879.
24. JSB, ILB to Eliza B., 23 November 1879, Ms 2633, f.143.

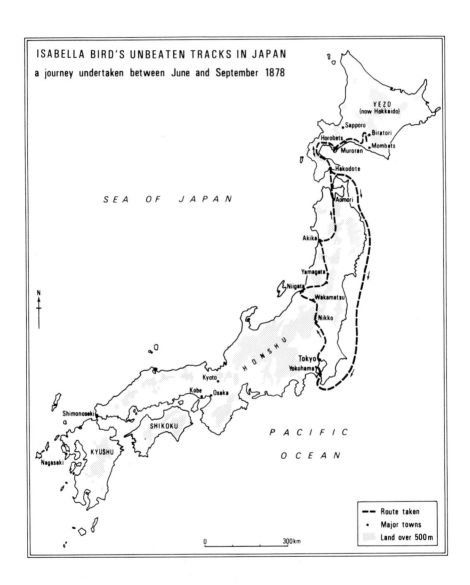

ISABELLA BIRD'S UNBEATEN TRACKS IN JAPAN
a journey undertaken between June and September 1878

YEZO
(now Hokkaido)

Sapporo
Biratori
Horobets
Mombets
Muroran

Hakodote

SEA OF JAPAN

Aomori

Akika

Yamagata
Niigata
Wakamatsu

Nikko

N

HONSHU

Tokyo
Yokohama

Kyoto

Kobe
Osaka

Shimonoseki

SHIKOKU

PACIFIC

OCEAN

KYUSHU

Nagasaki

Route taken
Major towns
Land over 500m

0   300km

56

6 *'Unbeaten Tracks in Japan'*

In the autumn of 1877 Isabella was in Edinburgh heavily engaged with the Grand Bazaar,[1] in aid of the National Memorial to David Livingstone[2] which was to take the form of a Medical Missionary College, but despite her busy days she felt emotionally drained and increasingly unwell. When Dr Grainger Stewart recommended a change of air she considered what to do and where to go. Her first thoughts were to ride in the Andes – where better to use her favourite Mexican saddle? But Mr Darwin[3] when applied to, 'was not encouraging' and so she turned her mind to 'the untravelled parts' of Japan.

In 1878 it was twenty years since the opening of the Japanese treaty ports, and ten years since the Restoration of the Emperor in 1868 which had ended the old isolationist regime.[4] It was always her ambition to search for the 'unbeaten' tracks in Japan, for despite some changes in Tokyo, Yokohama and Kobe, the old Japan survived unaffected elsewhere.

That she was successful in her ambition depended in part upon her contacts in Japan, for her social status at home enabled her to command no less than forty letters of introduction to her compatriots in Japan.[5] Through Lady Middleton and the Duke of Argyll she was provided with a recommendation to Sir Harry Parkes, the British minister,[6] and Lady Parkes – to whom her book was subsequently dedicated – who both welcomed her in May 1878 with kindness and enthusiasm, encouraged her in her ambition to explore unknown Japan and generously smoothed her way forward. After a brief stay at the Oriental Hotel in Yokohama she took the small train – on one of two railways then operating in Japan – to Tokyo where she settled at the British Legation from which, with the aid of experts like Ernest Satow, she organised her expedition.

Isabella had two principal concerns: the engagement of a servant interpreter and 'the Food Problem'. Her compatriots, (few of whom had ventured beyond the confines of the treaty ports), felt sufficiently expert to advise her that 'bread, butter, milk, meat, poultry, coffee, wine and beer are unobtainable'.[7] The foods which were available, 'rice, tea and eggs', with occasional fresh vegetables – that is Japanese food – was dismissed as 'fishy and vegetable abominations'. She decided on 'a modified rejection of all advice', carrying with her 'a small supply of Leibig's extract of meat, 4lbs of raisins, some chocolate both for eating and drinking and some brandy in case of need'. Otherwise she proposed to live 'off the country'.

It was Dr Hepburn, a Japanese specialist, who helped her to interview pro-spective guide/interpreters although most applicants were dismissed out of hand as being unable to speak English. Of those interviewed, one came so elegantly dressed in the western manner, with such an exquisitely starched shirt that he could barely bow adequately, another withdrew, horrified that there was to be no 'master'. A third might have been engaged but for the arrival of a fourth 'the most stupid looking Japanese I have seen'.[8]

A boy – Ito – who claimed impressive experience was apparently recom-mended by one of Dr Hepburn's servants. He was eighteen years old, was some 4ft 10ins tall and seemed 'strong-looking'; he had, he said, lived at the American Legation, been a clerk on the Osaka railway, and travelled through northern Japan with a Mr Maries, a botanical collector. He insisted that he could cook a little, write English and walk 25 miles a day. Although his references 'had been burned' recently in a fire at his father's home and she was nervous and suspicious of him, he was hired at a fee of $12 a month. In fact the partnership with Ito was to be a good one; he served her well.[9]

It has been suggested that Ito may have been the guide favoured by the Japanese authorities, that he was, as it were, 'planted' and that her incident free journey was dependent on Ito's ability to impress his authority, and that of the government he represented, on the local people as they travelled. In this context it is worth noting that she was fortunate, thanks to the personal representations of Sir Harry Parkes, to obtain a passport which allowed her to travel north from Tokyo, throughout Japan, and into Hokkaido, (then called Yezo), without specifying the route she was to follow. At this time foreigners were restricted to the confines of the treaty ports and, if permitted to travel more widely, were required to follow a previously agreed route. Was Sir Harry able to negotiate such a passport on condition that she took Ito as her guide?[10]

Apart from the Parkes', most westerners regarded the proposed expedition, of a woman alone into the interior of Japan, as a kind of madness. By June the weather was getting very hot and all who knew of her plans spoke discouragingly of the misfortunes – including the hordes of fleas – which would assail her. Lady Parkes rendered much practical assistance by providing two light baskets (as panniers for a horse), a travelling bed or stretcher, which 'being two and a half feet from the ground is supposed to be secure from fleas', a folding chair and an India rubber bath. These were handed over to Isabella as being necessary 'for a person in feeble health', and by 9 June 1878 her preparations were complete. Her kit weighed 110lbs and that of Ito's 90lbs, a weight which was 'as much as can be carried on a Japanese horse'.[11]

Her own outfit consisted of a short costume of dust-coloured striped tweed with strong laced boots topped by a Japanese hat, 'like an inverted bowl, of light bamboo plait, with a white cotton cover and a very light frame inside which fits round the brow and leaves a space of 1.5 inches for the free circulation of air'. Unfortunately there is no drawing of this useful headgear. She carried her money and her passport in a bag around her waist. The rest of her equipment consisted of her own Mexican saddle and bridle and a reasonable quantity of clothes, together with Mr Brunton's large map of Japan, Mr Satow's Anglo-Japanese dictionary and volumes of the *Transactions of the Asiatic Society of Japan.*[12]

She was also lucky in having at her disposal the nation-wide Land Transport Company (the *Riku-un-kaisha*), for which she had much praise, which in pre-industrial Japan arranged 'the transport of travellers and merchandise by pack-horses and coolies at certain fixed rates' and gave 'receipts in due form'. By using this Company she avoided having to negotiate with farmers directly for the hire of their beasts, and saved much irritation and expense.[13]

However for the initial stages of her journey she hired three *Kurumas*, the small light man-drawn carriages which were then a common form of conveyance. Her first stop was to be at Nikko, the great Japanese shrine, on the tourist route but on the threshold of unknown Japan, some 90 miles north of Tokyo. Traditionally *Kuruma* runners had trotted along virtually naked, embellished only with elaborate tattooing – usually designs of dragons or fish – but by 1878 the men were required by law to cover their nakedness with short blue cotton drawers and shirts. In northern Honshu Isabella's men – running naked for comfort – hastily scrambled into their clothes as the local police approached. The men wore traditional straw sandals which quickly wore out as they pounded along and so the frequent stops to fit new sandals, while irritating to the passenger, allowed a good rhythm to be developed and encouraged steady progress.

The first day's travel was to Kasukabe where they put up at a large *yadoya* or inn. Despite the fact that her room was 'up a step-ladder of dark polished wood' this first experience proved something of an ordeal because she felt vulnerable as invisible hands silently moved the *fusuma* or sliding paper screens allowing countless eyes to peer at the strange traveller.[14] In fact throughout her time in Japan she never escaped from or became inured to the curiosity of those who, never before having seen a foreigner, and a foreign woman at that, constantly crowded in on her in huge numbers. It was always the same, on the first approach to a town: as soon as she was spotted, the messenger would rush off and arouse the whole populace to view this astonishing sight. In Yusawa, Northern Honshu, a roof overburdened by the crowd which had scrambled up to see her, gave way. Fortunately the mass of bodies protected each other as they fell and no-one was seriously hurt. Although it was burdensome to be such an object of curiosity, Isabella quickly accepted that the attitude of the people reflected their isolation and wherever possible she stipulated that she rent a quiet room adjacent to or overlooking the garden.

The other hazard was the fleas, bed-bugs and mosquitoes which disrupted her nights and indeed sometimes affected her days. On this first night away she noted that the floors, covered with the traditional Japanese *tatami* 'as neat, refined and soft a covering for the floor as the finest Axminster carpet … unfortunately harbour myriads of fleas'.[15]

She also commented on the 'perfectly bewildering' noises which assailed her as 'On one side a man recited Buddhist prayers in a high key; on the other a girl was twanging a *samisen*, a species of guitar; the house was full of talking and splashing, drums and tom toms were beaten outside, there were street cries innumerable, and the whistling of the blind shampooers, and the resonant clap of the fire watchman who perambulates all Japanese villages and beats two pieces of wood together in token of his vigilance, were intolerable'.

Later, looking back with some sense of embarrassment at her early fears, she was to feel 'absolute security' from all dangers and rudeness in her travel of 1,200 miles through northern Japan. Yet this first night, when she feared for her safety, her money and her health, was a long one which she never forgot. After another night Isabella came to the approaches to Nikko and all her nervousness dropped away as she neared 'this Japanese paradise'. Nikko was approached by a grand tree-lined road, the *Reiheishi-kaido* shaded by fine ancient *cryptomerias*, 'this glorious avenue with its broad shade and dancing lights and rare glimpses of high mountains', had 'a deep solemnity'.

On 15 June she settled in Nikko at Kanaya's (still an hotel today), where the silence, after the previous din, was a wonderful release. She was enchanted. The house itself, an irregular two-storeyed pavilion, approached by a flight of steps, had a garden brilliant with peonies, iris and azaleas. The mountain behind provided a back-cloth and the stream which tumbled down bringing cold pure water made a magical feature for the garden.

She described her room carefully, writing, 'The whole front of my room is composed of *Shoji* which slide back during the day. The ceiling is of light wood crossed by bars of dark wood, and the posts which support it are of dark polished wood. The panels are of wrinkled sky-blue paper splashed with gold. At one end are two alcoves with floors of polished wood, called *tokonoma*. In one hangs a *Kakemono* or wall-picture, a painting of a blossoming branch of the cherry on white silk – a perfect piece of art which in itself fills the room with freshness and beauty …'[16]

The shrines of Nikko had been a holy place since the eighth century and they became even more so when in 1617 the founding father of the Tokugawa regime, Shogun Iyeyasu, deified under the name of the 'light of the east, great incarnation of Buddha', was buried there amid great

An avenue of magnificent *Cryptomeria* trees, which bordered the few great public roads then in Japan. The *Jinrikisha* was a small man-drawn carriage much used by foreigners.

ceremony. Miss Bird gave a vivid description of the tomb writing 'Within, wealth and art have created a fairyland of gold and colour; without, Nature at her stateliest, has surrounded the Shogun's tomb with a pomp of mournful splendour. A staircase of 240 stone steps leads to the top of the hill, where above and behind all the stateliness of the shrines raised in his honour, the dust of Iyeyasu sleeps in an unadorned but Cyclopean tomb of stone and bronze, surmounted by a bronze urn .... Slant rays of sun alone pass through them, no flower blooms or bird sings only silence and mournfulness surround the grave of the ablest and greatest man that Japan has produced'.[17]

Whatever discomforts she had suffered before she arrived at Nikko were as nothing compared with the hazards she was to face after she left. In a spirit of adventure she had decided to tackle 'an exquisitely picturesque but difficult route which seems almost as unknown to Japanese as to foreigners' up the course of the Kinugawa river, north over the mountains. She was aiming for the important town of Niigata (and a treaty port), on the Sea of Japan coast.

She left Nikko passing down the 'long, clean street' via the *In Memoriam* avenue, of wonderful cryptomerias, from which they turned off to the left, 'by a path like the bed of a brook which afterwards by a most atrocious trail wound about among the rough boulders of the [river] Daiya, which it crosses often on temporary bridges of timbers covered with branches and soil'.[18] Notwithstanding the slow pace and the discomfort, 'a mere flounder either among rocks or deep mud', the exhilaration of crossing the low spurs of the Nikkosan mountains and seeing nearby, 'brilliant azalea and syringa clusters', and in the distance great mountains, gave much pleasure as she basked in the June sunshine.

For this leg of the journey her local guide was a small woman who for three hours, leading two 'depressed-looking' mares, showed them the way to a mountain farmhouse. Isabella dismounted and took refuge on the veranda of the house, where she was regaled with weak tea and boiled barley, while the horses for the next stage were recovered from the mountains where they were grazing. When the horses did arrive there was trouble with the bridle upon which she intervened 'and put on the bridle myself'.[19]

The route she was following took her up the river valley. She was delighted as a steep rocky track brought them within the hearing of the Kinugawa, occasionally they caught 'magnificent glimpses' of the river 'turbulent and locked in by walls of porphyry, or widening and calming and spreading its aquamarine waters over slabs of pink and green rock – lighted fitfully by the sun or spanned by rainbows, or pausing to rest in deep shady pools but always beautiful'.[20] That the going was difficult is attested to by the fact that after eleven hours in the saddle they had covered eighteen miles.

Throughout her travels she was dependent upon Ito who despite his little vanities, was invaluable and learning all the time. He resisted her requests

A modern view of Kanaya's Hotel, Nikko, north of Tokyo.
Isabella Bird stayed in an earlier version of the hotel. The magnificent garden
grounds enchanted her, as they still do today.

that he interpret for her when she wanted to question the peasants to know more of their hard lives, preferring to put on the grand manner and introduce his lady to persons of consequence and authority. But every evening he came to her armed with his notebook to discuss the words which she had used that day the meaning and spelling of which were not clear to him. He challenged her about her use of some words, noting that 'You say, "Oh, what a beautiful day", while other Englishmen say "What a devilish fine day it is?" or "What the devil is that?"' He was advised that such talk was 'common' and so inappropriate.[21] As she noted shortly after they left Nikko, Ito already speaks 'better English than most interpreters' and she knew that she had been fortunate in hiring – as interpreter and courier but also cook, laundryman, general attendant – so keen and malleable a young man.

Ito was proud of his lady who followed his advice in matters of etiquette and behaviour and never disgraced him. Her high standards were exceptional, for she thought the Japanese to be 'so kind and courteous that it is truly brutal in foreigners not to be kind and courteous to them'. Ito related some awful stories of the bad behaviour of her compatriots as they proceeded 'roaring out *ohio* to every one on the road' and 'frightening the tea-house nymphs, kicking or slapping their coolies, stamping over white-mats in muddy boots, acting generally like ill-bred Satyrs, exciting an ill-concealed hatred in simple country districts and bringing themselves and their country into contempt and ridicule'.[22]

If she was embarrassed by these accounts of her fellow countrymen's boorishness, Ito was himself mortified by the poverty and degradation of the people through whose villages they were travelling. He insisted that people in Yokohama would not believe him if he described the squalor of the villages through which they passed. It was shameful he thought, that a foreigner should see such things.

One description of a village, among many, will allow the reader to experience a Japanese village as it was in 1878. As she wrote, 'A road, at this time a quagmire, intersected by a rapid stream, crossed in many places by planks, runs through the village. This stream is at once 'lavatory and drinking fountain'. People come back from their work sit on the planks, take off their muddy clothes and wring them out, and bathe their feet in the current. On either side are the dwellings, in front of which are much-decayed manure heaps, and the women were engaged in breaking them up and treading them into a pulp with their bare feet ... The younger children wear nothing but a string and an amulet. The persons, clothing and houses are alive with vermin and if the word squalor can be applied to independent and industrious people they were squalid'.[23]

The dirt and filth in which these Japanese peasants then lived distressed her. She knew that the absence of clean clothes, (garments when washed

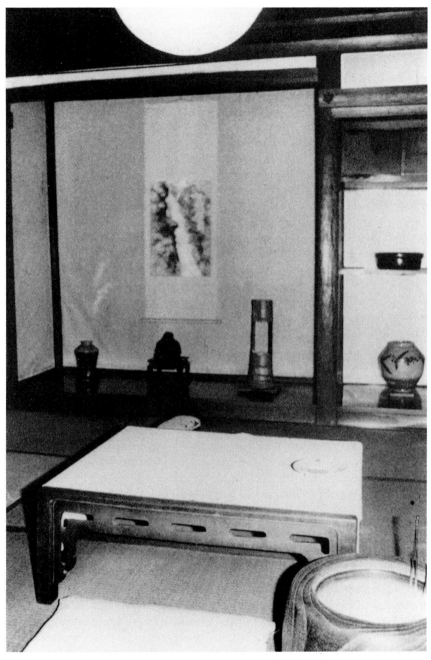

Isabella Bird's room, which overlooked the gardens, at the Kanaya Hotel, with *tatami* mats on the floor and traditional Japanese furnishings.

were dunked in the stream and rubbed with sand) with no proper washing of the person, as well as the constant attacks by myriads of biting insects, caused scratching leading to open wounds, ulcers and persistent skin infections. In the same village when she could not sleep because of the housemaster's son's cough she gave him 'a few drops of chlorodyne' which quieted him.

When in the morning she drew her screen she found virtually the whole population queuing up 'fathers and mothers holding naked children covered with skin disease or with scald-head or ringworm, daughters leading mothers nearly blind, men exhibiting painful sores, children blinking with eyes infected with sores, and nearly closed with opthalmia and all, sick and well, in truly "vile raiment" lamentably dirty and swarming with vermin, the sick asking for medicine ... Sadly I told them I did not understand their manifold "diseases and torments" and that if I did I had no stock of medicines ... To pacify them I made some ointment of animal fat and flowers of sulphur, extracted with some difficulty from some man's hoard, and told them how to apply it to some of the worst cases'.[24]

How such village people came to live in such conditions remained a puzzle to her. As she wrote, 'their industry is ceaseless, they have no Sabbaths, and only take a holiday when they have nothing to do. Their spade husbandry turns the country into one beautifully kept garden, in which one might look vainly for a weed. They are economical and thrifty and turn everything to useful account. They manured the ground heavily, understand the rotation of crops, and have little if anything to learn in the way of improved agricultural processes.' What she did not do was to enquire into the system of land tenure or the burdens of taxation under which these peasants lived. Even so conscientious a traveller could only hint at the ignorance and superstition which prevailed.

Her days varied with the quality of the horses and the difficulty of the terrain. Despite some depression when things went wrong she was usually excited by her journey and overawed by the beauty of the land. They journeyed north through the Sanno Pass, and skirted Wakamatsu;[25] was it Ito, the diplomat, who steered her away from this town, the last to oppose the new Meiji regime, where she might not have been well received?[26] From Tsugawa the river ran down to Niigata and Ito and his mistress were able to board a 'stoutly built boat' for the luxury of a river journey.

It was indeed astonishing to complete 45 miles in eight hours and arrive so speedily in Niigata. As she wrote, 'I enjoyed every hour of the day ... Pinnacles and needles of bare, flushed rock rose out of luxuriant vegetation. There were mountains connected by ridges no broader than a horse's back, others with great grey buttresses, deep chasms left by streams, temples with pagoda roofs on heights, sunny villages with deep thatched roofs hidden away among blossoming trees, and through rifts in the nearer ranges glimpses of snowy mountains'.[27]

In Niigata, she was welcomed to the Church Mission House by the Rev and Mrs Fyson[28] and in her book she did at this stage break off to insert a section on Missions in Japan. The missionaries, with a meagre 'success' rate, were the only elements of foreign life which persisted. Niigata, standing on the Shinano river which made its way to the sea through shifting sandbanks and shoals, had proved itself useless as a treaty port. The wet and misty climate in early July was intolerable; had she been there in winter, the damp cold and the heavy snow would have been even more discouraging. She was however delighted to find an excellent bookshop run by an articulate man who stocked Japanese translations of works by Huxley, Darwin and Herbert Spencer and who believed that, of these authors' books, the *Origin of Species* was the most popular. The bookseller also commented that there was by 1878 little demand for Japanese works such as a fine folio work on botany 'which gave root, stalk, leaf, flower and seed of every plant delineated ... drawn with the most painstaking botanical accuracy and admirable fidelity to colour'.[29]

Leaving Niigata and the relative comforts of a missionary home with some regret they moved north and inland where, although she revelled in 'the beauty and the wildness of that mountain route', walking over the difficult terrain and helping the *Kuruma* man up 'some of the steepest places' was exhausting. She was also suffering badly from insect stings and bites, which gave her fever and much swelling. Eventually she decided to consult a Japanese doctor, trained by the old methods who had none of the skills of modern science, who examined 'honourable hand' and 'honourable foot' with care and attention. He diagnosed a fever for which he prepared a 'vegetable febrifuge' and then compounded a lotion which he used to bathe the worst swelling. Over dinner to which she had invited him she enjoyed an interesting conversation with Dr Nosoki about the Chinese medicine which he practised, learning something of acupuncture as well as his views of the vegetable potions and lotions which he used. He had heard of chloroform but thought its use in childbirth must result in the death of either mother or child and therefore must be a device for keeping any population increase in check. As her arm improved following Dr Nosoki's treatment she was glad to give him credit.[30]

After more adventures, Ito and his mistress reached Hakodate on the southernmost tip of the island of Yezo (now Hokkaido) on 12 August 1878 having left Nikko on 24 June.

It was then something of a triumph to arrive safely in Hakodate, an important northern port of some 37,000 people, where she found much bustle and business. Although Hakodate was a treaty port and so open to outsiders, it was not so much the foreigners but the Japanese themselves who were active, for the new Meiji regime had determined to develop the northern

A view of a typical village street, similar to those which Isabella Bird knew. This is Hakone (c1870), showing the single storey thatched houses with a multi-purpose drain running in front of the houses.

island. Had Hokkaido remained empty it might have proved a temptation to the land-hungry Russians who had already expanded their empire across Siberia to the Pacific coast. In any case Japan herself needed room for expansion and proposed to encourage emigration from Honshu, the crowded main island, especially for unemployed ex-*Samurai* who were to be offered opportunities to establish themselves there as farmers. The government concentrated much money and resources into the Hokkaido development agency; there were many government officers and buildings in Hakodate, and inland, Sapporo was growing at a great rate.

But in Hokkaido there was a special objective – for which she subsequently became well-known – which was to visit the indigenous peoples of the island, 'the hairy Ainu' of whom, according to a 'rough census' of 1873, there were just over 12,000 remaining. On 17 August she left Hakodate and rode eighteen miles, enjoying the freedom given by the space in Hokkaido – she compared it in terms of remoteness to the Isle of Barra in Scotland – and both she and Ito revelled in the easy-going life. They took a boat from Mori, north of Hakodate across Volcano Bay to Harobets, just east of Muroran (see map) from where she travelled along the coast via Shiraoi to Sarafuto. Landing at Horobets from which she journeyed on to the Ainu village at Birafori, inland and upriver from Sarafuto, she was served and looked after by Ainu people.

At this time the Ainu appeared, to Europeans and to Japanese, as 'savages' and she tried without success to persuade Ito to be courteous, but he held stoutly to his view that 'they are just dogs not men'. They left Sarafuto with three horses and an Ainu guide and moved north into the forest. She found the track rough and irregular and something 'very gloomy about the solitude of this silent land, with its beast-haunted forests, its great patches of pasture ... and the narrow track ... on which the savages walk in their bare feet'.[31] When she finally arrived at Biratori, the largest Ainu settlement in the area, she found the village clean and the houses trim and in good repair. She was received graciously and with natural courtesy, welcomed to a large hut, with interior space of some 35ft x 25ft and a roof some 20ft high.

The visit to the Ainu was for the anthropologist the most important part of her Japanese trip. In the absence of their Chief she questioned them persistently about their lives and customs, watched the women preparing skins and making stews – the hot food simmering in a pot over the fire – saw the men returning from hunting and heard of their reverence for the Yezo Bear. She found that they did attempt to grow millet but that in the poor thin white sand which made up the soil in their forest clearings this usually failed, accordingly – although they were not nomads – after failing with millet crops in one place they would partly clear another small section and try to grow crops there.

She was not however welcomed by the Chief's mother who, sitting on the men's side of the fireplace 'splitting and knotting bark',[32] discouraged her family from confiding too much to the visitor. When the Chief returned it transpired that he had himself sent a message warning his people not to trust too much information to the foreign lady, for Ainu suspicion, living as they did some 100 miles east of Sapporo, was acute. They were terrified of the encroaching Japanese government who, like Ito, had little regard for these primitive peoples. As the agency *Kaitaikushi* was developing the potentialities of the area so the threat to Ainu culture and survival increased. Even Miss Bird, who was in general innocent of real Japanese intentions, was uneasy at their possible fate. Nowadays the splendid museum at Sapporo gives a vivid, and the only remaining, insight into the lives of the peoples of Hokkaido a century ago featuring not only the hard lives of the long-gone Ainu but also of those who replaced them, the new ex-*Samurai* settler-farmers.

Another major difficulty related to the Ainu's expectation that she could cure their illnesses. The most telling incident was that of a Chief's wife ill with fever to whom she administered some chlorodyne (which might have been expected to induce sleep and reduce pain) but the woman got worse and the unwilling 'doctor' feared they might blame her if the patient died. It was a worrying situation which was defused by giving the patient some brandy and some strong beef tea: to her relief after a remarkably long sleep the woman awakened 'decidedly better and quite sensible'.[33]

Miss Bird left the Ainu with regret – although sleeping in her clothes and having no water for washing had meant hardship.[34] It was a sad parting for clearly the Ainu who in their ceremonies presented their thanks to the sea, 'which nourishes us', and the forest 'which protects us' – as they said 'you are two mothers that nourish the same child' – were living a life of 'inherent barrenness', on borrowed time, and would soon disappear.

From time to time during her travels in Japan, and when with the Ainu, she does write of the fate of those not 'saved' by Christianity. Such comments are never obtrusive and reflect the 'missionary' pre-occupation of her readers at home rather than her own interests and do not in any way interfere with her careful unsentimental portrayal of primitive peoples.

She travelled back to base by land seeing more Ainu on the way and staying in the new Japanese settlements which would in course of time displace them. She hoped to slip back into Hakodate without being seen, dressed as she was in 'my old *betto's* hat, my torn green paper waterproof and my riding skirt and boots' which were 'not only splashed but caked with mud' but in the event she was spotted not only by Mr. Dening, the missionary, but also by the Consul and Dr Hepburn.[35] Despite her dishevelled state they must have marvelled at her courage and envied her her adventurousness.

In Hakodate on 14 September 1878 she parted from Ito 'with great regret';

was it not as she said wonderful 'that a lady with only a boy of 18 as interpreter can travel 700 miles through the interior not only without molestation but without any *attempt* at *extortion* as you will judge when I tell you that the whole hotel and travelling expenses of myself and servant, having either 2 or 3 horses always, only averaged 6/- shillings a day [30p]. The only annoyance has been the continual mobbing by polite crowds in regions where no European ... lady has been seen'.[36] Miss Bird had much for which to thank Ito, for her readers know of his constant support and encouragement while he performed sterling service steering her towards respectable *yadoyas* – the best resting places were often the brothels – and ensured that she suffered no embarrassment.

She wrote from Hakodate to warn Murray (her publisher) of her determination, despite previous disclaimers, to prepare a book on Japan. 'I have felt it impossible to write a book on this country but Sir Harry Parkes with characteristic impetuosity urges it by letter and promises all the aid which he and the staff at the Legation can possibly give. He says I have seen more of the interior of northern Japan than has been seen by any European, that no European has traversed a good part of the route and that I am giving months where other tourists have only given weeks ... I have no doubt I shall be concussed into making the attempt to write'.[37]

Isabella left Hakodate with Dr and Mrs Hepburn by sea in the *Hiogo Maru* on 14 September on a journey to Tokyo which should have taken 48 hours but which stretched to 72 as they encountered a typhoon. On reaching Yokohama they found much storm damage but she was soon re-established at the British legation where she stayed for about a month before leaving on the *Hiroshima Maru* (a large Japanese sidewheel, deck-over-deck, unrigged steamer). She stopped off at Kobe to re-establish links with Missionary friends, the Gulicks, from her Hawaiian days and then she explored Kyoto, Nara and the shrines at Ise as well as Lake Biwa and Osaka before sailing back to Tokyo.

She left Japan on this occasion by the S S *Volga*, her final entry read 'The snowy dome of Fujisan reddening in the sunrise rose above the violet woodlands of Mississippi Bay as we steamed out of Yokohama Harbour on the 19th [December 1878] and three days later I saw the last of Japan – a rugged coast, lashed by a wintry sea'.[38]

Notes

1. See Chapter 3: the autumn of 1877 was an anxious time, for John Bishop's proposal of marriage to Isabella had been shelved because of the distress caused to Henrietta (see Chapter 8 below).

2. David Livingstone (1813-1873), Scottish medical missionary and explorer who spent many years in Southern and Central Africa.

3. Charles Darwin (1809-1882) had travelled as naturalist in 1831 in HMS *Beagle* to South America and the Pacific. Subsequently his writing, particularly his book *The*

Origin of the Species by means of Natural Selection (1859) caused uproar in the scientific and religious world.

4. W.G. Beasley, *The Meiji Restoration*, 1963.

5. AS, p.100.

6. Sir Harry and Lady Parkes became personal friends of ILB. Sadly Lady Parkes died in Edinburgh in the Spring of 1880 (AS, p.114). Later after Sir Harry's death there was some talk about ILB writing his Life (JM, ILB to JM, 18 June 1887) but it came to nothing. See S. Lane Poole and F.V. Dickens, *The Life of Sir Harry Parkes* (1894).

7. ILB, *Unbeaten Tracks in Japan* (hereafter *Japan*), Newnes edition, 1900, pp.35-36.

8. *Japan*, p.34.

9. *Japan*, pp.34-35.

10. But see *Japan*, p.276 where ILB discovered that Ito had left his other employer, at $7 a month, because ILB was offering $12 a month.

11. *Japan*, p.36.

12. J.A. Lindo, 'Description of a trip to Niigata along the Shinshiu road and back by the Mikuni Pass', *TASJ*, Vol.111, part 1, (14 October 1874 - 23 December 1874), pp.48-80.

13. *Japan*, p.102.

14. *Japan*, p.63.

15. *Japan*, p.63.

16. *Japan*, pp.72-73.

17. *Japan*, p.78.

18. *Japan*, p.103.

19. *Japan*, p.104.

20. *Japan*, p.106.

21. *Japan*, pp.108, 209 and 210.

22. *Japan*, p.109.

23. *Japan*, p.108.

24. *Japan*, pp.114-115.

25. It was at Aizu Wakamatsu (in Fukushima Prefecture) where most of the city burned when the last stand was made in an attempt to save the Tokugawa Shogunate.

26. J. Blewitt, 'Beaten Tracks in Japan', *Bulletin of the Japan Society, London*, (1980), p.13.

27. *Japan*, pp.132-133.

28. Rev. P.K. Fyson, MA, represented the English Church Missionary Society, see Niigata Directory in *The Japan Directory*, 1878, p.22.

29. *Japan*, p.153.

30. *Japan*, p.185.

31. ILB gives a detailed account of the Ainu peoples, *Japan*, pp.287-362.

32. *Japan*, p.299.

33. *Japan*, pp.307-308.

34. *Japan*, p.334.

35. *Japan*, p.362.

36. JM, ILB to JM from Hakodate, 11 August 1878.

37. JM, ILB to JM, 11 August 1878.

38. *Japan*, p.463.

7 *The Golden Chersonese*

It was Henrietta Bird, the Classics student, who suggested the title *The Golden Chersonese*[1] – had not Ptolemy referred to *Aurea Chersonesus* and Milton translated this as the 'Golden Chersonese' – for the book which was written after her sister's brief excursion into Malaya early in 1879. This book resulted from an unplanned five week visit to Malaya,[2] which Isabella Bird made after her visit to Japan, at the invitation of British officials there.

It was not a destination which she herself had chosen, and while in Malaya she stayed comfortably in government officials' bungalows, bearing no responsibility for her travel arrangements. No doubt her company was a bonus to Britons marooned in such remote territory and they were pleased to offer hospitality to such a traveller. Because she was so brief a time in Malaya – and fully conscious of her own ignorance – she felt it necessary to educate herself and her readers regarding the Straits Settlements. As a result the book contains chapters on the facts and figures then applicable to the individual Straits Settlements and the author notes that the Malay Peninsula 'is probably destined to afford increasing employment to British capital.' No doubt for present day scholars her accounts may seem inadequate but historically they are of interest giving a useful contemporary account of how one intelligent sympathetic outsider saw Malaya in 1879.

The western Malay States, including Malacca, Penang and Singapore, with which Britain was involved at this time, had been subject to frequent civil war, attacks from Siam and endemic piracy; in 1867 the Settlements of Malaya had been created and the administration transferred to the British Colonial Office. Following the opening of the Suez Canal (1869), giving a quick direct route to the Far East, the British government expected an increase in trade and so accepted the need to play a more active role, although it was not until 1896 that the Federation, with its capital in Kuala Lumpur, was established. In 1879 at the time of her visit the British were busy establishing themselves and it was with the British Residents in Malacca, Sungei Ujong, Selangor, and Perak that she was involved. British interest in Malaya had sharpened not only because of the increasing traffic to the Far East but also because of the discovery of important tin deposits.

It was her good fortune to be the guest of Hugh Low,[3] who had gone to the East as a young botanist and had settled there, becoming one of the more

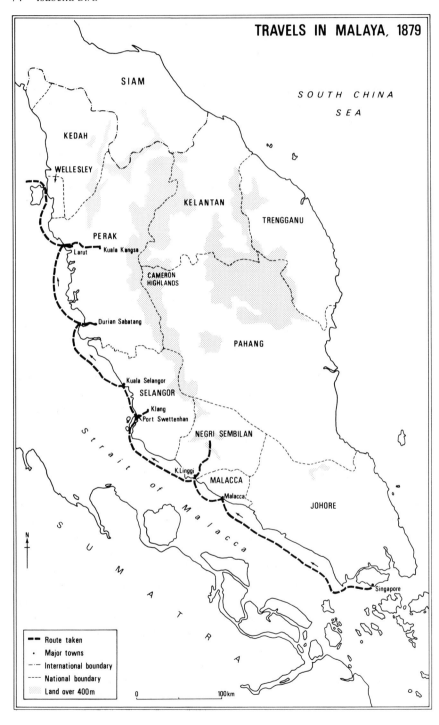

TRAVELS IN MALAYA, 1879

SOUTH CHINA
SEA

SIAM

KEDAH

WELLESLEY

KELANTAN

TRENGGANU

PERAK

Larut   Kuala Kangsa

CAMERON
HIGHLANDS

Durian Sabatang

PAHANG

Kuala Selangor

SELANGOR

Klang
Port Swettenhan

NEGRI SEMBILAN

K.Linggi

MALACCA

Malacca

JOHORE

S t r a i t   o f   M a l a c c a

S U M A T R A

N

Singapore

— — Route taken
•   Major towns
—·— International boundary
— — National boundary
▒   Land over 400m

0   100km

unusual of the British officials in Malaya. Shortly before Isabella's visit he had been appointed to the Residency of the then unknown jungle state of the Sultan of Perak. In appointing Residents the British were attempting to create conditions peaceful enough to stimulate trade, and at the same time introduce a system of 'Dual Control' which would retain 'Malay customs' and not interfere with local land holding, leaving most power in the hands of native rulers. At the very least they brought peace and stability to areas hitherto at the mercy of unruly elements, although Low was virtually alone in this huge area; the previous Resident had been murdered by the Malays in 1874. But Low who spoke excellent Malay, neither patronised nor despised the native peoples and was a keen exponent of the 'Residential System' which shaped the modern administration of Malaya.[4] She herself, who abhorred the high-handed behaviour which sometimes characterised the colonial administrator, was fortunate in being able to enjoy his hospitality. Of this, more later.

Miss Bird had left Japan on Christmas Eve 1878 arriving at Hong Kong (via SS *Volga*) some days later. After a brief interlude in Hong Kong, where she stayed with Bishop and Mrs Burden, she reached Canton on 1 January 1879. Despite the fact that she found the city 'intoxicating from its picturesqueness, colour, novelty and movement: "See Canton and die" I would almost say', she returned promptly to Hong Kong in order to catch the steamer bound for Europe and home.

The day before she left Hong Kong she had lunched with [acting] Chief Justice Snowden and he urged her to stop over at the Straits Settlements, lent her Newbold's *Malacca* to read and gave her introductory letters to the Governor and the Colonial Secretary at Singapore, where she arrived on 19 January 1879.

Because she had sailed from Hong Kong in the SS *Sindh*, a vessel belonging to the French *Messageries Maritimes* line, there was a twenty-four hour stay in Saigon in French Cochin China which she decided to visit.

In typical Birdian style she rejected a guide and alone 'walked about Saigon, saw its streets, cafés, fruit markets, bazaars, barracks, a botanic or acclimatisation garden, of which tigers were the chief feature'.[5] She then hired a *gharrie* (small man-pulled carriage) to drive out far beyond the town where she explored 'a labyrinth of lanes each with a high hedge of cactus'. She found the village of Choquan, 'every house of which was hidden by high walls of a most malevolent and obnoxious cactus, so as to ensure absolute privacy to its proprietors ... By dint of much peeping, and many pricks which have since inflamed, I saw that the poorer houses were built of unplaned planks or split bamboo, thatched with palm leaves, with deep verandahs, furnished with broad matted benches with curious, round bamboo pillows'.[6] While she was peering, a man came out of one house and his accompanying dogs attacked her, but the owner called off the dogs and as he was carrying a coconut she signed to him that she was thirsty. He gave her the coconut milk to drink and invited her in: 'This was rare luck' she exclaimed. Her extraordinary curiosity could always be relied upon. Throughout this long and vivid description of Saigon and its environs the temperature was well above 90°F.

Although she was nervous as to how this 'unexpected and hastily-planned expedition' to Malaya[7] would turn out, she was warmly greeted in Singapore by the Colonial Secretary and his wife who accommodated her in the official lodge from which she could walk and drive around Singapore. She was fascinated by what she saw, writing 'The city is ablaze with colour and motley with costume. The ruling race does not show to advantage. A pale skinned man or woman costumed in our ugly, graceless clothes reminds one not pleasingly ... of our dim pale islands. Every Oriental costume from the Levant to China floats through the streets – robes of silk, satin, brocade, and white muslin, emphasized by the glitter of "barbaric gold", and Parsees in spotless white; Jews and Arabs in dark rich silks; Klings in Turkey red and white; Bombay merchants in great white turbans, full trousers and draperies, all white, with crimson silk girdles; Malays in red *sarongs*; Sikhs in pure white Madras muslin, their great height rendered nearly colossal by the classic arrangements of their draperies; and Chinamen of all classes, from the coolie in his blue or brown cotton, to the wealthy merchant in his frothy silk crepe and rich brocade, make up an irresistibly fascinating medley'.[8]

Within a couple of days she was off in the *Rainbow*, a Chinese-owned boat, to the care of whose Welsh engineer she had been entrusted, en route for Malacca, where she was welcomed to the *Stadthaus* in the Governor's absence by his Chaplain. The presence of a continuous stream of native servants of different races in her room in Malacca came as a surprise. The Chinese attendant who looked after her clothes was particularly persistent even as she said 'Go', with much emphasis. 'I never get rid of him, and have to glide from my *Loloku* into my gown with a most unwilling dexterity'.

She was enchanted by Malacca, which had been colonised by the Portuguese in the sixteenth century and later taken over by the Dutch, before the advent of the British and so demonstrated by its people and its customs a mixed cultural heritage. She believed that the Malays appreciated the British because of their commitment to indirect rule, even so she wondered whether 'the Malays love us', for she doubted 'whether the *entente cordiale* between any of the dark-skinned Oriental races and ourselves is more than skin deep'.[9]

From Malacca an expedition was organised some 60 miles up the Linggi river into Sungei Ujong, a small protectorate which, with a Captain Murray as its Resident, was of interest to the British because of its tin mining. Murray, as Isabella noted, was 'very blunt, very undignified, never happy out of the wilds [but] thoroughly well disposed to the Chinese and Malays'. Although he had not succeeded in his efforts to speak the language, he was confident of his understanding of 'his' people and certainly convinced his guest of his effectiveness.[10]

From Sungei Ujong she moved north to the much larger state of Selangor – another tin-rich state. Later from her base in Larat (Perak) she was escorted around a tin mine by the Chinese owner. The mine was she reported 'like a large quarry with a number of small excavations which fill with water and are pumped by most ingenious Chinese pumps worked by an endless chain but there are two powerful steam pumps at work also. About four hundred lean, leathery-looking men were working, swarming up out of the holes like ants in double columns, each man carrying a small bamboo tray holding about three pounds of stanniferous earth which is deposited in a sluice, and a great rush of water washes away the sand, leaving the tin behind looking like "giant" blasting powder ... The tin is smelted during the night in a very rude furnace with most ingenious Chinese bellows, is then run into moulds made of sand, and turned out as slabs weighing 66lbs each. The export duty on tin is the chief source of revenue'.[11] She later took up residence at Klang and made a small excursion up river from the coast to Langat, to deliver a Mr Hawley to his post as a revenue collector. Although she had been favourably impressed by Mr Hawley's intelligence and energy as well as his amiability, she found it shocking to be leaving him alone 'in a malarious swamp'. There is a vivid account of the evils of being constantly plagued by mosquitoes, for she herself in spite of 'all her precautions ... am dreadfully bitten on my ankles, feet and arms, which are so swollen that I can hardly draw on my sleeves, and for two days stockings have been an impossibility and I have had to sew up my feet daily in linen'.

As she journeyed north in the care of other British colonial officials, she was struck not only by the health hazards presented by the climate but also by the danger which these people faced. At the Dindings, islands off the coast of Perak, they called at the site of the murder of the local British Resident apparently by a Chinese gang. In general she seems to have approved of most of the British administrators with whom she came in touch but she was not herself always approved. Major Paul Swinburne, 'a tall, slender, aristocratic looking man', 'who scarcely looks severable from the door-steps of a Pall Mall club', greeted her saying 'the sooner you go away again the better; there's nothing to see, nothing to do, and nothing to learn'.[12] She was especially interested in this unwelcoming man although his response to her presence was atypical.

By the middle of February 1879 she had made a difficult journey and was inland at Kwala Kangsa at the British Residency. Fortunately for this muddy route she was wearing her 'mountain dress'; as she said 'the identical mud-coloured tweed in which I waded through the mud of Northern Japan'. At another stage of the journey she was carried by elephant – not one resplendent with howdah and cloth of gold trappings – but one more prosaically decked with raw hide and two shallow baskets, held by rattan ropes. She had 'dropped' into one basket 'from the porch' and a young Malayan balanced her in the other. The elephant journey was eventful, for when the driver abandoned his post she was subjected to much anxiety and not a little danger as the elephant dashed off into the jungle for food prior to diving into a mud hole. As she was squirted all over with muddy water – and the young Malayan ran off – she ended up clinging to her basket which slipped badly to the side. She extricated herself and turned the adventure to good advantage, going to a nearby house where she 'hinted' that she would like a coconut. The house owner collected his ape or monkey and sent him up the coconut palm to gather one for the lady, who found the milk refreshing. She found the elephant and driver eventually but not before she had discovered that her boots 'were filled with blood'. She 'found five small brown leeches, beautifully striped with yellow' firmly attached to her ankles.[13] The leeches released their hold only when the elephant driver 'made some tobacco juice and squirted it' over them. But the elephant declined to carry her further and in the end she walked the last few miles and was glad to reach the residence at Kwala Kangsa.

Although the staff were there to greet her there was no sign of Hugh Low, the Resident. When she appeared for dinner, bathed but re-dressed in the mud-splashed tweed – her valise had not arrived – she was surprised and dismayed to find the table beautifully set with three places. She was requested to sit. No other human guests appeared but the staff brought in two apes, one large, one small which were established at the two other places and the meal proceeded. The animals were provided with curry, chutney, pineapple, eggs and bananas on porcelain plates. And so was the guest.

When the apes quarrelled, the larger Mahmoud attacked the smaller Eblis but she intervened and rescued the smaller animal. In due course after several days the Resident returned and to her chagrin Mahmoud and Eblis abandoned her utterly as they threw themselves in welcome upon their master. The friendly relationship with Hugh Low is emphasised by her host's remarking when the time came for her to leave that he had become accustomed to her presence. Hugh Low – by the nature of his job in an isolated place, a lonely man – added 'that you never speak at the wrong time. When men are visiting me, they never know when to be quiet, but bother one in the middle of business'.[14]

From her base at Kwala Kangsa she had an opportunity to go with another visitor on a 'shooting excursion' to a lotus lake 'at some distance'.[15] She much enjoyed this outing although less hardened travellers might have found it a gruelling experience. They crossed the Perak river and then walked before turning into the jungle where they waded 'through a stream which was up to my knees as we went, and up to my waist as we returned'. They went on through 'a doleful swamp' until they reached a 'smothered, reedy, ditch-like stream', in which there was an old dugout canoe half full of water. By careful balancing they managed to keep the canoe afloat and proceeded through swamp and lotus lake – 'covered with thousands of noble leaves and rose-pink blossoms' – until Captain Walker, the organiser of the trip, could climb into a low tree from which he could shoot teal and widgeon, while Isabella and the canoe proceeded ahead to force the birds to fly. Isabella found the swamp, the rising mist, and the failing daylight somewhat depressing as she had visions of King Arthur and would scarcely have been surprised had she seen 'the three fair queens in robes of samite mystic, wonderful'.[16] They returned to pick up Captain Walker but the branch on which he had been perched broke under him. Wet and sodden they worked their way back but it was all very difficult in the dark. When they finally reached the Residency, Hugh Low and his staff were out searching for them and Low was very annoyed that the party had been led on such a wild goose chase.

During the course of her stay she had a wonderful adventure in the jungle riding the Royal Elephant. Although in general, as she reported, in the forest 'the twilight was green and dim ... now and then there were openings where trees had fallen and the glorious tropical sunshine streamed in on gaudy blossoms of huge trees, and on pure white orchids and canary-coloured clusters borne by linas; on sun-birds iridescent and gorgeous in the sunlight, and on butterflies some all golden others amber and black, and amber and blue, some with velvety bands of violet and green, others altogether velvety black with spots of vermilion or emerald-green ... while sometimes a shoal of turquoise-blue or wholly canary-coloured sprites fluttered in the sunbeams; the flash of sun-birds and the flutter of butterflies giving an idea of the joy...'[17]

She was intrigued throughout this trip by the Malays, noting that their houses or *kampongs*, with simple mosques nearby, were usually built near the rivers. Foreigners were often embarrassed by the nakedness of native peoples but she was made of sterner stuff remarking that 'This *negligée* dress is merely a matter of custom and climate, for these people are no more savages than we are'. She learnt as much as she could of the Malays as Muslims, watched a Muslim funeral 'from a respectful distance', and decided it was wiser not to go into a mosque which were conical buildings usually raised on wooden pillars without minarets. The drum or gong used to call the faithful to prayer was usually housed separately in a small adjacent building. The mosque was served by one or two officials chiefly the 'Imaun' who 'performs the sacred rites of Islam'.[18]

One of the subjects on which she expressed unfavourable opinions to the Muslims was that of slavery, which she linked with 'debt slavery'. It was an awkward matter for the British keen to avoid interfering in 'Malay customs' and yet strongly opposed to slavery. The custom of holding as slaves those who were in debt led to many injustices; clearly opinions varied, some believing it to be 'a mild form of domestic servitude' others referring to 'evils and cruelties'.[19]

From Perak she rode 'on a capital pony' to Taipeng travelling with an un-armed Malay orderly, the royal elephant carrying her small luggage. As she wrote 'I met with no adventures on the journey. I had a delightful canter of several miles before the sun was above the tree-tops'.

There were also more ominous notes. The Resident at Taipeng, a Mr Maxwell, had spoken to a man who was travelling with his wife, enclosed in a *gharrie* with the husband walking by the side. The following night the woman woke with a scream and was soon in a trance and her husband knew that a devil had entered her. The wise man or sorcerer was called in and he spoke to the evil spirit asking, 'How did you come?' 'With the *tuan*, Mr Maxwell' answered the Spirit. 'How did you come from him.', the wise man asked. 'On the tail of his gray horse' came the answer. 'Where from?' 'From Changat-Jering'. This was known to be the home of many evil spirits. Fortunately the wise man was able to drive out the devil by burning strong smelling drugs under her nose. She felt that the Malays were very susceptible to belief in 'devils, familiars, omens, ghosts, sorceries and witchcrafts'.[20]

She enjoyed discussing Malay culture with Mr Maxwell, in which he was particularly interested, and in the case of proverbs they discovered that there were many which expressed sentiments similar to those she knew. She liked the reference to the person who is always chattering: 'The tortoise produces a myriad eggs and no one knows it; the hen lays one and tells the whole world'; or 'Freed from the mouth of the tiger to fall into the tiger's jaws'; or 'When the junk is wrecked the shark gets his fill'.[21] With Mr Maxwell she travelled to the coast again at Penang. She was struck by the 'dolefulness' of the mangrove swamp stretching for hundreds of miles along the coast: 'nothing but swamp and slime, loaded with rank and useless vegetation ... teeming with alligators, serpents and other vengeful creatures'.

On 25 February 1879 she sailed from Penang in SS *Malwa* 'and have ex-changed the sparkling calms of the Malacca Straits for the indolent roll of the Bay of Bengal. The steamer's head points north-west. In the far distance the hills of the Peninsula lie like mists upon a reddening sky. My tropic dream is fading, and the "Golden Chersonese" is already a memory'.[22]

The book on the Malayan adventure was not to be published until 1883. In the interval her sister Henrietta had died and she had herself married, becom-ing Mrs Bishop. *The Golden Chersonese* was reviewed, amongst a group of 'books for tourists', in *The Times* in July. The reviewer was pleased to know more of the Malaccan States and clearly relied on 'this most delightful of *raconteurs* for some adventures', comparing her favourably with Miss Gordon Cumming who is 'neither so daring nor so eccentric as Miss Bird'. There was a certain rivalry between these two travelling ladies although it seems likely that Miss Bird might enjoy being called 'daring' but she would hardly wish to be called 'eccentric'.[23]

Isabella's light-hearted account of her five week adventures in 1879 in Malaya, 'a beautiful and little travelled region', together with the compliments which she paid to those officials who looked after her, and the aura surrounding the title of her book, provoked from one reader a remarkable response. Emily Innes in *The Chersonese with the Gilding Off* (1885) wrote an account of life as she had seen it at first hand as wife of James Innes, one of the officials at Selangor. It tells a very different story.

When Isabella travelled from Penang to Kertang she commented that James Innes, a fellow passenger who served in Selangor from 1876–1882, seemed 'in dejected spirits as if the swamps of Durian Sabatang had been too much for him'.[24] Furthermore (in her letter to Henrietta) she noted that Innes seemed 'a man with a feeble, despairing manner and vague unfocussed eyes – I found Mr Innes a dreary and unintelligent companion'.[25]

Emily Innes, who had tried to learn the language and had shown herself courageous and resourceful, knew the loneliness of remote postings, and the dangers which were frequently faced. Unfortunately she was an embittered woman writing out of disappointment, for her husband was to resign from the colonial service in 1882 because of the corruption and nepotism which he believed he had encountered. She disapproved of Hugh Low who lived comfortably and was 'monarch of all he surveyed, he was better off and in a higher position than he could hope to enjoy in England'.[26]

Both Isabella Bird and Mrs Innes were received by the Sultan in his *balai* at Kuala Langat, although from the two descriptions the reader could not guess that both ladies were commenting on the same hall. For the exuberant Isabella 'the balcony of the audience-hall which has a handsome balustrade, was full of Malay followers in bright reds and cool white. It was all beautiful, and the palms rustled in the soft air, and bright birds and butterflies flew overhead, rejoicing in mere existence'. She also refers to the floor of the *balai* which was 'covered with fine matting nearly concealed by handsome Persian rugs'.[27] Mrs Innes remarks that they were received 'in a bare wooden shed, which was called a balai or hall of audience. It was a square building, with a tiled roof, a wooden floor, and a low wooden railing; there was no furniture in it but a few well worn mats and a European chair or two in very bad repair'.[28]

Emily and James Innes had read Isabella Bird's book, Mrs Innes noting that 'we felt as if we had known personally every creature, every thing and almost every mosquito she mentioned'.[29] But as Emily Innes commented, 'Miss Bird was a celebrated person and wherever she went was well introduced to the highest officials in the land; Government vessels were placed at her disposal, and Government officers did their best to make themselves agreeable, knowing that she wielded in her right hand a little instrument which might chastise or reward them as they deserved of her'. Mrs Innes had a point.

The author of *The Chersonese with the Gilding Off* considered that 'it may seem curious that notwithstanding the brilliancy and attractiveness of her descriptions, and the dullness and gloom of mine, I can honestly say that her account is perfectly and literally true. So is mine. The explanation is that she and I saw the Malayan country under totally different circumstances'.[30]

Fortunately for Isabella, the reviewer of Mrs Innes' book[31] in *The Times* did not connect *The Golden Chersonese* with Mrs Innes' book 'with the Gilding Off'. He concentrated instead on Mr Innes' 'hard treatment' at the hands of the colonial administration as well as the efforts of the various races including Malays, Chinese and Indians as they tried to adapt to the ever encroaching, ever powerful western world.

Isabella was always anxious about the Malayan book. She did write to John Murray nervously, '... it would be a very great convenience to me if I could see the papers on the protected Malay States in advance of publication [by John Murray]. In order to make my letters intelligible I am putting *a very short* chapter of notes on each state and it is desirable to make these as accurate as possible. I knew *nothing* about these states before I visited them and most people must be as ignorant'.[32]

No letter of Isabella's has been found in which she mentioned Emily Innes' book. But, sensitive as she was to public censure, she must have been mortified by Emily Innes' initiative. She herself had never written a book before on so slight an acquaintance with a country – through which she herself had not slogged and suffered over every inch of the ground – and she never did again.

Notes

1. ILB, *The Golden Chersonese and the way thither*, introduction by Wang Gungwu, Kuala Lumpur, 1967. 'Down to the Golden Chersonese', John Milton, *Paradise Lost, Book XI*.
2. For more general works see R. Allen, *Malaysia, Prospect and Retrospect: Impact and Aftermath of Colonial Rule*, (1968); R. McKie, *Emergence of Malaysia*, (1973), R.S. Milne and K.J. Ratnam, *Malaysia, new States in a new Nation*, (1973).
3. See J. Pope-Hennessy, *Verandah*, (1964), for insights into the career and character of Hugh Low.
4. See J.M. Gullick, 'Isabella Bird's visit to Malaya', *Journal of the Malaysian Branch of the Royal Asiatic Society*, hereafter *JMBRAS*, Vol.Lii, part 1, 1979, p.114.
5. *The Golden Chersonese*, (1967), p.96.
6. *The Golden Chersonese*, p.97.
7. *The Golden Chersonese*, p.108.
8. *The Golden Chersonese*, p.114.
9. *The Golden Chersonese*, Letter X, pp.142-153.
10. *The Golden Chersonese*, p.186.

11. *The Golden Chersonese*, p.289.
12. *The Golden Chersonese*, p.285.
13. *The Golden Chersonese*, p.301.
14. *The Golden Chersonese*, p.348.
15. *The Golden Chersonese*, p.340.
16. *The Golden Chersonese*, p.344.
17. *The Golden Chersonese*, pp.310-311.
18. *The Golden Chersonese*, p.314.
19. *The Golden Chersonese*, p.25.
20. *The Golden Chersonese*, p.353.
21. *The Golden Chersonese*, p.363.
22. *The Golden Chersonese*, p.368.
23. *The Times*, 21 July 1883, p.5, col.6. There are some papers of Constance Fredereka Gordon Cumming in the Gordon Cumming of Altyre and Gordonstoun papers, NLS.
24. *The Golden Chersonese*, p.276.
25. J.M. Gullick, *JMBRAS*, p.276.
26. E. Innes, *... with the Gilding off*, Vol.II, V, pp.133-4.
27. *The Golden Chersonese*, p.231 and J.M. Gullick, *JMBRAS*, Vol.LV, part II, 1982, p.102.
28. E. Innes, *... with the Gilding off*, Vol.I, p.91 and J.M. Gullick, 'Emily Innes, 1843-1927', *JMBRAS*, Vol.LV, part II, 1982, p.102.
29. E. Innes, *... with the Gilding off*, Vol.II, p.242.
30. E. Innes, *... with the Gilding off*, Vol.II, p.242.
31. *The Times*, 29 January 1886.
32. JM, ILB to JM, 12 Walker Street, Edinburgh, 12 December 1882.

PART III

1881–1904
FULFILMENT?

8   *Dr John Bishop's wife, widow*

On 8 March 1881, ten months after the death of Henrietta, her only sister –
and within six months of her fiftieth birthday – Isabella Lucy Bird became
the wife of Dr John Bishop who was some ten years her junior. The ceremony took place at St Lawrence Church, Barton on the Moor, Warwickshire,
close by the home of her cousin Major Wilberforce Bird,[1] who gave her
away in the presence of a few of her relatives. It was more of a wake than a
celebration, for the bride wore deepest mourning – a dress of braided black
serge with jacket and black hat relieved only by a 'gold necklet' sent by Mr
and Mrs John Murray.[2]

The day before her wedding Isabella was 'quite laid up with her spine'.
During her enforced idleness she wrote to thank Eliza Blackie, her 'dearly
loved and faithful friend' for 'all her loving letters which help to sustain my
failing heart'. She was exceedingly nervous but was pleased to report that,
'The dear soul arrived early on Saturday and so direct, gentle, unselfish and
well-dressed. I never saw him appear to so much advantage and my critical
family are all quite delighted with him!' The letter continued, 'Our marriage
is to be at 10.30 tomorrow, my cousin Mr Verney officiating. Major Bird
will give me away and there will be present my aunt, Mrs Merttins Bird and
her daughters, Mrs Wilberforce Bird, my hostess and my cousins, India Bird,
Bethie Verney and Professor Lawson ... the Church is in the park, one of the
smallest and quaintest in England – over seven centuries old and nearly dark
with stained glass among which the gridiron of St Lawrence, its patron saint,
is conspicuous. Pray for me darling tomorrow morning and for the loving
soul which at last has carried its point'.[3] Isabella's determination to have her
marriage celebrated in the presence of her relatives and with due regard for
all the proprieties is notable in view of her constant war against convention
in other areas of her life.

John Bishop[4] had become known in the Bird's circle as a young medical
man of promise. He had been born and raised in Sheffield but came north to
study, becoming M.B. and C.M. in Edinburgh in 1870, and gaining his M.D.
in 1873 with a thesis which won a Gold Medal. He had become a Fellow of
the College of Surgeons of Edinburgh in 1876 and of the College of
Physicians of Edinburgh in 1879. He had been accepted into the medical establishment and had served as a private assistant to Joseph Lister in the
Edinburgh Royal Infirmary where he was described as 'serious, middle-aged

and a most devoted disciple',[5] during the early days of antiseptic surgery.

In writing to Lady Middleton, Isabella described John Bishop carefully. 'He is about or a little under middle height, very plain, wears spectacles and is very grey but his face is redeemed by eyes which Sir Noel Paton says are "beautiful from their purity", and a high broad intellectual brow. He is very intellectual and studious, very receptive and appreciative intellectually, and very able, much cultured with very artistic tastes, but no artistic facility, passionately fond of nature, very diffident, not calculated to shine socially, or to produce a favourable impression *at first*, with a simple, truthful, loyal, unselfish nature and unfathomable depths of love and devotion. A character of truer simpler worth could not be found'.[6]

It was partly Dr Bishop's *gravitas* which appealed to the Bird girls, alone as they were without the benefit of support from male relatives. They both enjoyed his company. With Isabella he shared an enthusiasm for microscopic work and they worked together 'with the marvels of Atlantic oaze'[7,] while for Henrietta his quiet and unassuming temperament seemed to echo her own rather serious approach to life. Dr Bishop was strongly drawn to the older sister, he admired the gallant Miss Bird abroad – he had been amazed by her book on Hawaii – but he also understood something of the doubts and uncertainties which upset her life and saw how reliant on others she could be.

In the summer of 1877, when Isabella was 46 and John 36 years of age, Doctor John proposed. Isabella accepted. As she confided in John Murray, 'I hope you may be interested to hear (in advance of any announcement of the fact among my friends) that I am just now conditionally engaged to be married and that I am most anxious to regain my health, which has been failing again considerably, and not to be an invalid wife. I am thinking of going abroad to some region where I can live the same open air equestrian life which restored me before. It seems almost essential to visit my friends in the Sandwich Islands and if I go to that side of the world I should like to visit Japan. ... I have confided in you the reason of my projected tour before settling down to a stationary life – but pray regard the communication as confidential. I hope you have still romance enough to sympathise with a "love match".'[8]

It is presumed that John Bishop was the fiancé to whom she referred.

It was only when Henrietta was told of the secret engagement that Isabella realised how deeply her younger sister was affected. Isabella and John Bishop discussed the matter, decided that a public announcement was out of the question and the betrothal was shelved. Was there a note of panic in the next letter written to John Murray to enjoin his silence over the abortive engagement? As Isabella explained, writing from Braemar, 'thank you for your very kind wishes with regard to my engagement. My health is so bad that it can only be a conditional one so I would be glad that it should not be

St Lawrence's, Barton on the Moor, Warwickshire, where Isabella Bird married John Bishop on 8 March 1881.

Dr John Bishop, who had studied medicine at the University of Edinburgh, first proposed marriage to Isabella Bird in 1877. They married on 8 March 1881. Dr Bishop died at Cannes on 6 March 1886.

spoken about'.[9]

But for Henrietta the damage had been done, her health suffered and early in 1878 she was reported 'not well'. She never regained her good health even when staying on Mull. Isabella fled in February 1878, leaving for Japan and other points east not to return until May 1879. Over the winter of 1879–1880 Hennie agreed to stay in Edinburgh with Isabella but continued to long for Mull writing '*Winter* is the time to be in the Highlands and is the worst time in town'. The letter continued, '"She" is toiling to finish her book'.[10] What does the barbed 'she' suggest? On 1 April 1880 as a sick woman she travelled to Mull, remarking 'I never felt so weak on that voyage before', and despite a temporary improvement her condition worsened. Isabella arrived on 29 April and Dr Bishop on 30 April and they were both in attendance throughout May until Henrietta died 'of typhoid'[11] on 4 June 1880.

John Bishop wrote to John Murray from Tobermory two days later thanking the Murrays for the 'kindness and sympathy' which they had expressed earlier. As he explained 'The toil of the case prevented me from writing to you by return of post ... on Tuesday we had three hours of very arduous struggle for the patient's life followed by three days of brightening hope followed alas by four hours of toil in late morning ending in the departure of the spirit at 9.46 a.m.' John Bishop reported that Miss Bird was bearing her grief 'as a gentle Christian woman should'.[12]

On 16 June Isabella herself penned a letter to John Murray saying that Hennie's loss 'is all too terrible' for her sister had been 'The inspiration of all my literary work – my best public, my home and fireside my most intimate and congenial friend'.[13] But she also knew that with her sister's death the only obstacle to her marriage had been removed.[14]

The letter of 16 June is of special interest for it gives some insight into Miss Bird's opinion of her future husband as she wrote, 'it is impossible to speak too highly of the noble conduct of Dr Bishop, who with a large and increasing practice, out of humanity sacrificed everything for more than five weeks during which time he was never in bed, was doctor, friend, partially nurse and servant and at the last having risked his own life and made himself lame for life ... with the help of the nurse carried out the coffin ...'[15] Because Hennie's illness was labelled as 'typhoid' the local people would not help and because John Bishop had had a fall and broken his leg he was himself ordered to 'rest' and was thus able to spend his time on Mull nursing Hennie.

Whether Hennie's sadness over John Bishop was known to those in their circle of friends in Edinburgh is not clear, but Anna Stoddart in writing Isabella's biography (published in 1906) skilfully obscured and re-arranged the facts. She reported that John Bishop's proposal, in the summer of 1877, was rejected – despite the fact that it was accepted – on the grounds that Isabella 'was so deeply attached to her sister', 'all my world' and 'my pet to

The redoubtable Isabella Bird Bishop at the time of her marriage, March 1881.

be with whom is my joy'. In August (according to Stoddart) Dr Bishop was persuaded 'to let their friendship abide undisturbed by considerations which she was unwilling to face'.[16] That Anna Stoddart was able to gloss over these matters depended in part on the fact that she was in 1905 dealing with John Murray IV as publisher of her book. The revealing letters which Isabella wrote in July and August 1877 referring to a 'love match' and announcing her 'conditional engagement' were addressed to John Murray III who had died in 1892 long before Isabella's biographer set to work.

Isabella Bird and John Bishop became officially engaged 'to the great surprise of most of her circle',[17] in December 1880 some six months after Henrietta's death. Notwithstanding her earlier commitment (in 1877) to a provisional engagement, the prospective bride remained in a state of great emotional turmoil. She continued all through the autumn to deny any engagement, to fret about 'her great perplexity', to mourn for her dead sister. Was it the ghost of poor Hennie which haunted her? As she wrote to Mrs Blackie 'I feel marriage a most tremendous step to take without her and *with* her I never could have endured a third'.[18]

Sir Harry Parkes, whose own wife had died in Edinburgh at about the same time as Hennie, recommended the marriage, as did Lady Middleton, a friend of long-standing, who wrote that if love were there she would urge acceptance because 'the world would look upon it as the most natural end of his devotion to Hennie, that my social position by birth and my literary position were too firmly established to be shaken ...'[19]

It is clear that the attentions of John Bishop caused Isabella Bird to think seriously about her social position in the event of her marriage. For early in 1878, shortly after her abortive engagement the previous summer, she wrote – concerning introductions to people in Japan – to John Murray setting out her station in life as follows, 'my mother's family the Lawsons of Aldborough Manor and Boroughbridge Hall are one of the oldest families in Yorkshire, the property having come down from father to son for eight centuries and that my father's family the de Byrds, who unluckily in my great grand-father's time took the name Bird (for a property), are a very old Warwickshire family and that both by relationship and marriage are connected with several families of the English nobility'.[20]

John Bishop would appear to have come from a respectable family in Sheffield. His father had died in 1850, when he was nine, leaving the then useful sum of £1,291. Perhaps his mother, who survived her son John, encouraged her eldest child's ambition to take up medical training in Edinburgh. She had been left a widow in 1850 with three small children, and yet must have found sufficient resources to support, however slenderly, a student son for some years. Prior to the marriage John Bishop signed an Ante Nuptial Contract (dated 21 January 1881) by which he 'bound himself to lay out and invest in her name within six months from the date of his decease the sum of eight thousand pounds, the revenue to be paid to the said Mrs Isabella Lucy Bishop during all the days of her life and the capital to be at the disposal of the deceased'.[21] In working out the pre-marriage contract lawyers would no doubt take into account the strong possibility that John Bishop as the younger partner, would survive his wife, in which case the clause relating to her maintenance would not apply. In fact John Bishop had little time to accumulate any funds before his early death some five years later.

Although married status gave a woman added respect, as Mrs Bishop, had she been required to undertake the traditional wifely role, she might have been sacrificing a great deal. It is true that Isabella and John had considered the matter of her further travels and had agreed that should she feel the need she would go. Sadly, the marriage did not last long, for John Bishop became ill.[22] The few years they had together during the early 1880s were spent moving around southern Europe vainly seeking health.

Immediately after the wedding the Bishops travelled to Malvern, a nearby watering place; on 26 March 1881 they were back in Edinburgh at the marital home, 12 Walker Street, although as Isabella wrote, 'it will be long before I at least feel settled'.[23] There is a charming description by Anna Stoddart of the Walker Street drawing-room. Isabella, like many others, had succumbed to the Oriental craze, although in her case her Japanese items were beautiful pieces collected by her in the course of her travels. Her fine Satsuma and Nagasaki porcelain and her antique bronzes – representing twins, mythical heroes in Japan, one with arms and the other with legs, excessively long – were added to by 'Eastern cabinets and the palms which stood in the Daimyo's bath'. In addition to the Edinburgh house they still retained Henrietta's cottage on Mull, to which Isabella retired when she wished to mourn for her sister alone.

In Edinburgh, the King of Hawaii-nei lunched with the Bishops in Walker Street where he conferred on Isabella the Hawaiian Literary Order of Kapiolani,[24] later they were also guests of Mr and Mrs Macfie at Dreghorn Castle while the King was staying there. In the autumn they journeyed south and stayed at the Elms, Houghton, and Isabella escorted her husband around the scenes of her childhood and took him rowing on the Ouse.

It was at the end of 1881, when Isabella was alone on Mull, that John Bishop first became seriously ill. Bishop had a 'slight scratch' on his face and an infection was believed to have entered his system following an operation that he had performed on a foreign sailor in the Edinburgh Royal Infirmary. Isabella, delayed on the island by bad weather, was distraught; fortunately when she finally reached Edinburgh, John, although weak, was recovering. At the beginning of 1882 Dr Bishop was well enough to resume his hospital work and see his patients, later they had a break in the spring when they travelled South. After this John returned to work in Edinburgh while Isabella continued to the continent where she established herself with close friends at Cadenabbia in northern Italy only returning to London in July.

Wherever she travelled she was very busy with her literary work, for King Kalakana's visit had revived interest in her book on Hawaii – a new edition of *Six Months in the Sandwich Islands* was prepared. *Unbeaten Tracks in Japan* was also selling well. In addition she was working on the letters she had sent to Henrietta from Malaya. These eventually appeared as *The Golden Chersonese* – the title chosen by Henrietta and dedicated to her 'Beloved Memory'. During 1882 she became depressed, although as soon as she was engaged in thinking of others she was her more usual clear-headed practical self. In August 1882 she spent a month in Mull where she enjoyed entertaining friends and added tricycling to her accomplishments. She had appreciated advice from John Murray and 'Mr Browning' on the merits of various cycles especially as their advice saved her from buying one which would have been 'too slow for my somewhat fast notions of locomotion'.[25]

On returning to Edinburgh she found her husband clearly unwell; apparently the 'blood-poisoning' of the previous autumn was still present and still 'sapping at the quality of his blood'. From late 1882, although continuing to work, John Bishop was never well. In the late Spring of 1883 they went travelling in the south and west of England and thereafter Dr Bishop's health came to dominate both their lives. At the end of 1883, in London, he was visited by Sir Andrew Clark and by Sir Joseph Lister, his old professor, both of whom advised travel, for neither could recommend treatment which might reverse the illness.

The summer of 1884 was spent at Tobermory and as the patient rallied Isabella began to believe that her husband might survive. He was ordered to go south for the winter although the journey to Hyères, Southern France proved a sorry trial as on arrival the sick man was so exhausted that he lay 'scarcely noting who was there or what was done'. They remained in Hyères for some months although with the onset of the summer heat had to remove to the mountains at St Luc, Valais. In the autumn of 1885, still critically ill, John Bishop was brought down again and they settled at Cannes for the winter. In December 1885 he wrote, a sad stilted letter, using the 'friendly aid of an amanuensis', referring to the 'tender care and wonderful kindness' which he was receiving and referred to 'My dear wife and my excellent attendant who are much over worked' and also to 'a very able and most delightful medical friend in Dr Frank who with his wife the Lady Agnes are most assiduously kind. We have had the benefit of a consultation with Sir J. Frazer'.[26]

Writing from Hôtel des Anglais, Cannes, early in 1886 Isabella gave details of her day:

9 a.m.	Breakfast and read in bed until 10
10 – 10.30	go for half hour with John

11 – 12	am in my Salon where I write, prepare notes and receive selected visitors
12	lunch
12 – 12.30	with John, write for him or read to him
2.30	either drive or go to see a friend or do needed shopping
4.30 – 6 p.m.	literary work
6 – 6.30	with John, then dinner
7.30 – 8.30	with John
9 p.m. – midnight	bed
12 – 7.30 a.m.	with John, then back to bed

She concludes, 'I do not have 5 minutes in 24 hours'.[27]

It was a gruelling schedule. No doubt the precise times which are given reflected the arrival and departure of hired nurses or friends; she was herself apparently undertaking night duty on a regular basis.

The steady deterioration in John Bishop's condition called for bold measures for, on 3 January 1886, Sir Joseph Lister came out to join them. He found a 'sturdy young Italian peasant' who 'for a large sum of money' was willing to donate some of his blood to Dr Bishop. The blood transfusion was completed with great care, Sir Joseph being assisted by three other doctors in an exhausting process which lasted one hour and a half.[28] It would indeed have been a miracle had the operation succeeded for, despite the fact that anaemia had been identified by Thomas Addison in 1855, nothing was then known of the chemical failures in the body which led to anaemia or of blood[29] groups or of the dangers of using blood of the wrong group. The operation did not reverse the decline: John Bishop died of pernicious anaemia[30] at Cannes on 6 March 1886.

Isabella was distraught. Some days after the death she wrote about her husband to John Murray, 'I now see that his extraordinary patience, self control, cheerfulness and intellectual activity blinded all who were about him for the last eighteen months to the extent of his deprivations and suffering. He was always so happy, so interested in everyone and everything, so enthusiastic, so grateful and so full of purpose that it did not seem as if he could die'.[31]

As she wrote sometime later, 'I never think of myself as his widow always his wife. It was strange that so late in life and so unwillingly on my part, that unequalled unselfish devotion and his increasing beauty of character should win my whole heart and that then he should leave me'. 'The loss of him is simply *awful* – my own pure, saintly, heroic, unworldly unselfish devoted husband'.[32] It was ironic that such a romantic woman should, at the age of 50, marry a man ten years her junior whom she really only came to appreciate after she had lost him.

There seems no doubt that despite the discrepancy in their ages John

Bishop was determined to make Isabella Bird his wife. He found it exciting to be associated with a literary lady, he loved to read her travel books and articles and enjoyed her conversation laced as it was with anecdotes of her adventures. He sympathised with her ill health but believed that a contented married life might lead to improvement, he recognised her passionate nature and even when ill rejoiced saying, 'My bride loves me, I have not lived in vain'.[33] Their physical relationship can only remain a matter of conjecture given their ages, inexperience and increasingly poor health.

And yet there must remain a lingering doubt, was she really suited to the wifely role? Although she had devoted a good deal of her time to John Bishop during his long illness, she had also been away exploring Switzerland on various small expeditions, visiting friends, and performing other necessary tasks. Had John Bishop also recognised that despite her apparent invalidism his wife would always be driven by her bounding energy?

Another matter which arises relates to the constant removal of John Bishop from one location to another in southern Europe as they sought air good enough to restore him to health. Were the journeyings in fact done at Isabella's behest to satisfy her craving for change? What were the doctors thinking of depriving a sick man of his home and comforts for so long? Early in his illness the Bishops were advised to remain away for eighteen months, but the exile went on and on and John Bishop was never allowed to return home to Edinburgh.

John Bishop had taken 12 Walker Street as the marital home but did his wife ever accept this house as a permanent abode? As Anna Stoddart remarks, 'time and her husband's devotion had gradually strengthened her attachment to the house in Walker Street'[34] yet she found time in the spring of 1884, two full years before her husband's death, to come home to clear up and empty the house, storing furniture and valuables. Sadly, for the last twenty-four months of his life John Bishop, even had he been able to persuade his doctors and his wife to let him end his exile, had no home to which to return.

Mrs Bishop's pre-occupation with her husband's illness distracted her attention from her own health and she remained generally well although over the winter of 1882–1883 she was suffering from a spinal attack. On 1 June 1885 she came to London and under a general anaesthetic had an operation – also for the removal of a spinal tumour? – performed by Sir Joseph Lister. She wrote an extraordinary effusion on the effects of chloroform which was published in *Murray's Magazine*.[35] It should also be noted that some years after this operation she abandoned her custom of having all her dresses made with a 'Watteau plait' or pleat at the back to disguise her spinal condition.[36] Was this a belated acknowledgement that the Watteau plait in her dresses had never been necessary?

Under the terms of John Bishop's Will, Isabella as widow was executrix and sole beneficiary and received the proceeds from the estate, including the life assurance policies which totalled some £3,500. Two of these policies had been taken out in August 1877 immediately after Isabella had first accepted his proposal of marriage. Altogether John Bishop's total assets were just under £4,555 and all of these were consigned to Isabella under the terms of the Ante Nuptial Contract.[37] His library and surgical instruments were valued at rather less than £60. Although Dr Bishop's widow was the beneficiary of his modest estate, and his elderly mother received nothing, years later in her own Will Isabella did ensure that Dr Bishop's six nephews and nieces received legacies from her, ranging from £500 to £100 and totalling £1,800.

During the time immediately following her husband's death, finding Edinburgh 'the place of saddest reminders' she moved to London where she set up house at 44 Maida Vale, intending to offer a home to those out-patients attending St Mary's in Paddington who lived far away in the country, but this ambitious scheme quickly proved too exhausting and, like the Maida Vale house, was eventually abandoned. She herself registered for surgical nursing training and worked in the casualty department of St Mary's, becoming skilled in using splints and dressing wounds; she also took lessons in 'ambulance work' often spending up to ten hours a day on duty. She watched all sorts of operations including those involving amputations, hernia, trephining, and the removal of tumours and learned to nurse patients recovering from such treatments. She also learnt the new technique of putting a leg in plaster. In general there were few references to her hospital work in the correspondence which survives although she did, in June 1887 at the time of the Golden Jubilee of Queen Victoria, ask John Murray if she might 'bestow on the Matron of St Mary's Hospital' the ticket which he had kindly sent her for a place from which to view the procession on his balcony in Albermarle Street.[38]

Her own training as a medical auxiliary was part of her plan to help at small medical mission hospitals which she would provide as fitting memorials for her husband and sister. It was the medical aspect of the work which appealed, and she had at the Medical Mission Centre in Edinburgh an important source of information on this type of hospital as well as friends and colleagues of her husband who generated much enthusiasm for her initiatives. During the course of her journeys, observing and recording the customs and beliefs of the many people through whose lands she travelled, she had frequently regretted her inability to provide even simple remedies for sufferers amongst whom she had lived.

The attraction of Palestine, the Holy Land, was to Christians at this time very great. Mrs Bishop resolved to establish and equip a hospital in Nazareth of twelve beds, in which she herself would initially act as nurse to deal particularly with surgical cases. This hospital would be part of the medical mission already working there under Dr Torrance, a personal friend of Dr

Bishop's.[39] All her plans came to nought. The Turkish government, after much procrastination, refused permission.[40] She was forced to look elsewhere.

During 1888 she determined to travel to India leaving behind her 'the bitterness of death'. The voyage would be a turning point, 'a silent interval between the familiar life which lies behind ... and the strange unknown which lies before'.[41] In India she could set up her hospitals without political complications, and (although she did not say so) who knows, she might have Tibet and Persia and Kurdestan within her grasp.

Notes

1. AS, pp.143-146, PB, p.189.
2. JM, ILB to JM, 4 March 1881.
3. JSB, ILB to Eliza B., 7 March 1881, Ms 2634, f.29.
4. John Bishop (1841-1886), MD Edinburgh (1873), MB & CM (1870), Fellow Royal College of Surgeons, Edinburgh (1876), Licentiate of the Royal College of Physicians, Edinburgh (1879), Surgeon Medical Missionary Dispensary, Cowgate, author of chapter on 'Antiseptic Treatment' see *Medical Directory* (1885), p.1020.
5. R.J. Godlee, *Life of Lister* (1917), p.607, Joseph Lister (1827-1912) surgeon, studied at University College, London, served as Professor of Surgery at the Universities of Glasgow and Edinburgh where he developed antiseptic surgery, thus promoting a revolution in surgical techniques and making internal operations possible.
6. AS, p.146, Lady Middleton, a close family friend, was married to Henry Willoughby and had houses at Settrington House, Birdsall, Yorkshire, (near Mrs Dora Bird's family home) and Middleton Hall, Warwickshire, see *The Peerage, Baronetage and Knightage of Great Britain and Ireland*, (1858), pp.395-396.
7. AS, p.96, PB, p.183.
8. JM, ILB to JM, 'private', 27 July 1877.
9. JM, ILB to JM, 'private', 29 August 1877.
10. AS, p.115.
11. The diagnosis 'of typhoid' might be correct, although HAB's long lingering illness makes it doubtful. ILB suffered from 'typhoid' also (AS, p.109) in Egypt in 1879 on her way back from the Far East.
12. JM, JB to JM, 6 June 1890.
13. JM, ILB to JM, 16 June 1880.
14. ILB was the executrix and sole beneficiary of HAB's Will which had been drawn up shortly after their mother's death on 18 February 1867. She inherited some £6,450 (SRO, SC/70/4/184 and SC/70/1/201).
15. JM, ILB to JM, 16 June 1880.
16. AS, p.97.
17. A. Grainger Stewart, Obituary, *BEM*, November 1904, p.701.
18. JSB, ILB to Eliza B., n.d. but December 1880, Ms 2633, f.326.
19. JSB, ILB to Eliza B., n.d. but December 1880, Ms 2633, f.326.
20. JM, ILB to JM, 24 February 1878.
21. The information on the Ante Nuptual Contract and on John Bishop and his family comes from John Bishop's Will and Testament, SRO, reference SC/70/4/218 and SC/70/1/250.

22. JM, ILB to JM, 28 July 1883.

23. JM, ILB to JM, 26 March 1881.

24. AS, p.150.

25. JM, ILB to JM, 5 October 1882.

26. JM, JB to JM, 29 December 1885.

27. JSB, ILB to Eliza B., 9 February 1886, Ms 2636, f.160-161.

28. JSB, ILB to Eliza B., 9 February 1886, Ms 2636, f.160-161.

29. It was not until 1907 that Janssky discovered that there were four types of human blood.

30. Pernicious anaemia is now known to be due to the absence of secretion of hydro-chloric acid and other factors; eating liver, or nowadays, highly concentrated ex-tracts of liver, keeps the disease under control but does not cure it.

31. JM, ILB to JM, 18 March 1886.

32. JSB, ILB to Eliza B., Cannes, 1 May 1886, Ms 2636, f.212-213.

33. JSB, ILB to Eliza B., 44 Maida Vale, London, 28 February 1888, Ms 2637, f.151.

34. AS, p.164.

35. 'Under Chloroform, a psychological fragment' (*Murray's Magazine*, 1887, Vol.1, pp.327-330) was a long musing piece about her life experiences, and her faith. It begins with

> 'Sleep! Sleep!
> Can I ever wake again to weep?'

and ends

> 'Farewell for ever
> Doubt, mist and gloom
> Welcome for ever
> Truth light and home'

36. JSB, ILB to Eliza B., Tobermory, 27 December 1891, Ms 2638, f.294.

37. John Bishop's Will and Testament, SRO reference SC/70/4/218 and SC/70/1/250.

38. JM, ILB to JM, 18 June 1887.

39. 'The Hospital written of is a hospital of 12 beds which I purpose to put up as a Memorial to my husband in connection with a medical mission. The demand for one at Nazareth is great ...' JSB, ILB to Eliza B., Tobermory, 1 February 1887, Ms 2637, f.23.

40. AS, p.187.

41. AS, p.202, quoting letter to Mrs McDonald.

9 *From Persian Gulf to Black Sea, Mrs Bishop and 'the Great Game'*

The widowed Isabella Bishop had two objectives when she sailed for India in February 1889, she planned to set up memorial medical mission hospitals (see Chapter 13) and she hoped to resume her career – which had been abandoned for 11 years – as a daring traveller. Had she already decided to make the long and perilous journey from the Persian Gulf in the south through to Turkey on the Black Sea in the north? Did she then know that by traversing such territory she could hardly fail to involve herself in 'the Great Game'?[1]

The Great Game was the long undeclared struggle which lasted throughout the nineteenth century between Russia and Britain for influence and power in the lands of the Middle East which stretched from the decaying Turkish empire in the west through Persia to Afghanistan and Tibet in the east. There was in effect a buffer zone in Central Asia as Britain sought to protect India and the route to it, and the Russians strove to absorb as much land as they could into their ever-expanding empire. As the marauding Cossacks, at the forefront of the Russian advance, captured Tashkent, Samarkand and Bokhara so British officers, keen to escape from duties in the heat of India, mounted undercover operations designed to undermine Russian influence in countries north and west of India. It was a war, but undeclared and shadowy, and Isabella Bishop, no doubt innocently, was to some extent, involved in it.

In Simla in northern India in October 1889 she met Major Sawyer, an Assistant Quartermaster-General of the Indian Intelligence Service, and learned that he was about to set out on a military–geographical mission through Persia to Teheran. The Major agreed that she could join his party, a chance for which she had hardly dared hope, which would give her an opportunity to travel as a western woman in difficult country dominated by war-like Muslim peoples.

She had arrived in Karachi in March 1889 and quickly moved north by train, in enervating heat, via Rawalpindi into Kashmir. There she spent some time arranging for the establishment of the John Bishop Memorial Hospital. Finding that others could supervise the new building she soon organised a small adventure into Tibet.[2] This would be 'travel' rather than 'exploration' and along 'beaten' rather than the 'unbeaten' tracks she preferred, but she had not undertaken any strenuous travelling for eleven years and she needed to know, at the age of 58, that she was still capable of such effort. The hot season in India had brought the English in large numbers to Kashmir and she escaped eagerly, wearied by 'the clatter of English voices', from an area which had capitulated as she thought 'to lawn tennis and badminton'.[3]

When she left Sonnamarg her 'outfit' consisted of 'two servants, a Pathan soldier of the Maharajah of Kashmir's guard, three baggage ponies, an Arab horse, a small Cabul tent, and a shelter tent five foot square'.[4] She clearly relished the preparations for her departure, and felt that it would be exciting to be on the move again.

As she rode out of Kashmir she noted the three great steps up to Tibet through the Zoji La at 11,300ft, the Namika La at 13,000ft, and the Fotu La at 13,500ft altitude.[5] The Zoji La was an important crossing place used by many who wished to have access to Central Asia. It was certainly hazardous travel as the 'roads', in effect bridle tracks, had been with difficulty constructed along the sides of gorges, 'sometimes being blasted out of the edges of precipices from 1,000 to 3,000ft in depth, but oftener scaffolded – that is poles are lodged among the crevices of the cliff and are loosely covered with slabs or planks or brushwood.' The track was wide enough for one caravan but disaster threatened when two such convoys of men and beasts had to pass each other on the narrow dangerous edge. The 'twig bridges' over the mountain torrents were another hazard. She lost two animals crossing poor broken down bridges.

But it is clear from her description, as they undertook the 2,000ft climb to the Zoji La, that she was exhilarated by what she saw. 'It was sunrise', she wrote, 'and in the dewy, rose-flushed atmosphere, high above the pass a mass of grey and red mountains, snow-slashed and snow-capped, rose in peaks, walls, pinnacles and jagged ridges, above which towered yet loftier summits bearing into the heavenly blue fields of unsullied snow alone. Below as a last dream of beauty, stretched the Baltal Valley, green as an English lawn, starred with white lilies, and dotted with clumps of trees, which were festooned with red and yellow roses, white jasmine and clematis. Above the hardier deciduous trees appeared the *Pinus excelsa*, the silver fir and the spruces, higher yet, the stately grace of the disdar clothed the hillsides and above the forests, rose-tinted in the sunrise rose the snowy mountains of Tilais'. And she concludes, 'I never saw natural grass or forests again till I descended months later into the paradise of Kulu'.[6]

On the Tibetan side, even when she passed by in late June, she was confronted by 'much-crevassed snow-fields and decaying avalanches'. One day she crossed and re-crossed the Dras river no less than four times on 'snow bridges'. As she moved down to the 'valley bottom', at an altitude of about 10,000 ft, she found a dry barren area where, surrounded by mountains as it was, no rain could penetrate. The 'tasteless and unstimulating' cups of tea which were made from water which boiled at this altitude at temperatures between 187° and 195° Fahrenheit together with the violence of the winds and the fierceness of the sun's rays, were reminders of the inhospitable areas through which she was passing.

She was pleased when she reached an area where she found Tibetans, whose physical appearance, as compared with the Kashmiris, was not impressive but they were she averred, 'truthful, trustful and independent'. She liked being introduced to various village headman as she passed and was delighted when they admired her horse[7] and wished her a good journey.[8]

The Buddhist presence was much in evidence as she travelled in Tibet. Not only were there parties of *lamas* constantly on the move but so many of the hill-tops were crowned by monasteries or *gonpas*. These were, she wrote, 'vast, irregular piles of fantastic buildings, almost invariably crowning lofty isolated rocks or mountain spurs reached by steep rock stair-cases, battlemented towers with curtain walls above, temple domes, bridges over chasms, spires and scaffolded projections gleaming with gold, looking like the outgrowth and blossom of the rock itself.'[9]

When she arrived at Leh she was escorted to the shady bungalow of the British Joint Commissioner where she settled down happily. It was fun during the month of August as caravans arrived from Kashmir, Kabul, the Punjab and Lhasa, and merchants thronged the bazaars at Leh where 'the harsh dissonance of bargaining tongues rose high' and 'mules, asses, horses and yaks kicked, bit, squealed and bellowed'.[10]

She left Leh on a short three-week expedition to the mountain district of Nubra with a well-informed Moravian missionary. Travelling at an altitude of between 15,000 and 18,000 ft there were severe difficulties, as some of the men and animals suffered bleeding. They tried to ride yaks and although Isabella put her own saddle on her yak she did not succeed in taming it. Eventually she was forced to return to her own horse because 'some of my yaks shied, plunged and kicked, executed fantastic movements on the edges of precipices, bellowed defiance, knocked down their leaders and rushed madly down mountain sides, leaping from boulder to boulder till they landed me among their fellows.'[11]

As she came down the Lahul Valley she crossed into what was then claimed as 'British Tibet'[12] where she found the Moravian missionaries had made good progress in organising irrigation and the storage of water. She was happy to camp at Kylang for an extra three weeks as the harvest was brought in but then travelling, in leisurely fashion, she spent five weeks en route for Simla which she reached on 17 October 1889, where she acknowledged 'the amenities and restraints of civilisation'. The Tibetan journey had in one sense been an interlude, a reassurance to her as to her fitness, and a preparation for sterner days ahead, but it had had its moments as when in crossing the flooded Shayok river her borrowed Turkestan horse had failed to leap the bank and rolled over onto her as they both fell into the river. After 'a choking struggle and a moment of suffocation' she was dragged out, escaping with 'a broken rib and some severe bruises'. The horse drowned.[13]

It was a fortunate circumstance which enabled Mrs Bishop to join a semi-official party as a player, even if a minor one, and of the wrong sex, in the Great Game. Was the young Major persuaded by more senior officers to accept this highly regarded lady as a fellow-traveller? She certainly had a fine reputation; her books on her experiences in Hawaii, the Rocky Mountains, Japan and Malaya were her references. Nevertheless it might be thought unlikely that Major Sawyer would have volunteered to take a near-60-year-old woman with him through Muslim Persia on a long and hazardous journey in dead of winter. Even if he knew of her undoubted prowess on a horse he must have wondered how such a companion, a western woman unused to the demeaning attitudes constantly required of her sex in Muslim countries, would fare. Would she become a burden? Might she become a danger? Throughout this journey she travelled veiled and camouflaged, an appendage of the party with none of the freedom to which she was accustomed elsewhere. The Major, labelled by Mrs Bishop as 'the Sahib' because of the lordly disdain with which he treated the natives, was she believed 'as prickly and self-opinionated' as Curzon;[14] and as stubborn, resourceful and courageous as herself in the face of danger and hardship.

In the course of this winter journey the young officer and the adventurous lady came to respect and even like each other, so much so that after the Major's obligations to Mrs Bishop had been fulfilled they planned a further expedition together from Isfahan to the country of the Baktiari Lurs. Despite the hardships, Mrs Bishop had reason to be grateful to the Major whose tolerance allowed her to traverse areas in Muslim territory normally closed to western women.

By December 1889 she was hurrying to complete her arrangements in India to join up with Major Sawyer. She journeyed south by rail through Lahore to Karachi, and from there by boat westwards along the coast to Bushire. She travelled for part of the journey to Baghdad, with Hon. George N Curzon (later Lord Curzon). Curzon had been travelling widely in the Middle East trying to interpret the reality of the Russian threat to India. During the autumn of 1888 he had penetrated into Russian territory by travelling as far as possible along the newly constructed Trans-Caspian Railway in Asiatic Russia. His book, *Russia in Central Asia* was published at the end of 1889 while Isabella was in the Middle East. When Mrs Bishop and G N Curzon were fellow·travellers he was, as she wrote 'prospecting', and was preparing in his forthcoming book, *Persia and the Persian Question*, to draw attention to the broad strategic imperatives in the Middle East.

Mrs Bishop had no opportunity on this journey to travel quietly with her

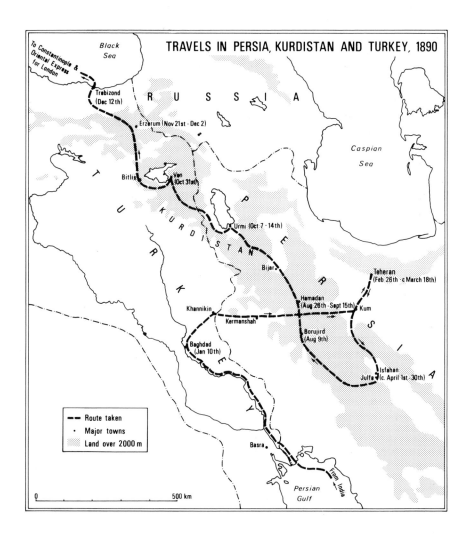

TRAVELS IN PERSIA, KURDISTAN AND TURKEY, 1890

Black Sea

To Constantinople &
Oriental Express
for London

Trebizond
(Dec 12th)

R U S S I A

Erzerum (Nov 21st - Dec 2)

Caspian
Sea

Bitlis

Van
(Oct 31st)

T U R K E Y

K U R D I S T A N

Urmi (Oct 7 - 14th)

Bijar

Teheran
(Feb 26th - c March 18th)

Hamadan
(Aug 26th - Sept 15th)

Kum

Khannikin

Kermanshah

Boorujird
(Aug 9th)

Baghdad
(Jan 10th)

P E R S I A

Isfahan
Julfa (c. April 1st - 30th)

Route taken
Major towns
Land over 2000 m

Basra

From India

0   500 km

Persian
Gulf

horses and her one servant interpreter for she was of necessity, for strategic and cultural reasons, attached to a larger party. She had to hire a servant and muleteers as well as five mules, two for riding and three for baggage, onto which provisions and brazier were strapped. In order to make things easier she put her clothes and possessions into native local made trunks and packed only a folding bed and a chair. For the first time she armed herself with a revolver.

They set out eastwards from Baghdad on 10 January 1890, she unwillingly riding a saddle mule at the beginning of what she called 'an awful journey'. Was it for security reasons that Major Sawyer determined to travel at the worst possible season when snow, bitter winds and enervating cold would necessarily assail them? Isabella did not mince her words, 'I never would have undertaken it had I known the hardships it would involve, the long marches, the wretched food, the abominable accommodation, the filthy water, the brutal barbarism of the people. We were detained four days by torrents of rain at Khannikin, the last town in Asiatic Turkey ... and soon after reached the snows of the elevated plateaux of Northern Persia, and have been marching day after day from eighteen to twenty-two miles with mercury at from four to twelve degrees below the zero of Fahrenheit through snow from 18ins to 3ft deep, sometimes getting on only one and a half miles an hour, and putting up at night either in cold, filthy, and horrible caravanserais with three or four hundred mules and their drivers or in Kurdish houses shared with mules, asses, cows and sheep.'[15]

As they progressed over snow-covered plateaux and through high windswept passes she added more and more layers of clothes in an effort to keep the cold at bay. From Kermanshah (2 February 1890) she described her travelling clothes, writing 'In addition to double woollen underclothing I put on a pair of Chitral socks over two pairs of woollen stockings, and over those a pair of long loose Afghan boots, made of sheepskin with the fur inside. Over my riding dress which is of flannel lined with heavy homespun, I had a long homespun jacket, an Afghan Sheepskin coat, a heavy fur cloak over my knees, and a stout "regulation" waterproof to keep out the wind. Add to this a cork helmet, a fisherman's hood, a "six-ply" mask, two pairs of woollen gloves with mittens and double gauntlets'.[16] She also commented on the problems of mounting and dismounting from horse or mule 'thus swaddled'. The use of the 'six-ply mask' although in this case intended for protection from the cold, was obligatory for a woman in Persia. Violence threatened if she, perhaps tempted by the warm sun, ever appeared uncovered.

To her horror she noted that the Persian women along the route wore nothing but cotton. 'Even in this severe weather', she wrote, 'the women of this region have nothing on their feet, and their short blue cotton trousers, short, loose, open jackets, short open chemises and the thin blue sheet or *chadar* over their heads, are a mere apology for clothing.'[17]

They rested for a while at Kermanshah before setting off again on 3 February 1890. The journey onward was, if that were possible, even worse as the passes were still thick with snow and the searing winds cut through everything. There were waterless regions of 'black rock and gravel' and deep mud in the Kavi or Great Salt Desert. Each day they 'rode and stumbled', camping in utter misery; each evening she made poultices and compresses for soldiers and muleteers, who were 'blinded by the snow and sick with fatigue.'

The accommodation in which they stayed offered no comfort. In one account she explained 'Crumbling difficult stairs at each end of a crumbling mud house led to rooms which barely afforded a shelter ... A man shovelled the snow out of my room, and tried to make a fire but failed, as neither he nor I could stand the smoke produced by the attempt. This imperfect shelter had a window-frame, with three out of its four wooden panes gone, and a cracked door, which could only ensure partial privacy by being laid against the posts from the outer landing, which was a flat roof. The wall was full of cracks through which the night wind rioted in a temperature 5° below zero.'[18]

One of the things which gave her most distress was her introduction (by the servants of the party) as a physician – *Hakim* – often when she awoke her room was packed with sick and ailing women and children. Nevertheless although she recognised the eye diseases, cataract and incurved eyelids (from the persistent wood smoke) she could do little to alleviate their misery and this made her feel 'like a brute for leaving them'.

Most of this journey she rode a variety of 'saddle mules'; some were better than others. Occasionally, usually in some crisis, she was allocated a good horse. One, 'a splendid Arab' had, she wrote, 'a neck clothed with thunder', a horse to make one feel young again, with his elastic stride and pride of bearing, but indeed, I 'snatched a fearful joy' for the snow was extremely slippery and thirteen Arab horses in high condition restrained to a foot's pace had belligerent views of their own, tending to disconcert the unwary rider.'[19]

One of the additional hazards of the journey occurred when their party confronted another caravan coming in the opposite direction. This could lead to chaos and indeed disaster as on a narrow track, with danger a step away on either side, neither would give way. One day when Major Sawyer's party had had 'a tremendous day's march, only fourteen miles in seven and a half hours of severe toil', they were all warned to keep together in case of difficulties with oncoming caravans. 'Difficulties indeed', Isabella cried, 'I was nearly smashed' as she continued, 'the rub came on a bank near a stream where there was a deep drift. I decided to give way' as the first sixty animals each bearing two heavy packing cases bore down upon her but her mule declined to step off the track. Only Major Sawyer's orderly saved her on this occasion from serious injury. As it was she lost 'her snowglasses' and sustained 'a number of bruises, a badly torn riding skirt, and a bad cut, which bled profusely', although quite quickly 'the blood froze'.[20] The snag about this type of encounter, which was not unusual as heavy snow held up several caravans which then, once the weather abated moved off in Indian file, was that any laden beast forced off the narrow track fell heavily and could not rise in the snow without being unloaded. When 60–100 animals were involved it could occasion gruelling hard work and many hours delay.

They arrived in Teheran on 26 February 1890. She was expected by the British minister, Sir H. Drummond Wolff, where as she explained, 'Arriving from the mud of the Kavir and the slush of the streets after riding ten hours in ceaseless rain on a worn-out horse, caked with mud from head to foot, dripping exhausted, nearly blind from fatigue, fresh from mud hovels and the congenial barbarism of the desert and with the rags and travel-stains of a winter journey of forty-six days upon me, the light and festivities were overwhelming'. Perhaps Sir Drummond Wolff had expected her earlier for he had that very evening arranged a large dinner party in her honour inviting to his table all those to whom she had had letters of introduction. It was in the end all too much and she was taken to her room where 'removing only the mackintosh cloak, weighted with mud which had served me so well, I lay down on the hearthrug before a great coal fire and slept until 4 o'clock the next morning'.[21]

Despite the fact that she was in her 59th year and had lost 32lbs in weight she had noted that 'I am really much better than when I left Baghdad ... I really like the journey except when I am completely knocked up or the smoke is exceptionally blinding'.[22]

Major Sawyer's account of the expedition is laconic although Mrs Bishop had noted that 'M—'s Herculean strength is not what it was', he himself makes no reference to his own health. The Major did however recognise the increasing strain on his party, writing (15 February) 'Followers all laid up. Horses Seedy'. Less cryptically he explained three days later that 'The followers are causing anxiety owing to their showing signs of pleurisy and pneumonia and general debility from recent trials from cold and snow'. On the last day he commented, 'the mud was painfully excessive and the British Legation was not reached until 8 p.m.'[23]

Whether Major Sawyer regarded himself as part of the Great Game or not, his written record of his findings were prosaic, not to say dull, referring to the geographical features including mountains, passes through them, rivers, whether dry or in flood, the soil and the possibility of building roads or railways through the territory. He also noted the presence of any local or Turkish military, and from the way he writes it is clear that he thought matters would be a lot easier if the British were to take over in Persia as they had done in India.

Notwithstanding her exhaustion on reaching Teheran, she rallied quickly.

Within three weeks of her arrival, plans were being made not only for a journey south (and away from home) to the Church Mission House at Julfa at Isfahan, but also from there north westward into the mountains of Luristan. This extra expedition, which would finally turn her footsteps towards home, was to be done 'within the protection of Major Sawyer's escort, but on such strict conditions as to leave her practically dependent on her own resource and courage'. Was Major Sawyer still engaged on secret, undisclosed adventures?

She left Teheran on 18 March on what was to be she said, 'so far a delightful journey'.[24] There were several features which gave her pleasure. The most important perhaps was the chance to speed ahead of her caravan on her 'handsome Arab' horse. It seemed so different from her struggles earlier in January and February, as she wrote 'the roads have nearly dried up, the country looks cheerful, travellers are numerous, the sun is bright, but the air is cool and bracing and the insects are still hybernating (sic)'. She had also made a fortunate appointment of Mirza Yasuf, who was to be with her for nine months, as her interpreter and personal assistant, although he had previously done no 'menial' service, he had wanted the job because he planned to get to England, and he proved satisfactory in all respects. This journey south giving her 'halcyon days of Persian travelling' succeeded so well largely because of the 'long gallops' which turned 'marches of from twenty-two to thirty miles into delightful rides of from three and a half to four and a half hours'.[25] What did the Persians think of this lady, smothered in the customary covering garments, galloping freely miles ahead of her 'caravan'?

Apart from her servants and baggage animals she was 'a lady travelling alone'[26] and as she moved south she found to her pleasure that she suffered no difficulties or inconvenience. As she discovered for herself, it would have been an entirely different matter had she not been attired in the shapeless over garments of a local lady. Because the day was warm, and she expected to arrive at Julfa Mission House, Isfahan, she 'had dressed with some regard for European sensibilities'. She was noticed immediately. The local boys shouted 'a Feringhi Woman, a Nazarene'; this brought men and boys calling her bad names and making 'fiendish laughs'. They also spat at her. She moved on as quietly as she could and no harm was done. But it was as she wrote, 'a bad half hour'.[27] On another occasion, suitably dressed in her 'shroud' as she called it, and followed by her servant, she had carelessly allowed her *chador* to slip. A boy 'looked quite into my shroud' and at once started shouting 'Kafir' – meaning infidel or Christian – fortunately there were few people around but she was discomforted reporting 'I did not run, but got back to the "hotel" as fast as possible'.[28]

Once she reached Julfa, the Armenian Christian part of Isfahan, she was in good hands staying at the Church Mission House with the Bruce family. As Dr Bruce wrote, 'we greatly enjoyed her sojourn with us for the month of

April 1890, for she took the keenest interest in the work of the mission and was a most delightful guest, whom it was a privilege to entertain.'[29] She met the local dignitaries, visited the famous sights and enjoyed mission outings, riding out to the yearly picnic of the Armenian congregation.

In the midst of all this cosiness Major Sawyer arrived making 'an immense sensation in this minute community, which vegetates in superlative stagnation'. As Isabella noted, 'His splendid appearance, force of character, wit, brutal frankness, ability and kind-heartedness make a great breeze'.[30] But the Major had come south from Teheran to collect Mrs Bishop for they were to set off on the expedition to the Baktieri country during which they were to be as independent as possible, but she was to be encouraged to camp each evening 'within the ring of his sentries'.

Without doubt the Major was a congenial companion; did she ever think of him as the son she did not have? She and the Major were, she averred, 'very good comrades' – as she wrote, 'he has shown a great deal of good feeling in some very difficult circumstances'. And as she continued, 'I hope and believe that in the wonderful journey before us nothing will happen worse than a little friction which will not affect the good companionship'.

She made extensive preparations, packing tins of preserved meat, milk and jam, tablets of soup, tea, candles and saccharin which made up rather more luggage than usual.[31] In addition she bought presents for the mountain people among whom she planned to travel. The Major was to be with her as far as Burujird; this was to be for her the first leg of a long journey home.

Mrs Bishop was by this time in something of a dilemma; yes, she was a traveller, and an intrepid one, but was she also a missionary, with medical leanings? While no-one would have considered soliciting Major Sawyer for medical aid, wherever she went the cry of *'Hakim'* or Physician went up and every day her camp was besieged by men, women and children. Messrs Burroughs and Wellcome had presented her with 'a beautiful medicine chest of the most compact and portable make ... containing fifty small bottles of their invaluable "tabloids" a hypodermic syringe and surgical instruments for simple cases'. 'To these I have added a quantity of quinine and Dr Odling at Tehran gave me some valuable remedies. A quantity of bandages, lint, absorbent cotton completes this essential equipment'.[32] But the local people rejected the 'dictum that a copious use of soap and water must precede all remedies'.[33]

The journey with the Major, which ended on 10 August 1890 when they reached Burujird, had been arduous and, with the increasing medical work, exhausting and frustrating. She parted amicably from the Major with whom she had shared 'difficulty, danger and privation' and he journeyed back towards the south-east reaching the Mission House at Julfa on 25 August[34] while she disbanded her 'caravan', for the muleteers from Isfahan would go no further.

At the same time, she resolved to carry through her long held ambition, to cross 1,000 miles through Kurdestan, Azerbaijan and Turkey to the north-west and aim for Trebizond, in Turkey on the Black Sea. Her route would lie through high mountain territory where snow blizzards and sharp frosts would necessarily assail her. In addition, the land she proposed to traverse was peopled by the most war-like and unruly Muslim people, amongst whom lived enclaves of systematically persecuted Armenian Christians. Despite her intelligence and her curiosity, what did Mrs Bishop know at this time of 'the Armenian Question'? Vaguely, she favoured the Kurds rather than the Armenians. It would have astonished her as she gathered her equipment in Burujird to know that no less a person than W E Gladstone would quiz her on her knowledge of the Armenian question when she did finally arrive home.

She left Burujird and travelled quickly on a fine horse 'Boy' in ten marches to Hamadan, where she stayed three weeks at the Armenian Mission House ill with a 'spinal collapse'. On 15 September 1890 Isabella left the security of Hamadan for the first stage of her journey to Trebizond. The outlook was not rosy for it was mid September and Hamadan, at an altitude of over 6,000ft, was already cold and her route lay across high mountain country. She was not well served by her *chardavar*, the muleteer, who forced her – he said for security reasons – to travel as part of a large caravan, which made both day travel and night rest continuously noisy and dusty. To add insult to injury, she was robbed of clothing, essential toilet items and her sketches, travel notes, pencils and gold pen.[35] Vexed by all these annoyances she determined to recover the initiative; this she did by sending a messenger, bearing her letters of introduction, to the local Governor, who, at Bijar despatched eight soldiers to guard her camp at night. Upon this the *chardavar* recognising her mastery, detached her small caravan from the large one and remained with her himself until they reached Urmi.

At Urmi she quickly re-assembled her caravan, employing Kurds for the next stage, although she found them 'insolent, violent, disobedient and indeed mutinous'. She left Urmi on 14 October 1890 and on the following day must have celebrated her 59th birthday with quiet satisfaction. As she travelled she met with Christian Syrians or Nestorians, and then began to realise the role of the Kurds as predators upon these despised Christians. These helpless Christian peasants, at the mercy of both marauders and misgovernment, were a revelation to her, as they preferred to be martyred for their Christianity rather than to succumb to the blandishments of Mahomet.

To the north west of Urmi she crossed into Armenia, and through much of this territory she was glad to have the protection of armed men sent to her by the local governors. After many adventures and many calls for assistance from British Vice-consuls and missionary families, she arrived safely in Van on 31 October[36] where it was a relief to find shops where she could buy

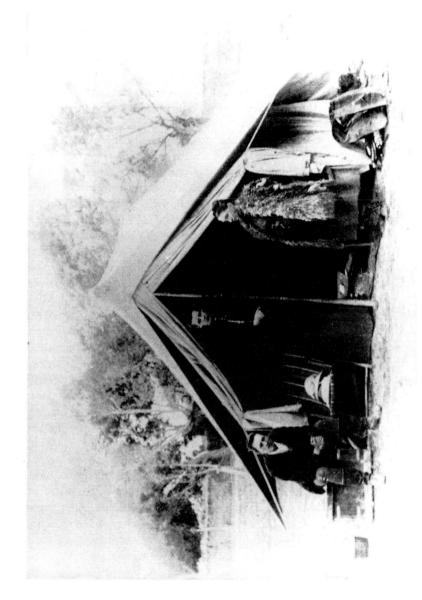

(l-r) Major Sawyer; Miss Bruce; Mrs Bishop
during a journey through Baktieri Lurs Country, Persia, in the autumn of 1890.

warm winter clothes and replace much of her stolen gear.

On 5 November she left Van for Erzeroum with replenished supplies and one Murphy O'Rourke, a Turk, of Irish parentage, as guide and interpreter. She enjoyed the ride to Bitlis where she stayed five days, although when she left on 13 November the weather was extremely cold and despite good servants this part of the journey was difficult especially as her caravan was threatened by brigands on occasion. Fortunately she had taken the precaution of hiring Kurdish watchmen to travel and protect her small group of travellers all of whom were exhausted by rain, snow and biting cold. It was a relief to reach Erzeroum[37] on 21 November after eight wearying days from Bitlis. She was forced to spend ten days in the town recovering and acquainting herself with the 'Erzeroum troubles' but also tracing Murphy who had decamped with her horse 'Boy'. Murphy, discovered drunk in a poor part of the town,[38] was restored to his duties and the party left for Trebizond on 2 December and although the weather was very bad she could hardly be lonely on the busy route to the coast. As the climbs on the hilly route were treacherous with ice she often walked 'Boy' up or down to avoid accident. She arrived in Trebizond on 12 December and one day later, during which she bade farewell to Mirza and Murphy, she embarked on the SS *Douro* for Constantinople. She boarded the Orient Express and reached Paris on Christmas Day, arriving in London on 26 December, where she breakfasted with Mr and Mrs Murray before leaving for Edinburgh where she was welcomed to Charlotte Square the next day by Professor and Mrs Grainger Stewart.

Anna Stoddard sums up Isabella's achievement clearly writing, 'with her quiet persistence, her unflinching courage, her power of command, her independence of luxury, her superb digestion which conquered strange food and endured its lack, and her splendid riding, she surmounted every obstacle, passed almost scathless through every jeopardy, observed, recorded and stored all that interested her and gained every objective attainable by the enterprise'.[39]

After this semi-secret journey she became fully conscious of the power struggle then taking place, as she wrote, she was being 'hampered by formerly unknown restraints' as she had been required to send 'the first half of the Baktiar journey to the Indian War Office' while as she remarked 'the second half will go this week'.[40] Her book *Travels in Persia and Kurdistan*, full of good descriptions and gripping narrative as severe weather threatened their progress, is a model of discretion. Major Sawyer, the anonymous 'M—', is referred to occasionally, but of the strategic importance of the area, nary a word.

Had she travelled safely because of her own courage and resourcefulness or because it was inconceivable that a woman could be any part of the undercover operation of the Great Game? She certainly was much better

Mrs Bishop astride 'Boy' at Erzeroum, Turkey, December 1890, with Mirza Yusuf (r) and Murphy O'Rourke (l).

informed as a result of her travels and had heard much of the Great Game. The conversation which she had with one *Hakim* (physician) expressed attitudes then commonly held in the Middle East. 'You are a powerful people', he said to her, 'but very slow. The people, who know nothing, have too much share in your government. To rule in Asia, and you are one of the greatest Asiatic powers, you must not introduce Western theories of government. You must be despotic and prompt, and your policy must not vibrate. See here now, the Shah dies, the Zil-i-Sultan disputes the succession with the Crown Prince and in a few days Russia occupies Azerbaijan with 200,000 men, captures Teheran, and marches on Isfahan. Meanwhile your statesmen talk for weeks in parliament, and when Russia has established her *prestige* and has organised Persia, then your fleet with a small army will sail from India! Bah! No country ruled by a woman will rule in Asia'.[41]

She had left Baghdad on 10 January and arrived at Trebizond on 12 December 1890. She had travelled 2,500 miles.

Notes

1. P Hopkirk, *The Great Game, on Secret Service in High Asia*, (1990), see also *The Times*, 5 May 1990.
2. See I L Bishop, 'A Journey through Lesser Tibet', *SGM*, (October 1892), pp.573–628, 'Among the Tibetans', *Leisure Hour*, (1893), pp.238–244, 306–312, 380–386, 450–456; and *Among the Tibetans*, (1894).
3. ILB, 'A Journey through Lesser Tibet', *SGM*, (October 1892), p.513.
4. 'Lesser Tibet', *SGM*, p.514.
5. 'Lesser Tibet', *SGM*, p.514.
6. 'Lesser Tibet', *SGM*, p.514.
7. Her horse was Gyalpo ' a beautiful creature' who 'left the mark of his teeth or his heels on everyone', *Leisure Hour*, (1893), p.238.
8. 'Lesser Tibet', *SGM*, p.517.
9. 'Lesser Tibet', *SGM*, p.517.
10. 'Lesser Tibet', *SGM*, p.517.
11. 'Lesser Tibet', *SGM*, p.521.
12. There was legally no such place as 'British Tibet' for Tibet had remained largely isolated, protected by its great mountains from the predatory advances of Britain, Russia and China (which had claimed suzerainty since 1720). Britain invaded in 1903–4 and Russia made a treaty in 1905.
13. 'Lesser Tibet', *SGM*, p.525.
14. G N Curzon (1859–1925) First Marquess of Kedleston, was in 1890 an ambitious young politician establishing his credentials as an expert on the Middle East. He became Viceroy of India in 1898.
15. AS, p.221.
16. *Journeys in Persia and Kurdistan*, Vol.I and II, Virago edition, 1988 and 1989, (hereafter *Persia*). *Persia*, Vol.I, Letter VI, p.132.
17. *Persia*, Vol.I, Letter VI, p.136.
18. *Persia*, Vol.I, Letter VI, p.130.

19. *Persia*, Vol.I, Letter VI, pp.113–114.

20. *Persia*, Vol.I, Letter IV, pp.90–91.

21. *Persia*, Vol.I, Letter VIII, p.181.

22. *Persia*, Vol.I, Letter VI, p.147.

23. H A Sawyer (Major), *A Reconnaissance in the Bakhtiari Country, S.W. Persia*, Simla, (1891), pp.31–33, (copy in RGS Library, London).

24. *Persia*, Vol.I, Letter X, p.211.

25. *Persia*, Vol.I, Letter X, p.221.

26. *Persia*, Vol.I, Letter XI, p.226.

27. *Persia*, Vol.I, Letter XI, p.244.

28. *Persia*, Vol.I, Letter X, p.219.

29. AS, p.225.

30. AS, p.227.

31. *Persia*, Vol.I, Letter XIV, pp.282–3.

32. *Persia*, Vol.I, Letter XIV, p.285, see also Chapter 13, note 30.

33. *Persia*, Vol.I, Letter XIV, p.322.

34. H.A. Sawyer, *A Reconnaissance in the Bakhtiari Country, S.W. Persia*, p.78 (copy in RGS library, London).

35. *Persia*, Vol.II, Letter XXV, p.171.

36. The Vice-Consul at Van said that 'he would have doubted the sanity of anyone who had proposed to travel from Urmi to Van by the route I took', *Persia*, Vol.II, Letter XXX, p.333.

37. *Persia*, Vol.II, Letter XXXIV, p.381.

38. *Persia*, Vol.II, Letter XXXIV, p.382.

39. AS, p.242.

40. JSB, ILB to Eliza B. Bournmouth, 21 February 1891, MS 2638, f.208.

41. *Persia*, Vol.II, Letter XXV, p.199.

10   *Korea, 'a mere shuttlecock'*

In January 1894 Isabella Bishop left her native shores for a period of travelling in the Far East which was to last for a total of three years and three months. Her journeys were in Korea[1] and China, while she retreated to Japan from time to time to rest and recuperate. As a result of these adventures she produced two books, one in 1897 on Korea[2] and the other in 1899 on the Yangtse basin of China. These reinforce the impression that, though she reported and wrote with her usual clarity and enthusiasm, she was by 1894 like the Flying Dutchman a wanderer prevented from settling anywhere permanently.

During these years Mrs Bishop paid four separate visits to Korea and spent a total of nine months there. She arrived first on 1 March 1894 and remained there until 21 June when she was 'deported' to China because of the threat of war,[3] then she was back for six weeks early in 1895 and again in October. Leaving for China at Christmas 1895, she returned in mid-October 1896 and remained in Seoul until the end of December 1896. At first she found the country depressing and monotonous; perhaps her unfavourable reaction was partly due to her sense of loss at hearing of the death of Miss Clayton, a dear friend of long standing. She explored widely and she became familiar with the urgent problems which faced this poor undeveloped country which lay helpless – a 'mere shuttlecock', as she noted, between Russia, China and Japan. Her experiences in Korea where she knew the King, and the Queen (before her assassination) as well as the representatives of the Western powers, forced her into an appraisal of political realities in the Far East in the late 1890s. *Korea and her Neighbours* is an account of her travels but also includes much on helpless Korea unable to respond adequately to political pressure from outside.

Korea had succeeded in maintaining its isolation as the Hermit Kingdom until 1876 when Japan forced a treaty on her; within six years, in 1882, China had imposed 'Trade and Frontier Regulations'. Subsequently, the door having been prised open, the United States (1882), Great Britain and Germany (1884), Russia and Italy (1886) and Austria (1892) all succeeded in arranging treaties. Korea was for these purposes treated as an independent state and not as heretofore subject to Chinese overlordship. The outcome of the treaties was that Seoul, together with the ports of Chemulpo, Fusan, and

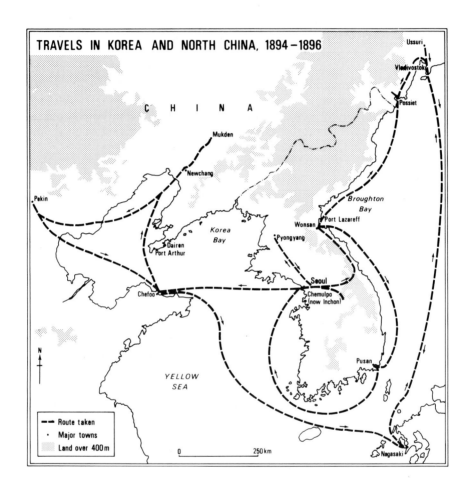

TRAVELS IN KOREA AND NORTH CHINA, 1894–1896

CHINA

Ussuri

Vladivostok

Possiet

Mukden

Newchang

Broughton
Bay

Pekin

Port Lazareff

Wonsan

Korea
Bay

Pyongyang

Dairen
Port Arthur

Seoul

Chefoo

Chemulpo
(now Inchon)

N

Pusan

YELLOW
SEA

Nagasaki

- - Route taken
·   Major towns
      Land over 400 m

0   250 km

Wonsan were opened to foreign trade, later in 1897 two other treaty ports, Mok-po and Chinnam-po were added to the list.

Once the treaties had been signed, some foreign representatives were accredited to Korea although the British merely asked their minister to China additionally to act as minister to Korea. Small settlements for foreigners were built in Seoul and at the treaty ports elsewhere. It was the Japanese[4] who took advantage of the new facilities having (in 1897) more than 10,500 nationals (out of a total of 11,000 foreigners) as well as 230 (out of 266) business concerns. At this time there were some 65 British subjects in Korea. It was also the Japanese who provided banking facilities as she noted, 'The fine Japanese *yen* or dollar is now current everywhere. The *Dai Ichi Gingo* and Fifty-Eight Bank of Japan afford banking facilities in Seoul and the open ports'.[5] It was a relief to have the benefits of Japanese banking at the treaty ports especially as she was to find no effective facilities for money exchange in rural Korea.

In the countryside in Korea in the late 1890s Mrs Bishop was subjected to much more personal harassment than had befallen her earlier. On one occasion 'young Mr Miller', the missionary accompanying her, was forced to confront one of her attackers as he 'very gently, without anger' dealt him 'a scientific blow on the chest'. This 'sent him off the road upon his back in a barley field'. This, as she remarked, almost apologetically, was 'Lynch law'.[6]

She also aroused hostility by her presence as a woman travelling openly and on several occasions in Korea she was subjected to an intense curiosity, which amounted to assault. At one inn she reported that 'The women and children sat on my bed in heaps, examined my clothing, took out my hairpins and pulled down my hair, took off my slippers and drew my sleeves up to the elbow and pinched my arms to see if they were of the same flesh and blood as their own'.[7] On this occasion her Chinese servant Wong restored order by turning out the crowd for the fourth time, and then advising her strongly to sit on her bed and clean her revolver. This proved effective. It should also be noted that during her travels in Japan (in 1878) her man Ito, as a Japanese, had greater authority than either Mr Miller (himself a suspect foreigner) or Wong, her excellent Chinese servant had amongst the Koreans.[8]

Prior to leaving for the Far East, Mrs Bishop had spent three years at home. As a famous speaker she had lectured on several occasions, for the Royal Geographical Society in London and for its Scottish equivalent in Edinburgh. Moreover, she spoke widely for the missionary organisations, lacing her message on spreading the Christian Word with her own remarkable travel experiences.

Her health remained precarious. In Edinburgh Dr Grainger Stewart, a close friend as well as her medical adviser, confirmed, by the end of 1893 'the inefficient action of her heart, an affection of the base of one lung,

Mrs Bishop's own photograph of Chemulpo harbour (now Inchon), Korea 1897, showing the primitive hovels on the shore and the local sailing ships in the harbour.

which retarded her pulse and enfeebled her breathing'.[9] It is not possible to judge whether in present day terms this diagnosis had any reality. As expected, Dr Grainger Stewart did not forbid travel, indeed he advised it. Clearly Isabella was making plans.

In January 1894, full of presentiments of death, perhaps not unusual even in a gallant 63 year old, she left England from the port of Liverpool. She was delighted to find that the Allan Line had – at their expense not hers – allocated her a deck cabin on SS *Mongolia* in which she travelled to Halifax, then across Canada; then finally from Vancouver Island to Yokohama. As her immediate destination was Korea she moved via Kobe arriving at Chemulpo (now Inchon), the port for Seoul, on 1 March 1894.

Without a Korean interpreter her first efforts to get away into unknown Korea proved difficult. The situation was saved by a young Presbyterian missionary, a Mr Miller, who volunteered to bring his own Korean servant and travel with her.[10] She quickly hired a small boat and with her tiny party set off to explore the northern and southern branches of the Han river which, rising in the mountains to the east dissects Korea and flows to the sea near Chemulpoo.

The boat – at 28 feet long and almost 5 feet wide – was topped by a ridge pole and sticks and a roof covered with 'mats of pheasant grass'. She had ordered the roof herself as an extra and it proved serviceable, although the rain penetrated quickly, and the wind blew it off from time to time. The bow of the boat was kitchen and poultry yard, the centre was for Mrs Bishop and the 'hinder division' was for Mr Miller. In her central section she had placed her 'bed, chair, saddle and luggage' but she also accommodated 'sacks, rice-bags, clothing and baskets' reducing her area 'to a bare 6 feet', while Mr Miller 'lived and studied' in a space of 7'x4'4" and he and Chinese and Korean servant slept in this section.[11]

During this river exploration of over five weeks duration, the boat was being propelled up the river against the current. Part of the journey was relatively easy through placid waters, during which two boatmen – one fore and one aft – paddled or poled. When they were mounting the rapids, progress was slow, they sometimes made 'only 7 miles a day and it often took two hours to ascend a few yards, two poling with might and main in the boat, and three tugging with all their strength on shore. Sometimes the ropes snapped, then the boat went spinning and flying to the foot of the rapid'.[12] Occasionally Mrs Bishop 'in great exigencies gave a haul herself' but usually – no doubt to the relief of her companions – she waded ashore in water-proof wellingtons and walked along the river banks enjoying the surrounding countryside while the men man-handled the boat.

There can be little doubt that storming the rapids in this way exhilarated and excited her. Despite the hazards she was thrilled, writing 'the river

The Sampan, with a grass roof, which Mrs Bishop hired to take her up the Han River, Korea in 1894. Not many travellers would have contemplated such a journey in such conditions. (Photograph by Mrs Bishop.)

occasionally compressed by its colossal walls, vents its fury in flurry and foam, or expands into broad reaches 20 or even 30 feet in depth, where pure emerald water laps gently upon crags festooned with roses and honeysuckle, or in fairy bays on pebbly beaches and pure sand. The air was full of gladness. The loud call of the fearless ringed pheasant was heard everywhere, bees hummed and butterflies and dragon flies flashed through the fragrant air. What mattered it that our ropes broke three times, that we stuck on a rock on a rapid and hung there for an hour in a deafening din and a lather of foam and that "we beat the record" in only making 5 miles in twelve hours'.[13]

They had explored the south branch of the Han river first and then – despite the boatmen's anguished protests – pushed their way up the North Han.[14] Within forty miles of the east coast they parted company with Kim the boatman and his boat and, hiring horses moved overland, via the Diamond Mountains, to the sea. They eventually found their way north to the Korean treaty port at Wonsan, on the Pacific coast. During a twelve day period, as guest of American Presbyterian missionaries, Mr and Mrs Gale,[15] Isabella travelled north to Broughton Bay and explored Port Lazareff before setting sail south around the coast intending to return to Seoul. At Fusan, on the south coast of Korea, she found Japanese troops and a gun-boat in the harbour. When she reached Chemulpo, the port of Seoul, on the early morning of 21 June 1894 she found 'the deadly dull port transformed' by the Japanese.

The British vice-consul was insistent that there was a Japanese invasion and that she could not land but must leave at once on the *Higo Maru*, the Japanese vessel on which she had just arrived, which was going on to Chefoo in China. She had left all her gear in Wonsan in anticipation of returning for an autumn journey. Nevertheless – with no clothing other than the heavy tweed suit she was wearing, and the temperature at 80°F – she agreed to leave.

When she landed at Chefoo, without money, documents or clothes, she had to walk in great heat to the British Consulate. Embarrassed by her predicament, Isabella 'hung about the gate of the British Consulate for some minutes before I could summon up the courage to go to the door and send in the torn address of a letter which was my only visiting card'.[16] Consul Clement Allan of course welcomed her warmly, escorted her to the bank and arranged for her to be given credit. She also received 'a bundle of summer clothes' from her female compatriots and, thus equipped, returned to the *Higo Maru* which continued on its way to Newchang in Manchuria. *En route* she was pleased to see the mouth of the Peiho river and the Taku[17] forts which had been the scene of several notorious military actions against the Chinese in the previous years.

Once in Newchang she resolved to travel north to Mukden where there was an important missionary hospital but, at the beginning of July when she was rested and ready to move, she found the country to the north flooded. She embarked on a difficult journey on 'a narrow pea-boat', with one sail and a matting roof, which had come from the north carrying beans, the staple crop. The small boat was often becalmed as it made its way in pouring rain across the flooded countryside, ignoring the actual course of the river.

On arrival, having been in constant misery for days, she was ill, but in the course of being carried on a springless cart into Mukden she was tipped out, splintering a bone in her arm and tearing fore tendons. Dr Christie, one of the Scotch missionaries, nursed her in his home and she soon recovered. She was much impressed with the medical and Christian work undertaken by Dr Ross and Dr Christie[18] who because they went to great trouble to study and defer to local habits and customs, had developed, over their twenty-two years in Mukden, good relations with the authorities.

Echoes of war soon reached Mukden and Mrs Bishop was put on a rain-proof junk for the journey back to Newchang. From there she continued travelling, moving on to Pekin, then north by boat to Vladivostok where she stayed a month exploring the area and considering the success of the Russians as colonisers of their newly acquired empire in the Far East. She was anxious to discover the circumstances of those Koreans whom the Russians had re-settled as farmers in an area which had been a forested wilderness as late as the 1860s. By the end of 1894 she found 'newness, progress and hopefulness' the characteristics of Vladivostok, which lay at the centre of 'Russia's vast growing, aspiring Pacific Empire'.[19] She could see for herself the strong military and naval presence.

She took a seven hour journey to Possiet Bay, in territory claimed by Russia but not far from the N E Korean border where she found prosperous Koreans producing beef cattle for the Russian forces. She penetrated along the Russo-Korean border, eleven miles inland from Possiet Bay and from this vantage point could command a view of China at its north-eastern extremity. Her boat was almost frozen in as the ice thickened but she was able to return to Vladivostok. Later she made an excursion up the Ussuri river where she found the temporary terminus of the Trans-Siberian railway which did not at that time reach the eastern sea. She left Vladivostok on the last Japanese steamer of the season and spent a little time in Nagasaki before returning to Korea in January 1895.

During the time spent in Eastern Russia in and around Vladivostok, Mrs Bishop saw much of Russian military and civilian officials. She formed a favourable impression of the Russians who were successful she believed because 'she is firm where firmness is necessary, but outside that limit allows extreme latitude, avoids harassing aliens by petty prohibitions and irksome rules, encourages those forms of local self government which suits the genius and habits of different peoples and trusts to time, education and contact with other forms of civilisation to amend that which is reprehensible in customs,

The Gate of Victory, Mukden, Manchuria 1894.
(Photograph by Mrs Bishop.)

religion and costume'.[20] Was her glowing endorsement of Russian policy altogether over optimistic?

On her second visit to Korea in January and February 1895 she did not move beyond the capital, Seoul, partly because she was staying in the British Legation during 'two exciting months'.[21] She returned to Korea in the autumn of the same year, and apart from a journey north to Pyong yang, remained in Seoul. Her interest was aroused by the power struggle then playing itself out around the persons of the King and Queen of Korea as the Japanese began to flex their new military and naval muscles. For the first time in the modern period a non-Western nation was a force to be reckoned with.

Mrs Bishop arrived in Korea (in 1895) in time to witness the ceremony on 8 January whereby the Japanese presented Korea with its 'independence'. The King of Korea had found reasons to delay this occasion – which also required that he renounce Chinese suzerainty – fearing to antagonise his ancestral spirits by his actions. But in the end the Japanese prevailed and in solemn procession the reluctant King took the oath. As was observed, 'The sky was dark and grim, and a bitter east wind was blowing – ominous signs in the Korean estimation'.[22]

As the King emerged from the palace gate there were 'Groups of scarlet and blue-robed men in hats of the same colors, shaped like fools' caps, the King's personal servants in yellow robes and yellow bamboo hats, and men carrying bannerets. Then came the red silk umbrella followed ... by a plain wooden chair with glass sides in which sat the sovereign looking pale and dejected'. The oath was taken in the sacred enclosure where the King and his attendants were grouped 'under the dark pines'.[23]

Shortly after this occasion Mrs Bishop was entertained at the palace at a private audience. During the following weeks she was received on three further occasions so that she was able to make a judgement of both King and Queen. The King seemed a weak, well-meaning man quite unable to respond in any effective way to the crisis facing his Kingdom, while the Queen, by contrast, was powerful and clever, of 'singular intelligence and force'.

She returned to Korea in early October 1895, having heard rumours, which proved to be true, of the Queen's assassination. In May 1895, after the Sino–Japanese War the Chinese had been forced by the victorious Japanese to sign the Treaty of Shimonoseki by which they not only promised to pay a huge indemnity but also ceded the island of Formosa to Japan. With such a prestigious settlement behind them the Japanese felt they had earned a free hand in Korea. The assassination of the Queen was engineered by malcontent Koreans with the connivance and encouragement of the Japanese. The Japanese government may not have been implicated in the murder although their representatives then in Korea were.

Following the excitement of the tragedy of the Queen of Korea, Mrs

Bishop, attended by Mr Yi, a Korean who spoke good English and was 'bright, courteous, intelligent and good-natured',[24] and by Im, a soldier-servant from the British legation, set out on a journey north from Seoul to Pyong yang. Near the latter town the Chinese and Japanese had fought during the recent campaigns and she was able to see the devastation of war at first hand. With her usual disregard for wintry and inclement weather, the party started on 7 November and travelled slowly north over irregular mountainous and forested country to Song-du a 'royal city' with a good trade in grain. Around 150 licensed growers also harvested large quantities of Ginseng which was processed by two manufacturers.

Beyond Pyongyang she made her way to the battlefield where she found a memorial to General Tso, the dead commander of the Chinese forces. The memorial took the form of a 'neat obelisk' on which the legend read 'Tso Pao-Kuei, commander-in-chief of the Feng-tien division'. She had met General Tso in Mukden, Manchuria, where she had found him on good terms with the Scotch missionaries.[25] It was, she remarked, 'less of a battle than a massacre ... before the morning, this force, the flower of the Chinese army as to drill and equipment, had perished ... It is estimated that from 2,000 – 4,000 men were slain'.[26]

They left north Korea by the *Hariong*, which they boarded regardless of the fact that it was already crammed with Japanese soldiers, for Mrs Bishop, knowing there was nowhere nearby to rest, insisted upon staying on the ship. Poor Mr Yi would certainly have been left behind shelterless had he not been in the company of such a masterful woman.

By the 23 October 1896, when she visited Korea for the fourth and last time, she found many changes. The King received her kindly, made her welcome on three occasions, and told her that he would like a British Minister accredited to the Korean court. She found the Japanese in control, and various Korean officers clearing up the dirt and rubbish of the back streets of Seoul. But she also found that the Russians were still much in evidence, for the King had fled to the Russian Minister at the time of the Queen's murder and had remained there for a year. Even after he had agreed to return to his palace he had demonstrated his independence of the Japanese by inviting the Russians to send a Military Commission to re-organise and train the Korean army.

Sir Walter Hillier paid a remarkable tribute to Mrs Bishop's understanding of Korea, writing, 'Those who like myself have known Korea from its first opening to foreign intercourse will appreciate the closeness of Mrs Bishop's observation, the accuracy of her facts, the correctness of her inferences. She has been honoured by the confidence and friendship of the King and the late Queen in a degree that has never before been accorded to any foreign traveller and has had access to valuable sources of information, while her presence in the country during and subsequent to the war between China and Japan, of

The South Gate, entrance to Seoul, Korea 1895.
(Photograph by Mrs Bishop.)

which Korea was in the first instance the stage has furnished her ... the opportunity of recording with accuracy and impartiality many details of an episode of Far Eastern history which has hitherto been clouded by misstatement and exaggeration. The hardships and difficulties encountered by Mrs B. during her journeys into the interior of Korea have been lightly touched upon by herself but those who know how great they were admire the courage, patience and endurance which enabled her to overcome them'.[27]

As she left Korea for the last time in December 1896 Mrs Bishop knew that the Koreans were victims. They could not escape from their strategic position as Russia and Japan struggled for supremacy. After the Russo–Japanese war, when Japan had ousted Russia from Korea, the full weight of Japan's efficiency would be turned on to the defenceless Koreans.

By 1906, Western commentators skilled in Far Eastern affairs knew of the régime which Japan had imposed on Korea; indeed the Japanese themselves knew how they were regarded. Two comments illustrate how justified Mrs Bishop was (in the 1890s) in fearing for Korea and the Koreans. In August 1906, Dr G T Ladd left New Haven, USA to spend some time in Korea at the request of Marquis Ito, then Japanese Resident General there. Ladd's brief was to advise Ito on how to 'encourage the Koreans to accept Japanese rule'. As Ladd noted, 'Complaints of various sorts were constantly being made, not only against individual Japanese but also against the Japanese administration, as unjust and oppressive to the Koreans, and as selfish and exclusive towards other foreigners ... Especially had such complaints of late been propagated by American missionaries[28] either directly or by letters and newspaper articles .... In this way exaggerations and falsehoods were spread abroad as freely as one-sided or half truths .... The Marquis Ito greatly desired to be absolutely just and fair and to prevent the mistakes so harmful both to Korea and Japan'.[29]

It is interesting to read the comments of B L Putnam Weale, an experienced Far Eastern commentator who wrote how, 'It is but 48 hours between the two capitals (of Japan and Korea) ... Thus everything has been made convenient for Japan's civilising mission. The capital of a distressful country has been brought as close as possible to the capital of a successful empire; yet up to now the result has been pure failure'.[30]

Japan annexed Korea in 1910.[31] It could be argued that the way had been cleared for this action by the Anglo–Japanese Alliance of 1902.

Notes

1. Lee J. Longford, *The Story of Korea*, (1911), G.N. Curzon, *Problems of the Far East, Japan–Korea*, (1894), J.S. Gale, *Korean Sketches*, (1898), *Korea in Transition*, (1909), C.I.E. Kim and H-K. Kim, *Korea and the Politics of Imperialism 1876-1910*, (1967).
2. ILB, *Korea and her Neighbours*, (1898), was re-issued in a facsimile edition by

Pacific Basin Books, Kegan Paul Inc., 1985, (hereafter *Korea*).

3. A little later *The Times* was reporting on 'the extraordinary secrecy in which the operations of the [Korean] war have been successfully wrapped up by the Japanese authorities', *The Times*, 29 November 1894.

4. Japan had territorial ambitions in Korea and Taiwan, as soon as their new military and naval strength could sustain them.

5. ILB, *Korea*, (KPI, 1985), p.20.

6. *Korea*, p.104.

7. *Korea*, p.127.

8. *Korea*, p.66.

9. AS, p.270.

10. *Korea*, p.66.

11. *Korea*, p.69.

12. *Korea*, p.93.

13. *Korea*, p.99.

14. *Korea*, p.106.

15. See Rev. J.S. Gale, *Korean Sketches*, (1898), and *Korea in Transition*, (1909).

16. *Korea*, p.185.

17. S.G. Checkland, *The Elgins*, (1988), pp.153-154.

18. In her Will she left 'to the United Free Church of Scotland the sum of Five Hundred Pounds (£500) the income thereof to be applied in aid of the permanent endowment of the Medical Mission Hospital at Mukden' (SRO, SC/70/7/27).

19. *Korea*, p.221.

20. *Korea*, pp.236-237.

21. *Korea*, p.269.

22. *Korea*, p.247.

23. *Korea*, pp.248-249.

24. *Korea*, p.283.

25. AS, p.287.

26. *Korea*, p.317.

27. *The Scotsman*, Obituary, 8 October 1904. Sir Walter Caine Hillier, KCMG 1897, CB 1903, late Consul-General Korea, 1891-6, and Chinese Secretary to the British Legation in Pekin, latterly British Adviser to the Chinese government. He had known Mrs Bishop well during her time in Korea, *Whitaker's Peerage, Baronetage, Knightage and Compassionage,* (1909), p.404.

28. The complainants included Rev & Mrs J.S. Gale with whom ILB had stayed at Wonsan.

29. G.T. Ladd, *In Korea with Marquis Ito*, p.4. Ito Hirubumi (1841-1909) had travelled widely in the West and was an expert on foreign affairs. As a consummate politician he had been Prime Minister three times before resigning from office in 1901. Thereafter he became involved with Japanese foreign policy, including being Japanese Resident General in Korea. He was assassinated in Harbin, Manchuria, in 1909 by a Korean nationalist.

30. B.L. Putnam Weale, *The Truce in the East and its Aftermath*, (1907), p.40.

31. When President Roh of South Korea visited Japan in May 1990 Emperor Akihito expressed Japan's 'deepest regret' for its colonisation of the Korean peninsula, *The Times*, 25 May 1990.

11 China, 'an elaborate and antique civilisation'

During her three-year stay in the Far East between 1894 and 1897 Mrs Bishop paid two visits to China.[1] She was in the Shanghai area visiting Hangchow and Ningpo for three months in the Spring of 1895, and made her major exploration of the Sze Chuan province of inner China during the first six months of 1896. It was a difficult period which culminated in the Boxer[2] Rebellion of 1900 when members of a Chinese secret society (I-ho t'uan) in northern China, took murderous action against foreigners, whose imperialist ambitions had been much resented for some years. Any foreign traveller in China in the late nineteenth century knew of the danger as small incidents quickly grew into something more threatening. The number of unpleasant encounters which she personally reports in her book *The Yangtze Valley and Beyond*[3] is quite startling.

There were two main reasons for Chinese hostility. Treaties had, for many years, been forced on China by well-armed Western powers by the terms of which Chinese ports were forced open for foreign trade. Initially, the treaty ports were on the coast at Canton, Amoy, Foochow, Ningpo and Shanghai but by the 1890s the importunate foreigner had demanded access to inland ports including Hankow and Chung King. The penetration of central China by Westerners 'aroused strong local hostility'. As was explained, 'each new treaty port enriches the Imperial government at the expense of the provinces and deprives a great number of officials of their "legitimate" perquisites or "squeezes" in favour, as people think of highly salaried customs employees'.[4] The siphoning off of local revenue, previously the perquisite of provincial officials, by imperial officers – and often foreigners at that – was a source of much discontent which could easily erupt into violence. When she arrived at I-chang, where she stayed with Mr Scholtz, the Commissioner of Customs, she was surprised to see 'cairns of stones' in the hall and elsewhere. These had, she was told, been used as ammunition and had been hurled through the windows of the house during an anti–foreign riot some days earlier.[5]

The Christian missionaries were also a cause of offence for not only were they believed to be an arm of imperialism, but their proselytising zeal implied criticism of those Confucian ideals by which the Chinese had lived for centuries. Missionaries, who usually lived unprotected yet conspicuous within Chinese communities, were particularly vulnerable to overt hostility.

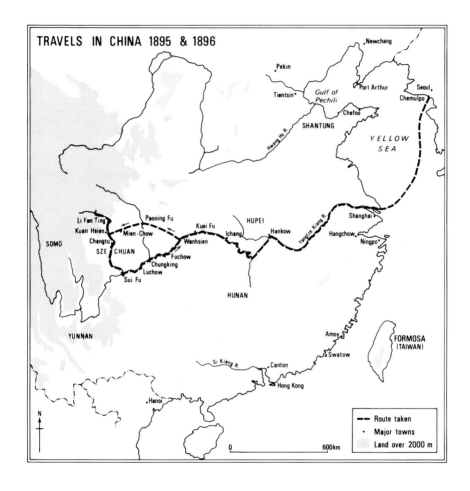

TRAVELS IN CHINA 1895 & 1896

Only members of the China Inland Mission went to the lengths of appearing 'all in Chinese dress'. This certainly made them less conspicuous but did it help? A month earlier there had been uproar in Wan Hsien; a deep well had run dry and everyone believed that the missionaries were responsible. Local people came in a mob to attack and only a respected mandarin persuaded them to withdraw. But the magistrate himself returned to claim that the Christian foreigners had stolen children 'to get their eyes and that their bodies were in the tanks at the back' of the house.[6] Part of the gulf of understanding between West and East was related to the superstition of the native peoples; eye stealing was one of the many evils regularly attributed to foreign missionaries in China. The magic of the intruders was capable of anything, therefore blame for any disaster could readily be placed on the foreigner who inevitably became the scapegoat.

So, although clearly an oversimplification, for the Chinese, the Western trader and the Christian missionary went hand in hand, both being supported by the superior armed force of Western gunboats.

Mrs Bishop also aroused suspicion because she was a foreign woman travelling alone, in an open chair, accompanied only by a handful of bearers. Respectable Chinese ladies would travel in a closed chair, in a convoy, properly guarded. Even if she had worn Chinese clothes everyone could see that she wore cheap cotton padded garments, topped by a Japanese hat; were she worthy of respect she would have been dressed in silk and would have been safe from prying eyes in her curtained chair. Clearly had Mrs Bishop adopted a safe posture hidden away as the Chinese would have liked she would have seen nothing of the countryside, nor learnt anything of the habits and customs of the people.

One of the most frightening incidents was in Sze Chuan when late one afternoon – being carried in her chair through the great gate into the city – she found herself surrounded by a 'dense and noisy crowd hooting and yelling'. She was bruised by the beating and, by a fluke, escaped into an inn where she was quickly bundled into a dark cupboard. The attack then began in earnest. The shouts turned into 'Beat her', 'Kill her', 'Burn her'. It was a terrifying incident and she was only saved on this occasion by one of her own bearers, who, after an hour of rioting, ran to the authorities with the news that the mob was 'murdering a foreigner'.[7] She was rescued, but it took her some time to recover.

The journeys in China were primarily an exploration of the Yangtze Kiang river basin (see map). She journeyed on the river as far as Wan Hsien then made an enormous detour northward and westward before arriving at Chengtu, the great city of the Sze Chuan basin. She then undertook a further adventure north-west from Chengtu up the River Min into territory bordering China's western frontier where the Mantze people lived on the edge of eastern Tibet. Finally from Chengtu she followed the river in a great sweep southward coming back eventually to the coast (see map).

She started her journey at Shanghai arriving there on this occasion from the north in a small Korean government steamer. She was delighted to see again along the British Bund 'the most approved and massive Anglo–Oriental architecture, standing in large, shady gardens, the Hong Kong and Shanghai Bank, the P&O office, the Canadian Pacific Railroad office, the fine counting house and dwelling house of the old and famous firm of Jardine Matheson & Co. and the long facade of the British Consular buildings with their wide sweep of lawns, being prominent'.[8] She praised the 'Model Settlement' of Shanghai with its Western municipal government, which provided pure water, efficient sewage disposal, and clean streets guarded by an excellent police force. She also commented on the extraordinary proliferation of leisure activities and the enthusiasm with which the Westerners pursued them.

Not all was sweetness and light, for Mrs Bishop spoke sharply about the British merchant community commenting that 'if men were to give to the learning of Chinese and Chinese requirements and methods of business a little time which is lavished on sport and other amusements there might possibly be less occasion for the complaint that large fortunes are no longer to be made in Chinese business'.[9]

Her biting words continued, 'Even in such lordly institutions as the British Banks on the Bund it seems impossible to transact even such a simple affair as cashing a cheque without calling in the aid of a sleek richly dressed Chinese ... who looks as if he knew the business of the bank and were capable of running it. It is different', she went on, 'at the Yokohama Specie Bank ... in which alert Japanese clerks manage their own affairs and speak Chinese'.[10] The theme of British reluctance to alter their business methods to accommodate their customers was one of which she was always conscious and to which she recurred.

When she was far away from Shanghai, in Sze Chuan province, she commented on the prospects for Lancashire cotton and found that 'the general verdict was that the widths of our cottons are wrong, and that widths about 15" cut to waste in making Chinese clothing. Another complaint was that our goods, put up as they are in wrappers intended to impose on "semi-civilised" people constantly make a display of colours which are in China "unlucky".' Another was that the printed cottons '...are coarse in pattern, colouring, and style more fitted for outside barbarians than for the refined tastes of a civilised people ... It is not that our cottons are too dear, but that the majority of people do not want them at any price. That is, that the strong heavy native cottons woven by hand, wear four times as long, and even when they are reduced to rags serve several useful purposes'.[11] The lessons which Isabella Bishop spelt out were never accepted by English cotton men and at this

Mrs Bishop's travelling party. She was sometimes required to take official guides with her. Note the small sturdy horses, the rough but padded dress of the men and the primitive houses in the background. (Photograph by Mrs Bishop.)

time– in the 1890s – the Japanese were busily providing Japanese cottons and ousting Lancashire cottons from China and other Far Eastern markets.[12]

From Shanghai she journeyed up the great river to Hankow, which is really three cities – the other two being Wu-Chang Fu and Han Yang – divided by branches of the river. The treaty port at Hankow had been opened in 1861 three years after Lord Elgin had made a daring voyage as far as Hankow in the *Furious*.[13] Here she found that the river – as she noted 'the glory of Hankow, as well as its terror' – was a mile wide. The river rose and fell depending on the rainfall and snow melt in the western provinces causing devastating floods, and often great loss of life. Sometimes the diminution of the flood waters could be anticipated when 'red' water washed down, for this was known to originate far upstream in the Red basin of Sze Chuan.

She found the principal streets of Hankow paved with large flagstones but remarked on the deep mud of other streets rutted by the heavy wheelbarrows used for transporting goods. The streets were crowded and nearly impassable as everyone struggled to make their way. The passage of a mandarin – with a look of 'unutterable superciliousness and scorn'[14] – sitting upright in his chair as he was carried through the throng by eight bearers assisted by many attendants, pushing through the jostling crowds, amazed her.

She left Hankow on the *Chang-wo*, a 'deck-over-deck, American built, stern-wheel steamer'[15] with six foreign missionaries and hundreds of Chinese aboard. The river was low and progress was slow, as sand and gravel banks impeded their way, so that when the boat sought deep water under the right bank, local people 'pelted them with mud and with such names as *Yang Kweitze,* 'foreign devils' or 'foreign dogs'.[16] There were dozens of Chinese junks – all engineless – and Mrs Bishop was full of praise for the masterly way they were handled by crews who manipulated the long bamboo poles which helped to stiffen the enormous sails, allowing them to manoeuvre their vessels out of danger.

Once they reached I-chang (opened to foreign trade from 1887) it was necessary for her to leave the steamboat and to hire a smaller boat in which to ascend the daunting series of gorges which separated the rest of China from the rich Sze Chuan basin. For over 100 miles the river was held in by the surrounding cliffs of hard rock which forced the water into narrow irregular channels. Boats from below were hauled up the rapids by hundreds of 'trackers' who with loops of rope around their bodies man-handled the boats up the foaming water.   ·

Although each boat carried as crew enough men to drag the boat through low water in ordinary circumstances, at every rapid many more had to be employed. Before the ascent they had the services of a man to bless the boat who bore a white flag bearing the message 'Powers of the water, give a lucky star for the journey' but once the propitiation of the river deities had

The Miton Gorge, Yantze Kiang, China
(photograph taken by Mrs Bishop).

been attended to they were ready. There were two dozen boats in the queue before them and they had to wait three days for their turn, but there was no disaster and after nearly six hours her boat cleared this particular series of rapids. It was felt that the dangers of the ascent of the Yangtze through the gorges fully warrant the vivid descriptions which have been given of them.[17]

In general the boat made each perilous ascent without its passengers, who were unceremoniously debouched onto the wet, slippery rocks at the side of the torrent. Isabella herself remarked that 'I never became used to the rapids and always felt nervous at the foot of each, and preferred the risk of fracturing my limbs among the great boulders and rock faces of the shores to spending hours in a turmoil, watching the fraying of the tow ropes'. She was frequently personally harassed as she waited on the rocks for her boat to be pulled up to the upper level. For the great ascent of the Hsin-tan rapids for which a pilot was necessary, she wrote, 'No-one can convey any idea of the noise and turmoil ... I realised it best by my hearing being affected for some days afterwards. The tremendous crash and roar of the cataract, above which the yells and shouts of hundreds of straining trackers are heard, mingled with the ceaseless beating of drums and gongs, some as signals, others to frighten evil spirits, make up a pandemonium which can never be forgotten'.[18] Eventually, after passing through quiet waters such as Coffin Gorge where they waited desperately for a wind, and several more cataracts, they emerged into the Sze Chuan.

At Wan Hsien she left the river for a huge detour across country to the north. During this journey she was in close touch with the members of the China Inland Mission some of whose members travelled various legs of the journey with her. She noted that every year each station of the China Inland Mission, received, carriage free, 'boxes of tinned eatables, sauces, arrowroot, and invalid comforts' from a Mr Morton of Aberdeen.[19] Some of these delicacies found their way into her baggage but in general, as she explained, 'the longer one travels the fewer preparations one makes and the smaller one's kit'. It was certainly a spartan existence which few travellers could have contemplated; every morning, for 146 days, she had 'a cup of tea made from "tabloids" and a plate of boiled flour, tea on arriving (at the end of each day's travel), and curried fowl or eggs with rice' every evening.[20] She bought from time to time Chinese cotton costumes and new straw shoes, and hoped by wearing such unobtrusive garments to blunt 'the edge of curiosity' of the people amongst whom she moved. This element of her journey 'began auspiciously with a dreamily fine day which developed into a red and gold sunset of crystalline clearness and beauty' but the travel arrangements were rough and she felt she had reached 'bed-rock'.[21]

She crossed rivers and mountains, moving over the pass of Fuh-ri-gan 'by a fine stone staircase of over 5,000 broad, easy steps with a handsome kerb-stone, all in perfect repair'.[22] With her keen eyes she spotted coal-miners 'crawling out of holes in the cliff side with baskets with black contents'. She came upon a gallery 'four feet high down which Lilliputian wagons ... descend from workings along a tramway only 12" wide. From some holes boys crept out with small creels holding not more than twenty-five pounds, roped to their backs and little room to spare above them'. She discovered that the coal seams were always worked on the level – never downwards – 'for fear of grazing the Dragon's back and making him shake the earth'.[23]

In course of time, and after several adventures, she arrived in Paoning Fu, around which there were perhaps some sixty Anglican missionaries working for various missionary societies and which was the chief centre of the work of the China Inland Mission (CIM). She was glad to accept the hospitality of the CIM which occupied some simple Chinese houses built around two compounds and was impressed by the devotion of these man and women who committed themselves so wholeheartedly to Chinese life. Their objectives, to learn Chinese, to dress in Chinese clothes, to observe Chinese deference as well as to work for the Christian mission were very demanding.

At this mission station there was no hospital and so it gave Mrs Bishop pleasure to provide the modest finance to fund the Henrietta Bird Memorial Hospital which was opened in one half of 'a noble Chinese mansion with a mandarins procession and great ceremony' some months after her departure (see Chapter 13).

She moved on westwards stopping at Mien-chow where she noted again while staying at Church Mission House the hazards of the missionary life where the two ladies required much fortitude to survive solitude and isolation although recently the local mandarin had protected them from attack saying dismissively, 'What does it matter? They are only women'.[24] Could women missionaries achieve much in Chinese society which had so little regard for the female half of the race? She pondered the wisdom of allowing married couples with children to commit themselves to the hazards of life in China at this time. Not unreasonably she believed that some children were so badly affected by the constant threat of violence that they should not be required to live in such conditions.

As she moved west and then south to Chengtu she was amazed at the richness of the great province of Sze Chuan isolated from the rest of China by the natural barrier of the Yangtze gorges and the surrounding mountainous terrain. It was an area containing some 4,000,000 people, of which almost half a million lived in the capital Chengtu. The land, rich and cared for, had been created by the engineering feats of Li Ping and his son (known only as 'The Second Gentleman') who had some two thousand years earlier drained the land and created a garden province.

Such well-cared-for land could produce as many as four crops a year including rice, opium, tobacco, sugar, sweet potatoes, indigo, rape and other oils, maize and cotton as well as mulberry trees for silk production and fruits of all kinds. The skilful water engineering, embodied in Li Ping's motto 'Dig the bed deep, keep the banks low',[25] so managed the water supply that the province had long been protected from drought and flood which continued to devastate other areas of China. The whole complex of water channels was kept clear by rigorous maintenance work which required some five or six feet of silt to be removed every year. It was the regular attention to the repair of the stone dykes and the existence of a short stretch of artificial river (the Min near Kuan Hsien) which, together with conscientious upkeep of the whole system, gave the Sze Chuan its enviable fertility and prosperity.

Mrs Bishop had looked forward to Chengtu, which had been recommended to her as 'a second Pekin'. She entered through the West gate, was relieved to see in the Tartar quarter, 'tall, healthy looking women with big feet' going about their business with 'something of the ease and freedom of Englishwomen'. The city had wide, well-paved streets which crossed at right angles, as well as a network of waterways crowded with craft all jostling to make progress. The city was encompassed by a 35ft high brick-faced wall with eight bastions which was some fourteen miles in circumference; in the wall there were four gateways which allowed the authorities to stop everyone and charge local customs for goods coming in. Chengtu, which bore, she thought, no resemblance to a European city, had great temples and fine public buildings and may have looked the same to her as it had to Marco Polo centuries earlier.[26]

After enjoying the sights of Chengtu, Mrs Bishop was intent on making a further excursion north and west (see map). She was recovering from one of the more serious attacks on her and so allowed others, including a Mr Kay, who with a good knowledge of colloquial Chinese, was to accompany her, to make the arrangements. This she was later to regret, as carelessness in recruiting coolies and bearers was to lead to difficulties later. She also regretted – as she was now moving into remote territory – that she had no reliable equipment for checking temperature and air pressure: her hypsometer (for calculating altitude by measuring the boiling point of water) had been 'rolled on by a pony'.[27]

Her party consisted of three bearers, for her carrying chair, two *chai-gen* (compulsory guides or attendants), five porters, Mr Kay and herself and their two personal servants. Their route was to take them up the valley of the Min river on a mountainous and circuitous road involving much climbing, but although very wet, the air as they moved upwards was cooler than in the valley and the scenery was magnificent. She found the bamboo bridges slung across the river beautiful but 'trying to the nerves' as the planks of the bridge 'tip up or tip down, or disappear altogether, or show remarkable vivacity

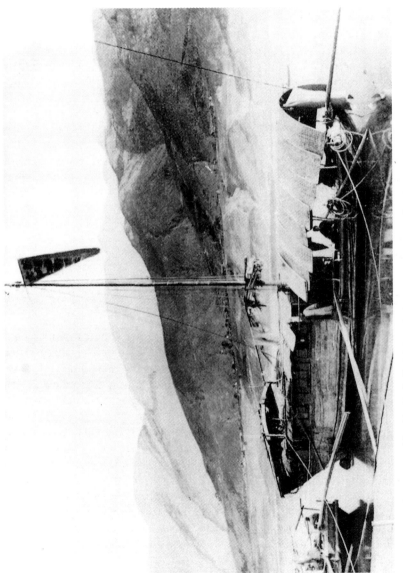

The *sampan* hired by Isabella Bishop for part of the journey up the Yangtze Kiang, China. (Photograph by Mrs Bishop.)

West Gate at Chiang-Ling Fu, China

when the foot is placed upon them, and many a gaping hiatus, trying to any but the steadiest head, reveals the foam and fury below'.[28]

For a fortnight they proceeded over this beautiful country as the road dipped and wound its way around mountains and over rivers; sometimes the road was 'scaffolded' – built out over a chasm on planks – or proceeded on steps cut into the rock. It was soon clear that one of the bearers was 'not up to his work' and because of the difficulties of the road they were only covering some thirteen miles during a nine hour day. As the road showed signs of deteriorating she wished she had had her Mexican saddle (which had been left in Korea) which would have enabled her to hire horses and dispense with some of the men who were unequal to this gruelling job of carrying her chair. As they moved further into the mountains they found the people more Central Asian than Chinese, and roofs were no longer of thatch but made of thin slabs of stone often held down in the face of threatening winds, by even heavier boulders. She noticed with approval that women were freer and could, like the men, cross the rivers by 'dangling from rope bridges'.[29]

Throughout this journey there was difficulty over the shortage of food, for in the mountains a party of twelve travellers proved an embarrassment. In one place the people made macaroni for them, cutting strips after the 'very close barley meal' had been rolled out thinly which was boiled and eaten with chopped peppers and onion. They also had sandwiches made with garlic chopped between 'layers of steamed paste'.[30] To feed her party at all required much negotiation. The poor supplies of food in the mountains caused unpleasantness; was this an artificial food shortage and part of the campaign to discourage her journey?

At Li-fan Ting they were told they could not proceed further, polite officials insisted that, for her comfort and safety, she must turn back, they barred gates and stationed sentries, 'the veneer of politeness disappeared'.[31] After a one day wait she decided to test the official resolve, there was a trial of strength, she managed to get into her chair, her bearers were told not to lift her, she told them to proceed. Mr Kay went ahead and opened gates, the officials did not interfere but followed them with imprecations.

Isabella had triumphed on this occasion and felt a 'pleasurable excitement' as they 'plunged into the unknown'.[32] Her curiosity had been aroused by the Man-tze people, apparently Tartars from Central Asia who lived on this western edge of China. She was by this time in Buddhist country with thick-walled stone buildings as she pushed beyond the confines of what was recognised as China.

They did hire mules and travelled further into a wild and untamed land, but food remained an acute problem, she reduced herself to tea and 'damper baked in the ashes' which could be pulled into 'long strings'. They were all hungry but they struggled on. At last she agreed they should turn back. The

Chinese had sent officials on ahead to discourage the Man-tze from helping her but once she had consented to withdraw 'salted goat, flour, honey and ancient and hairy butter'[33] were sent to her as a gift. It was a relief to be able to provide her men with a good meal.

To have succeeded in reaching Somo against all the protests of the authorities was quite a triumph. She abandoned further plans to travel by a river full of cataracts and gorges, down to Ta-tien-lu, (making another wide swing to west and south), partly because of her own weariness and partly because of fever and debility amongst the coolies. She and her men gathered their small equipment and left the 'deep blue glittering skies' of the mountains for lower Sze Chuan where in the heat of 'the Cloudy Province' they were pestered by mosquitoes and sandflies.

After a short rest she left Chengtu on 20 May for the 2,000-mile journey down the river to Shanghai. She hired a *wapan*, a small flat-bottomed boat with a matting roof where – with her cambric curtains erected for privacy – she began what was to be 'a delightful and propitious journey'. At first the boatmen had to man-handle the boat over sand and shingle but soon they joined the larger river where they were impeded by farmers who dammed the river frequently and charged a toll – exorbitant for westerners – before they could pass. She loved the hum of the water-wheels in series on the river bank and as the river became deeper and wider the *wapan* was able to make unhindered free passage.

The journey to Chia-ling Fu of 130 miles, where she stayed for a few days and changed *wapans*, had taken eighty hours. It was a cause of astonishment that the down-river journey was so peaceful and unremarkable when the inward journey by land had been so arduous. She stayed at Suifu and Luchow – where she visited another coal-mine nearby where workings were less extensive and where they were less superstitious about digging too deep and disturbing the Dragon – and eventually arrived at Chung King where she spent some time before leaving again in a hired *wapan*. Before she emerged at I-chang she had of course to brave the rapids up which she had earlier been hauled, but by June, the snows from the Asian High Table lands having melted, the water was some forty-five feet above its winter level. At Chung King the river, in winter some 800 yards wide, was by early summer two-thirds of a mile wide. She gives a graphic description of the downward journey, writing, 'When we reached the rapids, five men pulled frantically with yells which posed as songs, to keep steerage way on her, and we went down like a flash – down smooth hills of water, where rapids had been obliterated; down leaping races, where they had been created; past hideous whirlpools, where to have been sucked in would have been destruction; past temples, pagodas, and grey cities on heights; past villages gleaming white amidst dense greenery; past hill, valley, woodland, garden cultivation; and signs of

Mantze Rock Temple, extreme west of China

Isabella Bishop at Swatow, China with her camera and tripod.
(Photograph taken by Mr Mackenzie.)

industry and prosperity; past junks laid up for the summer in quiet reaches, and junks with frantic crews, straining at the sweeps, chanting wildly, bound downwards like ourselves; and still for days the Great River hurried us remorselessly along .... A pagoda or city scarcely appeared before it vanished – a rapid scarcely tossed up its angry crests ahead before we had left it astern'.[34]

She arrived below the gorges at I-chang some 56 hours – excluding overnight stops – after leaving Chung King. After the peaceful pleasures of being alone with her men on the *wapan*, she found 'the mirrors, enamels and gilding'[35] of the fine river steamer which carried her to Hangkow and Shanghai, distasteful.

But when she reached Shanghai (which she had left on 10 January) at the end of June 1896 she was in forgiving mood and had chosen to forget the unpleasant attacks upon her, writing that she was, 'truly thankful for the freedom from any serious accident and for the deep and probably abiding interest in China and the Chinese'[36] which the journey had engendered. It had been a memorable pilgrimage for a 65-year-old woman.

Not surprisingly she had her own opinion on the best ways to handle China, writing 'My own view is that to strengthen instead of weaken the Central Government is the wisest policy for all nations. We are all at present helping to disintegrate the Empire. In the weakness of the Peking government lies the weakness and possible abrogation of all treaty obligations'.[37] It was a prescient view but unusual even in a perceptive traveller at that time.

Notes

1. See A.H. Smith, *China in Convulsion*, (1901), Lord C. Beresford, *The Break-up of China*, (1899), J.B. Eamess, *The English in China*, (1909), P.A. Varg, *Missionaries, Chinese and Diplomats*, (1958), J.S. Spence, *The Search for Modern China*, 1990.
2. The 'Boxers', the I-ho T'uan Secret Society was partly religious and partly political. It was organised in 1896 by the Prefect of Shantung province and by 1900 it felt strong enough to go on the offensive. They attacked the foreign legation quarter in Pekin and murdered foreign missionaries and Chinese Christians in the countryside. Peace was restored, by the foreign powers late in 1900.
3. ILB, *The Yangtze Valley and Beyond*, (1899) re-issued Virago, (1985), hereafter *Yangtze*, see also A.J. Little, *Through the Yangtze Gorges*, (1888), E.H. Parker, *Up the Yangtze*, (1895).
4. *Yangtze*, p.151.
5. *Yangtze*, p.92.
6. *Yangtze*, p.172.
7. *Yangtze*, pp.215-217.
8. *Yangtze*, pp.17-18.
9. *Yangtze*, p.20.
10. *Yangtze*, p.21.

11. *Yangtze*, p.304.
12. For Japanese enterprise see H. Kawakatsu, 'International Competition in Cotton Goods in the late nineteenth century', D.Phil, University of Oxford, 1984, and A J H Latham and H. Kawakatsu, *Japanese Industrialization and the Asian Economy*, London 1994.
13. See S. Checkland, *The Elgins*, pp.162-163.
14. *Yangtze*, p.66.
15. *Yangtze*, p.79.
16. *Yangtze*, p.80.
17. See A.J. Little, *Through the Yangtze Gorges*, (1888) and E.H. Parker, *Up the Yangtze*, (1895).
18. *Yangtze*, pp.113-123.
19. *Yangtze*, p.191.
20. *Yangtze*, p.202.
21. *Yangtze*, p.202.
22. *Yangtze*, p.220.
23. *Yangtze*, p.220 and 223.
24. *Yangtze*, p.316.
25. *Yangtze*, p.337.
26. *Yangtze*, pp.349-350.
27. *Yangtze*, p.356.
28. *Yangtze*, p.359.
29. *Yangtze*, p.368.
30. *Yangtze*, p.369.
31. *Yangtze*, p.384.
32. *Yangtze*, p.388.
33. *Yangtze*, p.435.
34. *Yangtze*, p.491.
35. *Yangtze*, p.495.
36. *Yangtze*, p.495.
37. JM, Handwritten text of a lecture of ILB's dated 7 March 1899.

12 *The Final Fling in Morocco*

Isabella Bishop's last adventure was to North Africa in 1901 when, in her seventieth year, she spent six months between January and August travelling through the deserts and mountains of Morocco.[1] It was a memorable journey and she regained some of her old enthusiasm while living among the Arab peoples. But she kept only skimpy notes and did not intend to prepare a book, although she did have firm opinions which were aired in a strongly worded article in *The Monthly Review* of October 1901.[2] Morocco at the end of the century was a power vacuum, for no individual Sultan was strong enough to exert control over the whole country. Almost all the continent of Africa had by this time been carved up by the great powers; and in 1904 Britain agreed to waive her interests in North West Africa in France's favour in return for concessions in Egypt. Within months France and Spain agreed to 'share' Morocco, Spain to develop its interests in the north and France in the south of the country. Her writing reflected her pro-British stance but also gave a clear account of the then anarchical state of Morocco which presented so enticing an invitation to predatory European powers.

It was almost by accident that she went to Morocco. She had spent part of 1900 at Tobermory in her sister's cottage, but she was unhappy and decided to leave Mull 'forever'. She no longer found the island the paradise it had seemed believing, as Anna Stoddart explains, 'that the old piety, which made the West Highland Sunday a day of peace and worship, was almost extinct, and that unbelief was degrading the people whom her sister had loved and served'.[3] During March 1900, while walking near the cottage, she slipped and fell on the rocks, badly spraining her left knee and her right arm. She left Mull on 4 April, walking lamely. The slow recovery made it difficult to plan ahead but by the late autumn she thought herself well enough to travel. She still had her own home at Houghton in Huntingdonshire where she spent some time in the summer of 1900; while there she did enjoy the girlhood pursuit of rowing herself and her guests on the river, which she believed strengthened her arms.

Sir Ernest Satow, newly-appointed British minister to China, who had been a friend since her adventures in Japan in 1878 and who thought she would enjoy some months observing events 'behind the scenes', asked her to join him for the winter of 1900–1901 at the legation in Pekin. The Bishop of Calcutta was anxious for her to go to his aid in allocating famine relief

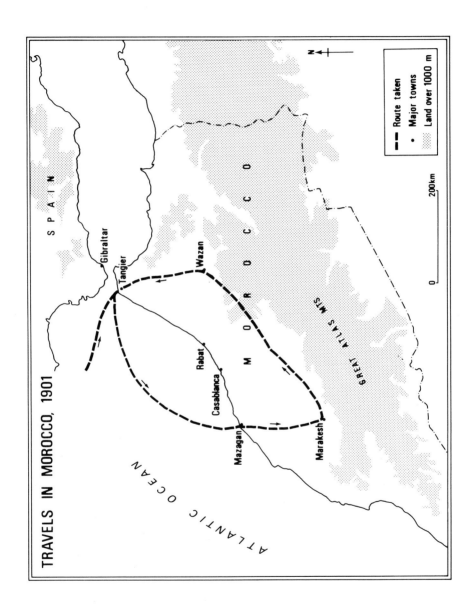

TRAVELS IN MOROCCO, 1901

supplies in India. No doubt it was pleasant to be asked to visit both China and India, but her lameness persisted and she decided that North Africa would be far enough.

She landed in Tangier on 4 January 1901 but immediately contracted blood-poisoning and was very ill with a high fever. That matters did not end badly may have been due to the intervention of Dr Roberts, who took her to his home at the Medical Mission Hospital and nursed her there. She recovered, and by March was able to leave Tangier by sea for Mogador and a two-month camping trip.

The sea journey and her landing was an experience in itself. As she wrote, 'it was a severe two days' voyage to Mazagan where the landing was so terrible and the sea so wild that the Captain insisted on my being lowered into the boat by the ship's crane in a coal basket. The officers and passengers cheered my pluck as the boat mounted a huge breaking surge on her landward journey. No cargo could be landed. I have never seen a boat in so rough a sea'.[4]

Nor when on 'dry' land were her troubles over. She had 'the worst servant I ever had' and when unexpectedly they found they had to camp they had not 'the necessaries'. As she reported, 'Before leaving the steamer I had a return of fever; and when the only camping ground turned out to be a soaked, ploughed field with water standing in the furroughs and the tent was pitched in a storm of wind and rain and many of the tent-pegs would not hold, and when my bed went down into the slush when I lay down, I thought I should die there – but I had no more illness and fever!'[5]

She was granted an audience in Marakesh by the Sultan there, before leaving for a two-month camping trip inland. Throughout this journey she was escorted by a Mr Summers whose 'capability, kindness and knowledge of the language and people' was to be a great comfort. Mr Summers arranged and paid for everything and she 'settled with him each week'. Whether the Moroccan adventures in the Spring of 1901 would have been possible without Mr Summers is a matter for conjecture.

But the Sultan's hospitality did not blind her to the evils afflicting the people. It was, she wrote, 'an awful country, the worst I have been in. The oppression and cruelty are hellish – no one is safe. The country is rotten to the core, eaten up by abominable vices, no one is to be trusted. Every day deepens my horror of its deplorable and unspeakable vileness. Truly Satan's seat is here'. Corruption and immorality were everywhere. She was critical of the religion which was, she thought, 'at once the curse of Morocco and the most formidable obstacle in the way of progress, chaining all thought in the fetters of the seventh century, steeping its votaries in the most intolerant bigotry and the narrowest conceit, and encouraging fanaticism which regards with approval the delirious excesses of the Aissawa and the Hamdusha'.[6]

Mrs Bishop writes movingly about the system of kidnapping for ransom in which those 'Kaids' in authority, (only because they have paid a heavy fee for their posts) and who are supposed to collect taxes and transmit them onward, throw into prison those 'likely to be squeezable sponges'. Most of these men were incarcerated – she was eloquent about the horror of prison conditions – purely because of the supposed willingness of friends to pay ransom money for their release. Although she herself had the use of a magnificent Arab horse, she claimed that in general, because of 'official robbery and the rapacity of the Court' that few good horses could be bought in Morocco. She deplored the fact that 'the Mares are execrable, and their progeny are soft, weedy, narrow-chested, good-backed brutes, without stamina and weak in the hind quarters'.[7] Anyone breeding good animals lost them to thieving, unscrupulous officials.

She noted with disapproval the system, which apparently provided a safe-guard against official greed, whereby those who had served could obtain 'Protection papers' from one of the great powers. France was apparently at this time busily engaged in giving some of its supporters in Morocco these 'Protection papers', favours which would in course of time be redeemed when France became the occupying power.

Notwithstanding her feelings at the cruelties of Moroccan life she was en-joying herself, writing from Zarktan Castle, 'You would fail to recognise your infirm friend astride on a superb horse in full blue trousers and a short full skirt, with great brass spurs belonging to the *generalissimo* of the Moorish army'.[8] And she could still laugh at herself noting that she had to mount her magnificent Arab charger by climbing a ladder held against its side.

With Mr Summers still in attendance she continued travelling, being based for some time at Marakesh. 'It was' she wrote, 'a splendid journey ... The bridle tracks on the Atlas are awful – mere rock-ladders, or smooth faces of shelving rock. We lamed two horses and one mule went over a precipice ... We had guides, soldiers and *slaves* with us. The weather was dry and brac-ing!'[9]

She was by this time some 500 miles south of Fez. Her comfort and safety may have been assured by Kaid Sir Hector de Vere Maclean, a Maclean of Loch Buie on Mull,[10] who had been for twenty-five years the officer in charge of the Sultan's forces. The young Sultan who employed Maclean received her 'on his throne on a high dais in pure white'. Mrs Bishop stood in front of the steps bareheaded but dressed in black silk 'the only European woman who has ever seen an Emperor of Morocco!' She wished this young Sultan long life and happiness, to which he riposted that he hoped that when his hair was as white as hers he might have her energy. She still took pride in her exploits, explaining that she was the first European woman who has ever entered the Atlas mountains or visited the fierce Berber tribes.

From Marakesh the party headed north, but within two days of Tangier they were pursued by armed and mounted Arabs and had to ride for their lives. She would have been disappointed had they not had any adventures but she was glad to be looked after by Dr Roberts again in Tangier until she crossed to Gibraltar on 8 July. She returned to her native shores for the last time in the summer of 1901 and so was at home to celebrate her 70th birthday in October.

Her article for the *Monthly Review* is a hard-hitting critique of a country ripe for take-over. The scandalous conditions in Moorish gaols had been taken up by the British Press; there was much public interest and concern. Her piece concluded by referring to various reforms in the tax collection system which were then planned although she believed that these suggested changes were a blind to deceive the Great Powers. As she understood the position, 'There can be no real remedy to the woes of Morocco which does not lay "the axe to the root of the tree", that is to the irresponsible power of the Court, which does not aim at the destruction of the present accursed system of mal-administration *root and branch*'.[11] Although Mrs Bishop would never have recommended foreign intervention – except that of Britain – the anarchical state in 1901 did lead to the intrusion of France and Spain into Morocco in 1904.

Notes

1. European interests in Morocco were not satisfied until 1904 (by an agreement of 8 April) when Britain accepted (in return for a free hand in Egypt) a French and Spanish sphere of influence in Southern and Northern Morocco respectively. During ILB's travels in 1901 there was much political confusion. See E.F. Cruickshank, *Morocco at the Parting of the Ways*, (1935), and M.M. Knight, *Morocco as a French Economic Venture*, (1938).
2. ILB, *The Monthly Review*, October 1901, pp.89–102.
3. AS, p.354.
4. AS, p.361.
5. AS, p.361.
6. *Monthly Review*, p.96.
7. *Monthly Review*, p.100.
8. AS, p.363.
9. AS, p.365.
10. AS, p.362.
11. *Monthly Review*, p.100.

Mrs Bishop in her version of Manchu dress, Edinburgh 1898.

PART IV

PERSONALITY, CULTURE AND SOCIETY

13 *A Professional with No Profession*

Although barriers were falling, as some persistent women mounted assaults on professional institutions previously exclusively male, no career was of right open to women during the nineteenth century. Isabella Bird was therefore, like other untrained women of the day, an amateur who by dint of perseverance and determination created her own professionalism.

She was born on 15 October 1831 into a country ruled by an unrepresentative Parliament – in which few men had the vote – which reflected the interests of the landed classes. At the time of her birth there was much civil unrest in towns across the country because the second attempt at a Reform Bill had been defeated in the House of Lords on 8 October – all twenty-one Bishops voting against.[1] The great Reform Act, which marked the beginning of modern British history and the slow transfer of power towards the common people, was finally passed in June 1832.

These reform movements were never intended to enfranchise women, whose rights by law and custom were then sorely circumscribed. Nevertheless the objectives of the Chartist movement[2] – active in the 1830s and 1840s – which included a demand for votes for all adult males, brought important issues to public attention. Soon there were those who had the temerity to urge votes for women. In 1867 – when Isabella was in her mid-thirties – John Stuart Mill[3] proposed an amendment to a Franchise Bill then being debated in the House of Commons, which by substituting 'person' for 'man' would have enfranchised certain women. Mill's amendment – greeted with incredulity and laughter – was soundly defeated. In the same year a Scottish Women's Suffrage Society[4] was formed in Edinburgh where Isabella then lived. Some progress was made when in 1882 important Married Women's Property Acts were passed applying to England and Scotland, which gave to married women legal rights to their own property previously denied. By 1904 when Isabella died women still did not have the vote, which came during the First World War, but the subject was being fully aired and could no longer be regarded as a laughing matter.

It is against this background that Isabella lived, and the fact that she fled so often to foreign parts reflects in part at least the frustrations which she felt. Would she, for example, given a different attitude to women in the society of her day, have pursued her early interest in chemistry? As it was she had no option but to organise her life to take account of the attitudes towards women in society which then prevailed. Moreover, although Isabella may not herself have thought consciously in these terms, remote foreign travel enabled her to assume an identity and gain an authority normally accorded only to men.

Her dissatisfaction with a conventional woman's life drove her to extraordinary lengths to achieve male goals of freedom, yet at home she accepted society as she found it, did not try to change it and so made her own bargain with its vagaries. Although not indifferent to the disadvantages under which women then laboured, she appreciated that she herself had succeeded in overcoming them. That she had been able to emerge successfully, as traveller and writer, depended partly on her social position, her father's indulgence and her modest financial independence and as well as on her own determination and well-honed manipulative skills. The two contradictory yet complementary *persona* which she sustained within herself, may initially have been difficult to develop but in the end they gave her an enviable *modus operandi*.

But Isabella was never insensitive to women's plight as they struggled against prejudice and disadvantage. As a young woman, in her *Notes on Old Edinburgh* (1869), she wrote harshly about those responsible for the inadequate provision of water in central Edinburgh which enforced 'female slavery of the most grinding description'.[5] Throughout her career, whether in her own country or elsewhere, she was always alert to the frequent mistreatment of women in society. Her books were attractive to women readers of her own time (and useful to us now) partly because of their detailed and sympathetic accounts of ordinary women's lives.

One remark, revealing of her attitudes, came in the autumn of 1880 when John Murray published, almost simultaneously, her book, *Unbeaten Tracks in Japan* and Sir Edward Reed's *Japan, Its History, Tradition and Religion.* John Murray, himself, congratulated her 'You have completely bowled over your male rival' while Sir Harry Parkes (then the British Minister in Japan) wrote to her, 'Your views are meeting with universal acceptance and Sir Edward Reed is nowhere!' Isabella commented: '*I think I have a lurking satisfaction in having vindicated a woman's right to do what she can do well* (author's italics) and in observing that all the reviews which have reviewed Reed's and my book together have attached more weight to my opinion and researches than to a man, KCB, FRS, and MP.'[6]

She was conscious of how disadvantaged as a woman she was, referring more than once to the honours and public rewards which were showered on men who had undertaken travel journeys no more dangerous and arduous than her own. As she wrote to Scott Keltie, then Secretary of the Royal Geographical Society in London, 'I lately opened the session of the Royal Scottish Geographical Society with an audience of 2,000, friendly, cordial, and afterwards went on (to give the same lecture) to Glasgow, Dundee and Aberdeen'; and she continued, 'I hear myself so continually spoken of as the "distinguished traveller" that I am arriving at the very natural conclusion that I am as well entitled to a medal as Mr Curzon or some others'.[7] The comparison with Lord Curzon[8] is apposite, for Curzon and Mrs Bishop had been fellow travellers briefly in the Middle East in 1890 and Curzon, then an ambitious young politician, was a recognised authority on the Anglo–Russian power struggle there. She may well have judged that she knew as much about the area as anyone else.

Curzon also figured prominently in the row which broke out following the unprecedented action by the Council of the Royal Geographical Society in electing some twenty-one women Fellows.[9] Mrs Bishop, proposed for the Fellowship by John Murray her publisher, was pleased with the honour in itself and delighted at the prospect of being able to use the map-making facilities available at the RGS. But once the general membership of the Society realised what had happened the storm broke.

It was argued that the Council of the RGS had exceeded its powers in electing as Fellows the twenty-one women. At a crowded extraordinary meeting fierce objections, raised by irascible retired admirals,[10] were made coherent by G N Curzon who rallied the opposition explaining that the 'emancipation of women would be not so much injurious to men as disastrous to women ... the rooms of the society were too small to be subjected to the overcrowding of ladies' – who in any case by their presence in the audience of the Society's lectures already 'exercised an influence'. He added that 'the great reputation of the RGS would be impaired by the admission of ladies' and in any case, 'Men traded on the initials FGS (Fellow of the Geographical Society) when they were abroad and he earnestly hoped that women would not do the same'.[11] The cheers which punctuated Curzon's speech were reflected in a close vote, 158 voting in favour of further women members while 172 voted against. For some years no more women were elected.

It is only fair to say that Curzon did pay tribute to 'the great work done by Mrs Bishop', 'who is already a Fellow' and said he was not opposed to the 'admission of really competent and distinguished women'.

On 27 May 1893 after receiving a circular from the Geographical Society Isabella wrote, 'I don't care to take any steps in the matter, as I never took any regarding admission. Fellowship, as it stands at present, is not a distinction and not a recognition of work, and really is not worth taking any trouble about. At the same time the proposed action is *a dastardly injustice to women*' (author's italics). When in July the vote came to deny Fellowship to any, other than those twenty-one women already elected, Isabella was indignant writing, 'I am much astonished at the retrograde movement of the RGS. Still I think it is better to exclude women altogether than, while admitting us, to create invidious distinctions in the membership. I suppose that the matter will not be allowed to rest here. I don't think that a

Fellowship, which is chiefly a matter of £.s.d., and is not a recognition of work done, is worth much at any rate'.[12]

Despite her off-hand manner over this matter, she was secretly delighted to be a Fellow not only of the Geographical Society in London but also to be the first woman Fellow of the Scottish Geographical Society in Edinburgh. On her memorial stone in Dean Cemetery, Edinburgh, the letters FRGS and FRSGS are proudly entered after her name.

The ambivalence which she felt is summed up in a letter to her intimate friend when she wrote 'I have a degree of legitimate pride in having made my own position as a writer and traveller by careful work without the aid of any-one and without sacrificing the delicacy of a woman'.[13]

On 10 April 1902 she lectured at (Royal) Holloway College on 'Where are the Women?' as part of a (missionary?) Conference presided over by Dr Marshall Long. The girl students presented her with an address of thanks which they all signed. In July 1903 she again lectured to 80 returned lady missionaries of the Church Missionary Society, with Mr Baring Gould in the chair. Tantalisingly, no record of these speeches, some of her last, has been found.

What then were the gifts which this woman had which would enable her to command a role, other than the domestic one, in Victorian society? With her keen eyes for close observation, her skill at eliciting information and her vivid descriptive writing, as well as her courage and daring, there could have been many career outlets open to her. Her interests ranged widely and included anthropology, botany, history – especially perhaps politics and power – in the countries which she had visited, as well as writing, photography and medicine.

It was always a major concern of this doughty traveller to search out primitive peoples as yet unaffected by 'civilisation', and from time to time she donned the mantle of the anthropologist and went to live with indigenous people. In 1878 she pushed into remote Hokkaido to join the indigenous Ainu people; in Persia in 1890 she made a special excursion through the Baktieri country seeking to understand the customs and mores of the Baktieri Lurs; in 1896 in the far west of China she pursued the Mantze peoples to the borders of eastern Tibet. During the four visits which she paid (between January 1894 and March 1897) to Korea she learned much of the primitive peasants whose way of life, unchanged for centuries, was about to vanish as the invading Japanese took over.

The Ainu[14] of Japan were found in Hokkaido and further north in the island of Sakhalin. They were believed to be a tall, strong, hirsute people, dependent on, and worshipping both land, on which they hunted bear; and sea, from which they gathered fish, thus providing all their needs. While she stayed with them in their huts she found them generous and hospitable, although in her case fearful that she was in some way connected with the encroaching Japanese developers. Later her writing on the Ainu people was much commended in scholarly circles.

In the Baktieri country in 1890 she found the people (at Killa Bazuft, Bazuft Valley) semi-nomadic, moving with their flocks and yet also cultivating crops. The details of their arable farming are given in precise Birdian style, 'They plough with a small plough with the share slightly shod with iron; make long straight furrows, and then cross them diagonally. They do not manure the soil, but prevent exhaustion by long fallows.... In reaping they leave a stubble five or six inches long. There is a good deal of spade husbandry in places where they have no oxen, or where the arable patches are steep. The spades are much longer than ours, and the upper corner of the sides are turned over for three inches. A spade is worked by two men, one using his hands and one foot, and the other a rope placed where the handle enters the iron, with which he gives the implement a sharp jerk towards him. In the higher valleys they grow wheat and barley only, but in the lower, rice, cotton, melons, and cucumbers are produced, and opium for exportation. They plough and sow in the autumn and reap on their return to their *yailaks* (summer quarters) the following summer'.[15]

She was cautious in describing the lives of the Mantze peoples – to the Chinese, *Mantze* means barbarian – in the extreme west of China because she did not in this case leave the rest of her party and stay alone with them. She was therefore relying in part on other commentators and only gave statements, as she explained, that 'at least four persons are agreed upon'.[16] She found the Mantze living – in four tribes totalling some 20,000 people – under the rule of the *Tu-tze* or tribal chief who was based at Somo. The *Tu-Tze* at this time exercised great power, not only of life and death, but also of taxation, requiring his people to pay some thirty percent of their produce to help him to raise the annual tribute required by China. These semi-autonomous tribes were believed in Pekin to be important as guardians of this part of China's western borders.

The Mantze were Buddhists and she found much evidence of religion in their country where Buddhas were often carved into the rock face and every family prayed to have one son who would become a Lama, a priest. She also noted the prayer wheels (which she had earlier seen to the far west in Tibet) at every house blowing merrily in the mountain winds. She was heartened by the freedom accorded to Mantze women who were 'on terms of absolute equality with men, possessing legal rights to property'[17] free to take on jobs such as muleteers and who were not, surprisingly, excluded by their sex from the supreme job of *Tu-Tze*.

In Korea[18] in November 1895 she saw three funerals (which always interested her) in one day. As her travelling companion at this time was a Korean she was able to learn a great deal about burial customs. She believed that, anthropologically speaking, it was important to record these ceremonies because they would almost certainly disappear as the Japanese imposed their own rule on Korea.

By the standards of anthropologists today her findings may seem modest but at the time she was a pioneer. Reviews of her work usually appeared in *Nature*, a journal which had been founded in 1869 to give a higher profile to scientific research.[19] In 1875 her *Six Months in the Sandwich Islands* was discussed, especially from the point of view of volcanoes and the disappearance of native peoples. As the writer commented, 'We recommend Miss Bird's delightful book to all who wish for a full and graphic account of the present condition of the Sandwich Islands and Islanders'.[20] In 1881 *Nature* noted that 'To the ethologist (sic) Miss Bird's notes on the Ainus ... will prove of special interest'.[21]

Throughout her journeys Isabella Bird was a keen amateur botanist. She noted whether a plant was economically important – yielding a cash crop – or purely decorative. At Hilo, on the island of Hawaii early in 1873, thrilled with all she saw and experienced, she wrote to her sister, 'I cannot convey to you any idea of the greenness and lavish luxuriance of this place, where everything flourishes, and glorious trailers and parasitic ferns hide all unsightly objects out of sight. It presents a bewildering maze of lilies, roses, fuschia (sic), a clematis, begonias, convolvuli, the huge appalling looking granadilla, the purple and yellow water melons, also varieties of passiflora, both with delicious edible fruit, custard apples, rose apples, mangoes, mangostein guavas, bamboos, alligator pears, oranges, tamarinds, papayas, bananas, bread fruit, magnolias, geraniums, *ohias* (Metrosideros polymorpha) *Kamani* trees, *Kalo* (Colocasia antiquorom [arum esculentum]) *noni*, (Morinda citnofolia) and quantities of other trees and flowers, of which I shall eventually learn the names, patches of pineapples, melons and sugar cane for children to suck and sweet potatoes'.[22]

She was only too conscious of the contrast between the luxuriance of nature on Hawaii and the dullness at home. She refers to 'the *Pandanus odoratissimus* in the palm-house of the Edinburgh Botanic Gardens, which is certainly a malignant caricature, with its long straggling branches, and widely scattered tufts of poverty stricken foliage. The bananas and plantains in that same palm-house represent only the feeblest and poorest of their tribe. They require not only warmth and moisture, but the generous sunshine of the tropics for their development. In the same house, the date and sugar palms are tolerable specimens, but the cocoa-nut (sic) trees are most truly "palms in exile".'[23]

In Korea she noticed the cultivation of hemp, an important fibre which she saw was used for 'mourners wear, bags and rope'. As she reported, 'In my walks along the river I had several opportunities of seeing the curious method of separating the fibre, rude and primitive, but effectual. At the bottom of a stone paved pit large stones are placed, which are heated from a rough oven at the side. The hemp is pressed down in bundles upon these and stakes are driven over the hemp and earth over all, well beaten down. The stakes are then pulled up and water is poured into the holes left by them. This, falling on the heated stones, produces a dense steam, and in twenty-four hours the hemp fibre is so completely disintegrated as to be easily separated'.[24]

In 1892 Isabella Bishop discovered photography, and her attempts to master this craft were to excite her in her later years and bring her great pleasure. From Seoul in Korea in 1897 she confessed, 'that nothing ever took such a hold on me as photography has done. If I felt free to follow my inclination I should give my whole time to it'.[25] In accordance with her endeavour to be a good amateur she enrolled for a course of lessons with Mr Howard Farmer at the Regent Street Polytechnic and she returned to Mr Farmer for further guidance whenever she was in London.

She was quite taken up with the idea of using her own illustrations, writing from Chengtu, Sze-chuan, 'Illustrations by a cheap process seem a great feature in books of travel now. I don't think that I mentioned that I have a number of my own photographs for this purpose'.[26] Her luggage was enlarged to take account of her camera, which added '16 pounds weight', and other equipment. These were not the days when neat rolls of film were carried home to be developed professionally, for this dedicated lady was her own technician. One of the most entertaining accounts of her photographic prowess comes while travelling on the river Yangtze just before the Chinese New Year in January 1896, when she noted, 'that the most successful method of washing out "hypo" was to lean over the gunwale and hold the negative in the wash of the Great River rapid even at the mooring place, and give it some final touches in the filtered water', (which she had obtained by using the pocket filter which she carried). As she commented 'This chilly arrangement was only possible when the trackers (who dragged the boat up the rapids) were ashore or smoking opium at the stern. Printing was', she continued, 'a great difficulty, and I only overcame it by hanging the printing frames over the side. When all these rough arrangements were successful, each print was a joy and a triumph, nor was there any disgrace in failure'.[27]

She confessed to 'a feeling of complacent superiority, of the amateurs who need "dark rooms, sinks, water laid on", tables and other luxuries. Night supplied me with a dark room; the majestic Yangtze was "laid on"; a box served for a table; all else can be dispensed with'.[28] In view of her own re-sourcefulness, one wonders how she responded to the cameras of the Sultan of Marakesh which she saw at his home in Morocco in 1901. As Anna Stoddart reported the Sultan 'had just had two photographic cameras made for him by Adams of Charing Cross Road. One of 18 carat gold cost 2,000 guineas, and the other of silver £900'.[29]

Isabella Bird was also involved with medicine and nursing which she learnt during her time at St Mary's Hospital in London, but this was largely undertaken immediately after her husband's death and was a symbol of her status as a doctor's widow in mourning. Although she talked of using the nursing training by serving in one of the mission hospitals she set up in memory of her husband and sister, she never put these plans into action. When she was travelling she always carried a medicine chest and as a result she was frequently appealed to by sick people. In Persia in 1890 she had a fine Burroughs and Wellcome Medicine Chest (gifted to her by the company) and her fame as a *Hakim,* or doctor, spread rapidly. On one occasion, when amongst 'the great Baktieri tribes' she was taken to see the Chief's son who was 'so dangerously ill of pneumonia that she went with him to his house and put on a mustard poultice and administered some Dover's powder'.[30] It was a difficult dilemma which she faced, for even by using some of her scanty hoard of drugs she might exacerbate an illness, and she knew she could never treat the hordes of people who clamoured for her help. This was professionalism of an involuntary kind.

If Isabella Bird had been alive today, would she have been a foreign correspondent bringing reports of wars and famine into a million homes? She certainly always acted as the professional even when in 1872, before she had learned that she needed the stimulus of danger to achieve good health, she spent two miserable months in the depths of despair in Australia. Notwithstanding her remarks about a 'too hideous' continent, some five years later she prepared no less than nine articles for the *Leisure Hour* in 1877[31] under the title of Australia Felix. Her pieces describe various aspects of life in Victoria with vigour and enthusiasm although she does not gloss over her dislike of the flies, the heat and the dust which haunted her while she was there.

On one occasion only she was 'commissioned' to report as a 'foreign' correspondent when in 1887 John Murray asked her to go and write on the state of Ireland for *Murray's Magazine.* It seems likely that Murray's request was deliberately arranged to encourage her back to work after her husband's death in 1886. Murray's ulterior motive in this matter is borne out by a sentence in one of Isabella's letters when she writes from Ireland, 'I am surprised to find that my powers of endurance are not diminished'.[32]

At that time the political problems in Ireland were acute. Charles Stewart Parnell,[33] the Irish leader, nicknamed 'the uncrowned King of Ireland', had decided to support W E Gladstone, who, as Prime Minister, sought to end the continuing Irish problem by bringing in (in 1886) his first Home Rule Bill which was, notwithstanding much support, defeated. At the same time, Parnell was accused of being involved in the violent campaign of the Irish Land League. It was at this stage that Murray asked her to go to Ireland and report on attitudes there for *Murray's Magazine.*

Isabella arrived at Wexford Station on Christmas Eve 1887 and plunged herself at once into Irish affairs. She was told 'You've come to Ireland at a warm time', although as she noted 'snow was falling briskly at the time'.[34] Her experiences were mixed, depending upon whether she was with the Protestant minority or with Catholics. One day, trying to arrange transport for the following day's journey, she asked 'for a car'. 'No, I could not get one'. I showed him a letter which I carried. 'That name commands our respect', said the car hirer, 'you will get your car'.[35] She noted Irish pride in those imprisoned for political acts writing, 'Dear indeed to the Irish heart is the man who has been in jail for a political offence'.

She found Mr Parnell universally revered. In Arklow she was told that he was 'loved like the Blessed Mother of God'. She quoted from a speech of Parnell's at Ennis in September 1880, on how to treat the man who has taken a farm from which another has been evicted. Parnell said, '... you must show him on the roadside when you meet him: you must show him in the streets of the town: you must show him at the shop counter: you must show him in the fair and in the market place and even in the house of worship, *by leaving him severely alone*, by putting him in a moral Coventry, *by isolating him from the rest of his kind as if he were a leper of old*, you must show him your detestation of the crime he has committed'.[36]

Despite Parnell's supremacy in 1888 he was brought down within three years by the divorce action of Captain O'Shea against Mrs Kitty O'Shea, citing Parnell as co-respondent. Parnell married Mrs O'Shea in June 1891, and died, aged 45, in October 1891.

At the end of her reports she noted that she had 'fulfilled the promise made in the first paper not to inflict my own opinions on the reader but to content myself with reporting facts or what were given to me as such. I must however be allowed to add that I do not believe that any Land Act however liberal, can relieve or content the peasant farmers of Ireland, crushed and swamped as they are under a load of debt, unless it is accompanied by an Arrears Act, dealing with arrears which have accumulated under rents which are now judged unfair'.[37]

Later in northern Korea, in October 1895, she gave a graphic, if hearsay, account of the battle of Pyongyang in which the Japanese had routed the Chinese army. But as she herself saw, 'Even in my walks over the battlefield, though the grain of another year had ripened upon it, I saw human skulls, spines with ribs, spines with the pelvis attached, arms and hands, hats, belts and scabbards'.[38]

By virtue of long days and weeks walking or riding over politically sensitive territory, Miss Bird became an expert on foreign affairs especially as they related to the Middle and Far East. Her unparalleled journeys through Persia, Kurdestan, Turkestan to Turkey in 1890 gave her first hand knowledge of a strategically important but little known area. She had been deeply affected by the persecution of Christians in Asiatic Turkey and had written two forthright articles which, under the title of 'The Shadow of the Kurd', were published in the *Contemporary Review* in May and June 1891.[39] Her subject had aroused great interest in W E Gladstone, who, always sensitive to talk of Christian persecution, had wanted to meet her. John Murray arranged a dinner at which Mr Gladstone quizzed Mrs Bishop on the Kurdish atrocities amongst Nestorians and Armenians. Not to be outdone by the great man she provoked a full half hour lecture in return when she asked 'but what was the Nestorian controversy?'

As a result of this exchange, and in response to general interest, on 18 June 1891 she appeared in Committee Room 15 of the House of Commons before an audience of members of both Houses – and their wives – to answer questions on the atrocities in Kurdestan. A hundred years later it is difficult to realise how unusual a proceeding this was, elevating a woman into the role of an expert. She was kept busy between 5–6.30 p.m. by a large audience from both Houses of Parliament impressed by her 'gentle voice, dignity of bearing, modesty and clearness of statement'.[40] Later *The Times* published an article of hers on the Baktiari peoples on 26 August 1891. She also lectured (25 August) to the British Association (Geography, Section E) at Cardiff. Her subject being 'The Upper Karun Region and the Bakhtiari Lurs'.

As a lecturer Mrs Bishop had a remarkable career. She had initially a curiosity value at a time when women were virtually unknown as speakers, but contemporaries were also curious about her because of her experiences as a traveller. Announcements that she was to speak often produced a large expectant audience in a packed hall; which from all accounts was not disappointed.

Her main professional interest was to transform her adventurous journeys into entertaining and engaging travel books. But she always supplemented this by writing Journal articles which had the effect of building up an ever wider readership for her books. As a girl she had been rebuffed in her first attempts to write for *Blackwood's* and other serious Journals; as an experienced writer of mature years she could place her articles almost wherever she wished. She was a regular contributor to the *Leisure Hour* and gave much support to the new *Murray's Magazine* launched in 1887.

John Murray, her publisher, who treated Isabella Bird as a professional, was keen to encourage her to go her independent way. He liked the way she wrote up her adventures and the vivid way in which she reported on her triumphs or disasters. Murray belonged to a publishing world which was unusual in that it did not discriminate against those women who could write books which would sell well.

But clearly Murray's instincts in accepting her work were right. He was on to a winner. When, for example, *Unbeaten Tracks in Japan* was published in the autumn of 1880 it was received with critical acclaim. Isabella expressed herself astonished, noting that, 'Forty seven reviews vary from *The Quarterly* downward and ranging from enthusiastic eulogy to praise without a drawback'. John Murray, himself apparently bowled over, wrote to her, 'How can I convey to you the tidings of your own praises which are resounding everywhere here and with a unanimity of which I have had no previous experience in my long career as a publisher. The demand for a third edition within a month of such a book as yours is I think quite unprecedented'.[41]

When John Murray III died in 1892, Isabella wrote to the family 'Thoughts of kindness and help, of giving pleasure to others seemed to come so naturally to your father, and made him so loveable ... How his geniality, brightness and enjoyment of the Society of his friends, and the way in which he made people acquainted with each other, made those gatherings in Albermarle Street as Mr Gladstone said 'The most charming in London ...'[42]

John Murray, himself a moderate in politics and religion, understood the likes and dislikes of the middle class readers for whom he catered. He appreciated their enjoyment of books on travel, exploration and discovery and found in Isabella a fine examplar of the adventurous author. John Murray IV (1851–1928) continued the family's connection with this famous lady.

In financial terms the arrangement between author and publisher was for the author generous. Of the profits which accrued, Isabella, as author, was to receive two-thirds,[43] the remaining one-third to go to John Murray. Despite fluctuations she was receiving a steady income from this source between 1880 and 1904 and on her death in October 1904 she bequeathed the copyright of all her books to John Murray IV 'free of duty and as a gift to you personally'.[44]

It is clear that Isabella Bird was a good woman of business who gave full attention to her financial affairs. On 10 January 1889 prior to her departure for India she executed a 'factory and commission' in favour of Dunce Forbes Dallas, Solicitor, Supreme Courts of Scotland. By this Dallas was appointed her 'factor, commissioner and attorney, to manage my whole business affairs in this country as he shall think proper and expedient'. In the course of a long and detailed document Isabella gave Duncan Forbes Dallas full powers to act for her and to handle her estate in the event of her death.[45] It is not known whether this 'factory and commission' remained in force or was renewed to cover other journeys. Duncan Forbes Dallas was still influential later, and he was named as one of the executors in her Will. Subsequently Anna Stoddart, when writing *The Life of Isabella Bird*, became alarmed as Mr Dallas wrote to her twice asking to see her work. Miss Stoddart urged John Murray IV on no account to accede to Mr Dallas' request to see 'either MS or proofs' before publication. She added that if Mr Dallas got sight of her MS 'then all four (executors) are equally entitled and that would indeed be terrible'.[46]

When Isabella Bishop died in 1904 she left an estate of over £33,000,[47] on which duty of over £1,500 was paid. It was a very large sum, reflecting the great success of her writing career and the care with which she had husbanded her resources. Some £1,500 of this money had come by inheritance from her mother, another £6,500 from her sister and some £4,500 from her husband,[48] but most of the accrual represented profits from her own work. In addition to her income from John Murray she must have received substantial sums for the many articles which she wrote for journals and magazines. She may have started as an amateur but it is certainly as a professional that she died.

Notes

1. *The Times*, 12 October 1831, reported particularly violent riots in Derby and Nottingham, where the Hussars were trying to keep order.
2. The Chartist movement had six aims, all but one of which have since been accepted, they were universal manhood suffrage, abolition of a property qualification for those standing for Parliament, annual Parliaments, equal representation, payment of MPs and voting by secret ballot.
3. John Stuart Mill (1806–1873) published *The Subjection of Women* in 1869, a seminal work.
4. E. King, *The Scottish Women's Suffrage Movement*, (1978), L. Leneman, *A Guid Cause*, Aberdeen, (1991), and E. Gordon, *Women and Labour in Scotland, 1850–1914*, Oxford, (1991).
5. ILB, *Notes on Old Edinburgh*, (1869) p.7.
6. JSB, ILB to Eliza B., 17 November 1880, Ms 2633, f.308.
7. Royal Geographical Society Archives, ILB letter, 4 December 1897, from Tobermory to John Scott Keltie, Secretary.
8. George Nathaniel Curzon (1859–1925), First Marquess of Kedleston, educated Eton and Balliol College, Oxford, sometime Under-Secretary of State for India, Under-Secretary of State for foreign affairs, Viceroy of India (1898–1905), Foreign Secretary (1919–1923).
9. The ladies elected as Fellows of the RGS in 1892 were:

> Mrs Isabella Bishop (née Bird)
> Mrs Zolie Isabella Colevile
> Miss Maria Eleanor Vere Cust
> Lady Coterell Dormer
> Miss S. Agnes Darbishire
> Mrs Lilly Grove (later Mrs James G. Frazer)
> Miss E. Grey
> Mrs Edward Patten Johnstone
> Mrs Beatrice Hope Johnstone
> Miss Julia Lindley
> Miss Kate Marsden
> Mrs Julia Mylne
> Mrs Elizabeth Prentis Mortimer
> Mrs Nicholas Roderick O'Conor (later Lady O'Conor)
> Mrs Mary Louisa Porches
> Miss Christina Maria Rivington
> Mrs French Sheldon
> Miss Florence M. Small and
> Lady Fox Young
> > *RGS*, Minutes, 6 July 1892.

10. The controversy over the admittance of lady members provoked some comment:

A Song of the RGS

"The Admirals are routed and the ladies remain Fellows of the Geographical Society"
Westminster Gazette;

Air 'The Admirals Broom'

Oh, there were three Admirals brave and bold
All Fellows of the Royal Geographical and
they cried Fal-lal and likewise Fiddle-dee-dee,
In the stentor-style of the quarter deck,
The question was, to decide if female FRGSs
could turn out true successes
and *they* shook their fists and cried
let them darn socks, boil 'taters' or make tea
But out from us they go! What *can* she–
creatures know of Geo–gra–phee?
                Punch or the London Charivari, 17 June 1893, p.285.

11. G.N. Curzon's speech was reported in *The Times*, 4 July 1893.

12. AS, p.267.

13. JSB, ILB to Eliza., 17 November 1880, Ms 2633, f.308.

14. ILB, *Japan*, Letters XL–XLV, (Newnes ed.), (1900), pp.292–355, see also J. Batchelor, *The Ainu of Japan*, (1892).

15. ILB, *Persia*, (Virago ed.), vol. II, Letter XVI, p.9.

16. ILB, *Yangtze Valley*, (Virago ed.), Chapter XXXIII, pp.437–446.

17. Review of the *Yangtze Valley*, *Nature*, Vol. LXI, November 1899 to April 1900, pp.252–254.

18. ILB, *Korea*, (KPI, 1985), Chapter XXIV, pp.283–291.

19. R. MacLeod, 'The Genesis of Nature', *Nature*, Vol. 224, (1969), pp.323–40, 'The Social Framework of nature in its Fifty Years', *Nature*, Vol 224, (1969), pp.323–40.

20. *Nature*, Vol. XL, 25 February 1875, p.322.

21. *Nature*, Vol. XXIII, 4 November 1880, pp.12–15.

22. ILB, *Hawaii*, (KPI, 1985), p.59.

23. ILB, *Hawaii*, (KPI, 1985), p.60.

24. ILB, *Korea*, (KPI, 1985), p.95.

25. JM, ILB to JM, 23 January 1897.

26. JM, ILB to JM, 11 April 1896.

27. ILB, *Yangtze River*, p.152.

28. ILB, *Yangtze River*, pp.152 and 191.

29. AS, p.362.

30. ILB, *Persia*, Vol.I, p.309; Dover's Powders, from Thomas Dover (1664–1742) who developed it; contained 10% opium, 10% ipecacuanha and 80% sulphate of potassium. Her list of remedies included 'Mustard plasters, Dover's powders, alicylate of soda, emetics, poultices, clinical thermometers, chlorodyne and beef tea', (ILB, *Persia*, Vol. I, p.156 and 285, see Chapter 9, pp. 99-114).

31. 'Australia Felix', *Leisure Hour*, (1877), see bibliography for page numbers.

32. JM, ILB to JM, 14 January 1888.

33. Charles Stewart Parnell (1846–1891), the Irish politician, became member of parliament for Meath and a prominent member of the Irish Home Rule party. In

1886 he joined Gladstone to turn out the Conservative government on the promise of an Irish Home Rule Bill, which was defeated.

34. 'On Ireland', *Murray's Magazine*, Vol.3, (April, May and June, 1888), I, p.467.
35. 'On Ireland', pp.472–473.
36. 'On Ireland', p.473.
37. 'On Ireland', p.835.
38. ILB, *Korea*, p.318.
39. AS, p.246, *Contemporary Review*, (May, June, 1891), pp.642–654 and pp.819–835.
40. AS, p.248.
41. JSB, JM, quoted in ILB to Eliza B, Tobermory, 17 November 1880, Ms 2633, f.308.
42. G. Paston, *At John Murray's ...*, p.298,
43. Some of the income she received from John Murray is listed below. But these figures are not complete.

Sandwich Islands	(1876)	£ 93. 0s.2d.
Rocky Mountains	(1880)	£665. 6s.5d.
Japan	(1880)	£162.16s.5d.
Golden Chersonese	(1883)	£389. 8s.0d.
Persia	(1891)	£356. 8s.9d.
Korea	(1897)	£576.14s.1d.
Yangtze	(1899)	£506.17s.7d.

Source: John Murray Archives. (My thanks to Virginia Murray for her help).

44. JM, W. Brabant (Solicitor and Executor) to JM, 1 March 1905.
45. SRO, RD 5 2229, pp.213–9. My thanks to David Brown.
46. JM, AS from yarrow Cottage, Kelso, to JM IV, 5 July 1905.
47. Isabella Lucy Bishop, Last Will and Testament, SRO 70/7/27.
48. The reference numbers for the Wills of her mother, Dorothy Louisa Bird or Lawson – SRO SC 70/4/105 and 70/1/131; of her husband John Bishop – SRO SC 70/4/218, SC 70/1/250 and of her sister Henrietta Amelia Bird – SRO SC 70/4/184 and SC 70/1/201. My thanks to David Brown.

14 No Missionary She

Isabella Bird was ambivalent in her attitude to the Christian mission movement which was then very powerful throughout the world. Her lack of conviction on these matters stemmed partly from the dramatic events in Birmingham[1] in her girlhood when her father, zealous in the mission field at home, had been attacked for his persistence about Sabbath Observance and partly from her own increasing uncertainty about her own faith.[2] Her father's lack of success in the Church of England and his sympathy with the Scottish Presbyterian Church were reflected in his older daughter's underlying anxieties on these matters. She came to the view that it was a mistake to make judgements or to attempt to interfere in the lives of others of different standards and values.

Moreover it was her own non-judgmental attitudes which made her such an exemplary traveller. Whether she was in the Polynesian Islands, Japan, Northern China, the Malay Peninsula, Northern India, Kashmir, Western Tibet, Central Asia, Persia, Arabia or Asia Minor she was curious about the peoples and respectful of their customs. She moved along unknown ways rather as an anthropologist seeking to learn, than as a missionary seeking to convert. It was her tolerance which made her so notable an observer. As she commented, 'My object was to live among the people ... I have lived much in their own houses and among their tents'.[3] Her sensitivity made her nervous of the Christian invasion for she feared the intrusion of the Christian missionary who despite his conviction that he brought salvation must necessarily be destructive of the mores of the society in which he worked. She dreaded the complications which could result from the attitude of the missionary, ignorant of the political implications of his involvement.

When, as an older woman, in her later years she became a partial convert to the mission cause, she was acting as sole representative of her father, mother, sister and husband, all of whom were dead. Even then as a famous speaker at missionary rallies the forthright – and critical comments – which peppered her addresses show clearly that the ambivalence remained.

She had herself been deeply moved by an incident in Armenia in 1890, when she had met and had been entertained by a group of Nestorian Christians who had lived long under the persecution of their Muslim overlords. In a subterranean dwelling she was beset by Christian priests and deacons beseeching her to send them a Christian teacher; when she demurred, they murmured, 'But England is a rich country'. Mrs Bishop was touched by a Christian people who had held fast to their faith despite centuries of oppression, and although these people were not analogous to those 'heathens' for whom the Christian missionaries were working she felt that Nestorian faithfulness was a sign to her.[4]

There were two other matters which also swayed her towards a more ready acceptance of overseas mission work. The first was the ill-treatment of women. She was particularly saddened by attitudes to women in Muslim societies – perhaps she came to believe that the Christian mission would improve their lot. The other concerned the lack not only of medical treatment but also of any idea of basic hygiene in the areas through which she had travelled. Wherever she had been, she had been appalled by the crowds which had besieged her begging for medical aid, and despite her reluctance she had been forced time and again to deploy her scant medical resources for the benefit of local populations. It was these concerns which encouraged her to support missionary affairs.

John Bishop, for five years Isabella's husband, was a staunch supporter of the Edinburgh Medical Missionary Society which had been founded in 1841 to provide medical care, laced with the Christian message, for poor of the city. Most of the staff at the dispensary, where Dr Bishop himself worked in a part-time capacity,[5] were young men and women themselves training as doctors and nurses who intended to enter the mission field. When David Livingstone died in Africa in 1873, it was resolved to establish in Edinburgh the Livingstone Memorial Training Institution. At Dr Bishop's behest the Bird girls became involved with the fund-raising for this project, which in December 1877 was focused on the Grand Bazaar.

Bazaars launched with aristocratic patronage were at this time a common form of activity for the aspiring middle classes. In this case the support of Princess Louise, Marchioness of Lorne, and one of Queen Victoria's daughters, was secured, together with that 'of 43 Scottish notables'. The Bazaar, appropriately for Christmas shopping, took place on 13, 14 and 15 December 1877 and was an enormous success. Hennie edited the *Bazaar Gazette* which 'took immensely' and was available each day at 3 p.m. Isabella not only wrote the *Bazaar Guide*, of which 2,000 copies were sold, but also helped Lady Paton to run the picture stall which raised £630 – Sir Noel Paton had already honoured them with the gift of one of his own paintings. Altogether 'the Bazaar was', as she wrote, 'a most splendid success, and the very pleasantest thing of the kind I was ever at'.[6]

But the medical mission was itself an aberration from the original missionary purpose, which was to teach the gospel in a pure form without offering any concessions in the shape of medical treatment or any other 'sweeteners'. Christ's ringing command 'Go ye into all the world and preach the gospel to every creature' said nothing about carrying medical supplies and rules of hygiene as part of the Christian pack. Yet there can be no doubt that the provision of medical care not only eased the lot of the missionary but was more readily accepted by native peoples than any other form of Christian endeavour.

In India where Mrs Bishop first set up hospitals in memory of her husband and sister, there were few problems for the Christian missionary, in the sense that the British, as overlords, saw to it that conditions were favourable. She sailed for India on 9 February 1889 and arrived at Karachi on 21 March from where she travelled northwards, stopping only at Lahore, in blazing heat, to look at native and missionary hospitals. At Sialkot[7] she visited Dr Whyte's hospital and dispensary before travelling on to Rawalpindi, and from thence into Kashmir. At Srinagar she was welcomed to the residency and looked after by medical missionaries including the Drs Arthur and Ernest Neve and Mr Knowles.

Once in Kashmir, where the climate was hot, but pleasant and manageable, she travelled around searching for a suitable site for her husband's memorial hospital. She was often escorted by Dr Arthur Neve who was impressed by her skilful adaptation of her costume to take account of local customs. As he reported, astride her horse she used a semi-Persian costume, with 'a dark divided skirt, long tea-coloured cloak, *pagri* and blue veil' so she could pass without hostile comment through crowded bazaars or open country.

She was gratified when the local Rajah arranged that his Council give her a piece of land, which seemed ideal for the hospital just outside Islamabad. After the disappointments of Palestine it was exciting to make such good progress so quickly. She was very pleased, writing, 'It is beautifully situated within these lovely waterways, yet within five minutes of the centre of the town and has three large chenar trees upon it. It is 240ft x 273ft. On it will be built an out patient department, a waiting-room, consulting-room, operation room, and dispensary, two pavilions, 50ft long, to hold thirty-two patients, and a *serai* or guest-house for patients friends who come to nurse them and cook for them.'[8]

Work started immediately on the John Bishop Memorial Hospital under the supervision of Dr Arthur Neve, who wrote enthusiastically of his task, 'Excellent limestone for all building purposes was quarried locally and the bricks were made on the spot. Brick-kilns and lime-kilns were soon in full swing'.[9] He also reported on the impossibility, due to the low level of the rivers in the summer season, of floating the timber down to the door. Although later rebuilt on the same site the newly finished hospital was, shortly after completion, washed away by the surrounding rivers in flood. Despite being a memorial to John Bishop the hospital, run by the Church of England Zenana Missionary Society (later handed over to the care of the Church of North India) was always for women and children.

As she herself was not needed at the site of the hospital a brief expedition to Tibet was soon organised (see Chapter 9). It was on her way back from Tibet, while she was in Simla, that she made contact with Major Sawyer whose agreement that she should join his party and travel with him in Persia put her under some pressure. She had therefore little time to deal with the problem of finding a suitable site for the Henrietta Bird Memorial Hospital. So, acting with great speed she found and bought 'a disused hotel at Bias, near Amritsar'.[10] Anxious to get away, she left funds for the adaptation, modification and equipment of the old hotel to Dr Martyn Clark whose medical mission work she admired.

Isabella's commitment to the Medical Mission might have ceased once the arrangements for the two hospitals in India were completed in 1889. But later in the 1890s she was to extend her patronage to China, Korea and Japan.

China in the late nineteenth century, as Sherwood Eddy proclaimed, 'was the goal, the lodestar, the great magnet that drew us all to the Christian mission cause in those days'.[11] Following the re-negotiation of further treaties with the foreign powers, the Chinese were forced to accept a Christian missionary presence to allow foreigners to live in inland cities, and to permit Western ships to ply the Yangtze River. Although these regulations were included in the treaties to facilitate trade, they undoubtedly encouraged Christian missions to penetrate inland China in the knowledge that ultimately they had behind them the authority of the foreign powers who had signed the treaties.

The optimism of the early missionaries in China from the 1840s was not borne out; their words fell on stony ground. The Chinese as a people were hostile, regarding missionaries as agents of imperialism sent to subvert their country and their values. The *literati* – the class from which mandarins were drawn – who had obtained their superior and well-paid posts at least in part because of their understanding of Confucius learning were never converted to Christianity. This meant that the Christian teachers were forced to concentrate on poorer people, who might have many reasons, including hunger, for accepting the new religion. These converts were sometimes called 'rice Christians'.

The dedication of the missioner was attested by the harsh treatment which they received which, in accordance with their Christian commitment, did nothing to temper their enthusiasm. As one recalled 'We were mobbed in the fu city, mobbed in the district cities, mobbed in the large towns. We got so used to being pelted with mud and gravel and bits of broken pottery that things seemed strange if we escaped the regular dose ... We went out from our homes bedewed with the tears and benediction of our loved ones, and we came back plastered over, metaphorically speaking, with curses and objurgations from top to bottom'.[12] Mrs Bishop spent four months in 1896 exploring the basin of the Yangtze River. Earlier, in 1895, she had spent a shorter time in the coastal ports of China visiting Swatow, Amoy, Foochow, Hangchow and Shanghai. Both these journeys had been mission-oriented; missionary families had welcomed and cared for her wherever she had stayed.

Mrs Bishop knew full well, and had herself frequently experienced, the opprobrium accorded to the foreigner. In one small town where she was refused accommodation she 'had to urge her treaty rights'[13] and once in her room the local people besieged her, broke down the door of her room shouting 'foreign devil', 'horse-racer', 'child-eater'. Eventually an official arrived and dispersed the crowd. Missionaries who lived remote in Chinese towns faced this kind of treatment regularly on a day to day basis.

She became an expert on the varied approaches of the different missionary societies in the Far East. She found that Bishop Bickersteth in Japan, although responsible for uniting three streams of Christianity into *Nippon Sei Ko Kwai*, the Holy Catholic Church in Japan, was strongly in the Anglican tradition, while Bishop Corfe in Korea was markedly Anglo-Catholic in character. Bishop Cassels of the China Inland Mission had just been consecrated the first Anglican Bishop in Western China. Isabella's interest in the medical aspect of the mission movement encouraged her to support all these different Christian traditions.

She was particularly impressed with the work of the China Inland Mission (CIM) in the Sze Chuan area for she thought that the CIM had tackled the problems facing the missionary living in the interior of China. As she approached the town of Paoning Fu she noticed 'two Chinese gentlemen', who proved to be Bishop Cassels and Rev Williams, both of the China Inland Mission, who had walked out to welcome her. The determination of those employed by the CIM to dress as Chinese and become Chinese in every way was admired, although she worried as she considered the implications for women. As she explained

> The ladies of this mission lead what I should think very hard lives, owing to their painful deference to Chinese etiquette, and their great desire to avoid doing anything which can give offence. As for instance, they never walk out without an elderly Chinese woman with them, or are carried in closed chairs.[14]

The China Inland Mission, founded by James Hudson Taylor, had five main principles and was in its day reformist. The mission was to be interdenominational, although conservative in theology; anyone, even those of humble origins with little formal education, could become missionaries; and the aim of the work was evangelical; education and medical work could be undertaken but they would not hide 'the central and commanding purpose'.[15] Finally the direction of the mission was to be in China, and there missionaries would wear Chinese dress and as far as possible identify themselves entirely with the Chinese people'.[16]

Hudson Taylor employed powerful, evangelical imagery when addressing student volunteers in Detroit in 1894. 'The gospel must be preached to these people in a very short time, for they are passing away. Every day, every day, oh how they sweep over ... There is a great Niagara of souls passing into the dark in China. Every day, every week, every month they are passing away! A million a month in China are dying without God'.[17] Others felt that Christian missionaries could never take on the burden and the guilt of failing to convert the Chinese millions, although clearly it was a haunting message with which to assail possible missionary recruits.

In 1896 in China she provided £100 for the Henrietta Bird Hospital in Paoning-fu, Sze Chuan. Indeed as she wrote to Mr Murray,

> I have seen nothing to change my opinion that medical missions are the most effective pioneers of Christianity ... Mrs Murray will be interested to hear that owing to the low price of silver, which at once doubles ones income, and the literally boundless hospitality I have met with, I have been able to build three hospitals containing altogether 160 beds – one under Bishop Corfe at Seoul, another under Bishop Cassels at Paoning-fu, Sze Chuan, another at Chow-fu and an orphanage for twenty-five earthquake orphans at Tokyo, under Bishop Bickersteth. These are my memorials of my husband, my parents, and my sister, and you can imagine the pleasure they give me.[18]

Once the money for the Mission Hospitals had been promised, the benefactress left to continue her travels for it was not part of her strategy to stay and help run them although earlier she had taken some of her nursing training specifically for this purpose.

The Far Eastern expedition during which she gifted money for charitable purposes in China, Korea and Japan had lasted over three years. She arrived back in London on 19 March 1897, after which she lectured widely at the Royal Geographical Society, and at evangelical meetings at Exeter Hall – as well as attending a 'Queen's Drawing-room'. She also spoke on behalf of the Church Missionary Society before dashing north to Edinburgh for the General Assembly of the Church of Scotland in May.

As a speaker in the mission cause she did not mince her words. In reflecting on the problems of presenting Christianity in China she was blunt noting that, 'It is not alone that it comes, as they think, to subvert their social order, corrupt the morals of their women, destroy their reverence for parents, old age and ancestors, and to introduce new and hateful customs; but its ideas have a Western dress, its phraseology is foreign, and the pictures with which it illustrates its teaching are foreign, indecorous in costume and pose, and odious, so much so, that in the Hang Chow Medical Mission Hospital it was found desirable to take them down to avoid the blasphemous and unseemly criticisms which were made upon them, and to present our Lord and His Apostles in Chinese dress and surroundings'.[19]

The corollary to this was to work through a 'native agency' which would present Christianity 'without the Western flavour'. 'Could', she asked, 'our Prayer Book, so intensely Western in its style and conceptions, metaphysics and language and adoration, and its ideas, many of them so unthinkable to the Eastern mind, remain the only manual of public devotion?'[20] These remarks quoted from Anna Stoddart's early *Life* (1906) are a reminder of how powerfully felt were Isabella's reservations about the missionary world.

But her strongest words were reserved for matters relating to the employment of women as missionaries, for she noted that women's work 'was beset with special difficulties' in the China Missions. She believed that Chinese etiquette, 'as to what is seemly for a woman' did encourage propriety, and that any young foreign woman who disregarded Chinese susceptibilities did so at her peril. She recognised the good work which could be done by 'educated ladies' but commended especially the work of women who sprang from 'humble social grades'.

She took issue with those foreigners in the treaty ports in China who also had strong views on the appointment of women missionaries to inland stations. Mrs Bishop thought that these young women – who were not to be under thirty years of age, and who understood the Chinese language and customs, dressed in Chinese clothes and had a senior Chinese woman to guide them – could be left in charge of a mission station. On the matter of young women who were affianced to young missionaries she was firm; they should come out to China and live under someone else's care for a year or two before marriage, only then would they be more of a help than a hindrance to their husbands.

After her return to the United Kingdom in 1897, she found herself involved in the Mission Movement not only as a speaker but also as an adviser. As a famous woman traveller with recent first hand knowledge of countries – which others could only theorise about and whose generosity had funded mission hospitals – she had an authority which none could gainsay. She did not hesitate to use it. It must have been hard for the ladies of the various women's missionary committees, in London, to hear such strongly held opinions – expressed in however soft a voice – by so experienced and knowledgeable a lady. The missionaries were regarded in China as agents of Western imperialism and as such they were feared and hated. After much unrest the Dowager Empress of China, on 24 June 1900, issued a decree – carried out by 'The Boxers'[21] who were particularly active in Shantung and Chihli provinces – ordering the killing of the foreigners. In Pekin, the legations under siege in July, were relieved in August by an army of the foreign powers. By the end of 1900 the Boxer movement in China was defeated.

Inevitably the Christian mission movement had suffered heavy losses as many, including Chinese Christians, Western missionaries and their families, had been killed. Of the Protestant foreigners some 188, including 53 children, had perished while many more had suffered grievously on long journeys escaping out of China. After the rebellion was over, foreign groups demanded compensation for the loss of life and damage done to property: only the China Inland Mission which, because its missionaries were so scattered had lost many good people, declined to make any claim against the government.

The Boxer revolt coming within three years of Mrs Bishop's departure from China reinforced her own clearly expressed unease at the role of the Christian missionary. Critics asked why should those from the West assume that their ideals and values were best? Some believed that Chinese hostility was entirely justified, and a movement developed to encourage mission work along more humanitarian lines which would ensure that they should aim more generally to improve the society in which they were working. Perhaps if emphasis were put on education, and health care for women and children, then the Chinese government would also begin to consider the education and health of its people. Captain A T Mahan,[22] the influential American historian, suggested that the West and China had a common interest to encourage 'regeneration promoted from within'.

Under the terms of Mrs Bishop's Will[23] substantial sums, totalling nearly £8,000, were left to missionary and charitable societies; some of these monies were specifically ear-marked for the support of the Bird and Bishop Memorial Hospitals. The Church Missionary Society received £2,500 which included funds to set up a permanent endowment to sustain the John Bishop Memorial Hospital at Srinagar, Kashmir. The China Inland Mission received £500 to support the Henrietta Bird Memorial Hospital at Paoning Fu, China. She also left £500 to the United Free Church of Scotland to endow the Medical Mission Hospital in Mukden. And the Edinburgh Medical Missionary Society received a total of £1,800, some of which was ear-marked for 'a John Bishop Bursary' which students of the EMMS would compete for annually. In addition the Zenana Bible and Medical Mission, otherwise known as the Indian Female Normal School and Instruction Society was left £500.

Mrs Bishop's view of the missionary movement was coloured by her own loss of faith as well as by her anthropological leanings which made her wary of any clumsy intrusion into the lives of primitive peoples. That she became a patroness of the Medical Mission movement reflects not so much her own views but her respect for the workers in the mission field and her determination to find a suitable memorial for her dead husband and sister.

Notes

1. AS, p.14, PB, p.167.
2. On 23 August 1888 she was baptised by total immersion by Mr Spurgeon of the

Baptist's Metropolitan Tabernacle, South London. She was not, and did not wish to be admitted to the Baptist Community but she was in great confusion writing '... The Church of my father's has cast me out by means of inanities, puerilities, music and gabblings and I go regularly to a Presbyterian Church where there is earnest praying, vigorous preaching and an air of reality', JSB, ILB to Eliza B, 28 February 1888, 44 Maida Vale, London, Ms 2637, f.151.

3. ILB, *Heathen Claims and Christian Duty*, (1894), p.6.

4. AS, pp.235–236.

5. Edinburgh had been an important centre for Medical Mission work since 1841. The work there was supported by several strongly evangelical medical professors at the University of Edinburgh who volunteered their services. See O. Checkland, *Philanthropy in Victorian Scotland*, (1980), Chapter 4.

6. Livingston Memorial Training Institution Bazaar, December 1877, AS, p.95.

7. AS, p.204.

8. AS, p.206.

9. AS, p.208.

10. AS, p.219.

11. S. Eddy, *Pathfinders of the World, Mission Crusade*, (1945), p.508.

12. H.P. Beach, *Dawn on the Hills of T'ang or Missions in China*, (1905), p.104.

13. AS, p.245.

14. *Yangtze River*, p.288.

15. S. Neill, *Christian Missions Overseas*, p.334.

16. Neill, p.334.

17. Quoted in P.A. Varg, *Missionaries, Chinese and Diplomats*, p.68.

18. JM, ILB to JM IV, 15 March 1896.

19. AS, p.338.

20. AS, p.339.

21. The 'Boxers', a Chinese secret society, I-ho T'uan, partly religious and partly political, were organised by the Prefect of Shantung in 1898, enraged by the increasing infiltration of their country by the ever-pressing foreigner. See Chapter 11 above, Note 2.

22. Alfred Thayer Mahan (1840-1914) emphasised the significance of naval force in world history. His books became classics and were very influential.

23. SRO, SC 70/7/27.

15 *'The invalid at home and the Samson abroad'*

Following the death of Isabella Bishop in October 1904 – within days of her 73rd birthday – A Stodart Walker[1] contributed a note to the *Edinburgh Medical Journal* under the heading of 'Mrs Bishop'.[2] This unusual entry was explained by the fact that she was the widow 'of a well-known Edinburgh practitioner' and that she herself was concerned with 'the establishment of medical missions'. The real reason for the note was Mrs Bishop's notoriety in medical circles in Edinburgh as 'the Invalid at home and the Samson abroad'.

It was not, the author believed, a question of dual personality, more 'the environment' which brought out her unusual strength. Mrs Bishop had, it was conceded, 'a large storehouse of energy'. And yet it was puzzling, 'When she took the stage as a pioneer and traveller, she laughed at fatigue, she was indifferent to the terrors of danger, she was careless of what a day might bring forth in the matter of food; but, stepping from the boards into the wings of life, she immediately became the invalid, the timorous, delicate, gentle-voiced woman that we associate with the Mrs Bishop of Edinburgh'.[3]

Perhaps the *EMJ* dismissed Isabella's multifaceted personality too readily, for it was in exploiting this that she achieved so rich and rewarding a life. Over a period of 30 years from 1873, Isabella abroad allowed her stronger self full reign as she entered without question into the male world of adventure and daring, while at home she hid her other self behind a mask of respectability as she quietly retreated into her conventional female self of soft voice and 'natural ill-health'.

That this pattern was able to evolve was a reflection of the way in which illness dominated the lives of so many middle class Victorian women. Whether this constant pre-occupation with health was rooted in the frustration felt by many at the limitations imposed on their lives is a matter which cannot be pursued here. As a 'delicate' child who is believed to have had (at the age of 18) an operation for the removal of a 'fibrous tumour' from the region of her spine,[4] Isabella Bird had good reason to place herself in her doctor's hands.

At home she suffered from enervating illness. She lay in bed – usual at the time, but very weakening – her doctors, always attentive, saw her day by day sink further into lethargy and immobility. Was she guilty of a kind of malingering? Or, dosed with bromides and other drugs, was she suffering from iatrogenic or doctor induced illness?[5]

In course of time, when both patient and doctor were exhausted, relief was sought by ordering the patient to take a change of air. In Isabella's case she rose from her sickbed and set off, still suffering, only recovering her zest for life when in acutely uncomfortable and potentially dangerous situations. It is argued here that although the conventions were strictly observed – the orders came directly from her male medical advisors – they were themselves but the instruments of Isabella's determination. That doctor and patient were in a sense in collusion comes as no surprise; it was standard practise at this time for medical advisers to recommend a change of air to comfortably off patients.

What is remarkable, in view of the invalidism at home, is the strength and energy which she demonstrated when she was abroad. Once translated into the milieu in which she felt she thrived, no one could show more endurance and fortitude. And in this foreign world where she felt so happy there is no greater demonstration of her skills than in her horsemanship. She was a brilliant rider who relished days, weeks and sometimes months in the saddle slogging across difficult and dangerous territory. Accounts of horses whether handsome, wilful, intelligent, stubborn or broken-down and badly treated, which she bought, or borrowed, enliven the pages of all her books.

And yet with her horse-riding she made an unpromising start, for like all ladies in 'civilised' society, when she first arrived in Hawaii early in 1873 she rode side-saddle, keeping skirted legs discreetly hidden on one side of the horse and ensuring that spine, body and legs were uncomfortably twisted. After a particularly excruciating mountain journey in Hawaii, Luther Severance, her American host, insisted that she would be safer and more comfortable on a Mexican saddle, riding astride the horse. This type of saddle, widely used in the Americas, had a large horn so placed at the front that the reins, if not needed to guide the horse could lie there and in an emergency the rider could hold on. For Isabella the adoption of a Mexican saddle on which she rode astride was a revelation. Several of her subsequent journeys depended for their success on her horse-riding skills as she coped with asses, horses, often wild and hardly broken – and even yaks in Tibet – onto which she attempted unsuccessfully to secure her Mexican saddle. On many occasions her proficiency and sensitivity to the horse enabled her to escape from dangerous accidents with only bruises to show.

Once astride her horse she was forced to wear trousers. On Hawaii it was the ladies riding costume, which consisted of 'full-Turkish trousers and jauntily made dresses reaching to the ankles',[6] which she adopted. Wherever she went thereafter, once removed from prying eyes at home, she adopted some kind of garb which included trousers. Although she certainly achieved male freedom by riding astride a horse, did frilly trousers worn under thick skirts constitute cross-dressing? So narrow were the conventions of the day that her

Mrs Isabella Bishop at her writing desk.
(Photograph: Elliott & Fry, Edinburgh.)

riding costumes became, at home, a matter of public comment and unwished-for notoriety and although she was herself sensitive about such criticism, her Rocky Mountain travelling dress was displayed with her approval at the National Health Exhibition in 1884.[7]

It was on Hawaii in 1873 that she first learned how to use horses to corral cattle. On that first occasion she was nervous, as she was riding an unshod horse but the leader of the cowboys shouted to her to keep close behind him, as she did. 'Putting our horses into a gallop we dashed down the hill ... then another tremendous gallop and a brief wild rush, the grass shaking with the surge of cattle and horses. There was much whirling of tails and tearing up of the earth – a lasso spun three or four times around the head of the native who rode in front of me, and almost simultaneously a fine red bullock lay prostrate on the earth'.[8] In this case the captive was intended for the pot and Isabella declined to witness its final moments.

In the autumn of 1873 in the Rocky Mountains she paid $8 a week for the use of a horse and for her board and lodgings. But during this wonderful period it was her own horse Birdie who gave her most joy for 'She is the queen of ponies, and is very gentle, though she has not only wild horse blood but is herself the wild horse. She is always cheerful and hungry, never tired, looks intelligently at everything and her legs are like rocks ... She is quite a companion, and bathing her back, sponging her nostrils, and seeing her fed after my day's ride, is always my first care'.[9]

There were also occasions in Estes Park when she was invited to help drive the cattle because Griff Evans, her host, 'needed another hand'. On one occasion they were out all day, covered a distance of nearly thirty miles which was as she said 'one of the most splendid rides I ever took'. They were driving in the magnificent high country of Colorado where 'the sun was hot, but at a height of 8,000ft the air was crisp and frosty, and the enjoyment of riding a good horse under such exhilarating circumstances was extreme'.

When they first saw 'a thousand Texan cattle' they were feeding in the valley below, but hearing the men and the horses they took fright and dashed off. This caused Griff Evans, the leader, to urge 'Head 'em off boys' and 'all aboard, hark away' and 'away we went at a hard gallop down-hill. I could not hold my excited animal, down-hill, up-hill, leaping over rocks and timber, faster every moment the pace grew, and still the leader shouted "Go it, boys" and the horses dashed on at racing speed, passing and re-passing each other, till my small but beautiful bay was keeping pace with the immense strides of the great buck-jumper ... and I was dizzied and breathless by the pace at which we were going. A shorter time than it takes to tell brought us close to and abreast of the surge of cattle'.[10] Her host congratulated her on her courage and said she was 'a good cattleman'.

After halting and holding the herd pinned in one of the valleys, she was required to leave Birdie and mount a *bronco* which was especially trained in cattle-driving, in 'doubling back like a hare' when it was necessary to turn wayward animals. She had particular difficulty with a cow and her calf, but in the end they completed their task of corralling the animals and then had an exhilarating gallop home.

Perhaps the most extraordinary and lyrical description of a horse is that of Gyalpo in Tibet: 'Badakshani bred of Arab blood, a silver-grey as light as a greyhound and as strong as a cart horse. He was higher in the scale of intellect than any horse of my acquaintance. His cleverness at times suggested reasoning power and his mischievousness a sense of humour. He walked five miles an hour, jumped like a deer, climbed like a yak, was strong and steady in perilous fords, tireless, hardy, hungry, frolicked along ledges of precipices, and over crevassed glaciers, was absolutely fearless, and his slender legs and the use he made of them were a marvel to all. He was an enigma to the end. He was quite untameable, rejected all dainties with indignation, swung his heels into people's faces when they went near him, ran at them with his teeth ... would let no one near him but Mando ... he was as good as a watchdog and his antics and enigmatic savagery were the life and terror of the camp.'[11]

She also knew how to look after horses, frequently intervening to save the horse from thoughtless and ignorant men. She found it very difficult to tolerate ill-treatment of horses, finding journeys with beaten, half-starved animals distressing. On Hawaii she paid a young guide to lay off 'an old big, wall-eyed, bare-tailed, raw-boned horse, whose wall-eyes contrived to express mingled suspicion and fear, while a flabby, pendant lower lip, conveyed the impression of complete abjectness',[12] in the hope that before the time of rest ended the 'owl-hawks will be picking at his bones'. The panache which she showed in riding and managing horses gave her status and respect when travelling amongst any horse-riding people.

The other health matter which arises relates to her ability to survive and flourish while travelling, despite the many diseases including malaria, hepatitis and dysentery which might have been expected to assail her. In many countries, with no knowledge of hygiene, she ate locally prepared food, drank the water of the region – although it might have been boiled – and suffered innumerable mosquito and other insect bites. The only protection which she would be expected to have would be vaccination against smallpox. She certainly lost weight on some journeys and it seems likely that, being a plump woman, she possessed useful reserves which were utilised when she suffered hardship when travelling.

But leading two such different lives brought its own problems, for friends whether at home or abroad knew only one Isabella; those in England or Scotland were in tune with the Isabella of fragile health, while those who knew the vigorous energetic woman abroad rarely saw her at home. In Edinburgh one missionary, with whom Isabella had stayed on Hawaii, could hardly 'recognise in the exhausted invalid the adventurous, high spirited, lively and amusing traveller of Hawaii'[13]

Letters from a contented Isabella abroad to friends at home, who knew only the poorly lady, were difficult to write. The problem is illuminated by two letters written at about the same time in August 1878 from Hakodate, Hokkaido, the northern island of Japan. To her sister (the recipient of the continuous diary which would later become her book on Japan) she wrote 'I am enjoying Hakodate so much that though my tour is all planned and my arrangements all made I linger on from day to day.'[14] To her intimate friend in Scotland she wrote, 'Nothing in Japan pleases me *one half* as well as the strolls around Altnacraig (in Scotland) in the long twilight of our beautiful June. If I am spared I shall never again cross any sea other than the Channel. My spine is so much worse that I cannot ride and without that I should prefer Mull. My journey so far has been a great disappointment as far as health goes.'[15]

Despite the gloomy tone of her letter to those in Scotland, her journey had been unprecedented over a difficult route rarely before traversed by a Westerner. Moreover she was very pleased with herself, writing to her sister, 'I feel a somewhat legitimate triumph at having conquered all obstacles, and having accomplished more than I intended to accomplish when I left Yedo.'[16] She also noted, at the same time, 'After being for two months exclusively among Asiatics I find the society of English people fatiguing and *chattering*. My soul hankers for solitude and freedom'.

The inconsistency of her position requiring that whenever she was abroad enjoying herself she was forced to write to friends at home, in disparaging terms, lamenting both health and journey, was particularly stressful in the case of her close confidant Mrs Blackie in Edinburgh. During 1873, her wonderful romantic year in Hawaii and in the Rockies, she never wrote to Eliza Blackie at all. Clearly the strain of writing suitably pessimistic letters proved more than she could cope with during a time of great personal happiness.

The development of her double persona was forced on Isabella Bird by the social conditioning of the time which denied a constructive role, other than that of wife and mother, to middle-class women in Britain. Because she had used her illness as a weapon, and had to be ordered abroad by her doctors for her health, she was forced to conform to what was expected of her when she returned. Without doubt it was a skilled performance although the costs to her were high.

The switchback life which Isabella had coveted and indeed achieved abroad made her restless and unsettled at home. She was always on the move and became, especially after the death of her relatives, 'of no fixed address'. Whenever she wanted to get away from Edinburgh it was, she said, too full of sad memories. She had in the past taken houses in London, including the house at 44 Maida Vale (1887), which proved a heavy burden for not only 'was it the sight of her husband's possessions' which saddened her but 'I have no heart to make it pretty, feeling that I cannot stay in it'.[17] Later, in 1898, she again 'settled' in London at 20 Earl's Terrace for 'This little house had ... a sort of homey, old fashioned look'. On this occasion the whirl of entertainment to which she was subjected in London proved to be too exhausting and was used as the excuse to move on.

It is true that she rented and tried to settle at Hartford Hurst, Wyton, near her girlhood home at the Rectory, on long lease from March 1899, but it too was given up. Dr Ritchie, of Edinburgh (who had succeeded as her chief physician on the death of Professor Sir Thomas Grainger Stewart) agreed with his colleagues 'that the situation close to the Ouse, the overflowings and mists from which saturated soil and atmosphere, rendered the house unwholesome and devitalising'.[18] One can almost hear the conversations between patient and doctor, as Isabella fed her ideas on the house to her medical advisors and the doctors obligingly re-issued them to her as informed medical opinion. At the beginning of 1903 she gave up Hartford Hurst, her last home, having already written (23 December 1902) to a friend that her furniture and things would be dispersed 'as I am not likely to have a house again'.

She returned to Edinburgh in August 1903, seriously ill. On 1 September 1903 Drs Gibson, Fordyce and Affleck, as well as Dr Ritchie, visited her in consultation. They concluded that she was affected by heart trouble – thrombosis was feared – yet she left the Nursing Home, at 11 Manor Place, in which she had been resident, saying 'I am not going to be a cipher any longer'.[19]

In her last letter to John Murray IV, written in a very shaky hand she explains, 'These are the first lines I have attempted in ink since 20 August 1903 and I think I have only written pencil notes during the same period. My severe heart disease obliges me to be completely flat in bed and as I am deplorably weak writing is almost impossible. This is the more vexatious as this, after over 30 years of varied hard work without a holiday has put my brain into excellent working order and has completely renovated my memory'.[20]

As she lay unable to rally her strength, she considered her life, its triumphs and its disappointments. How circumstances would have changed had she married as a young girl as she had hoped; then, armed with a quiverful of children, her life would have developed along entirely different lines. She smiled as she pictured Mountain Jim who had been, despite his reputation as a desperado, such a wonderful companion, well able to challenge her as a horsewoman in the magnificent Rocky Mountain country of Colorado and yet equally attractive when in reflective mood, reciting favourite poems or singing to her. She thought of John Bishop, her husband for a brief five years, of how he had tolerated her wilfulness and how by his steadiness, devotion and integrity he had caused her to love him.

She was, she knew, determined, self-centred and manipulative and yet, how else could she have overcome the stultifying conventions of the day? If she wanted any sort of meaningful life, what other course had been open to her? Was she not a famous Victorian who had entertained, educated and amused a wide public who had admired her daring as a traveller, relished her books, enjoyed her journal articles and listened enthralled to her well-presented lectures?

How she would have revelled in some official recognition of her achievements; alas, the honorific Dame Commander of the British Empire, which would have given her intense pleasure, and which she undoubtedly deserved, was not to be introduced until 1917. And yet she is now being recognised as an early feminist. It is one hundred years since her original books were published by John Murray; all her travel books have been re-issued and are still available – an accolade beyond her wildest dreams?

Friends bearing flowers, plants and palms rallied round; Dr Whyte, Dr Macgregor, Canon Cowley Brown, Miss Lorimer and Miss Stoddart were among her regular visitors. She often held the flowers in her hand and remembered the roses, tulips, anemones and Christmas roses of the cottage garden at Tobermory and the rectory garden at Wyton, while occasionally her mind went back to Tattenhall, her grandparents home, and to Taplow Hill. She was nursed by Blair (by then Mrs Williamson), a former maid, together with cousins and devoted friends as they tried to tempt her appetite, once so robust – now so wayward – with delicacies of food sent in from the country.

In the Autumn of 1903 she was removed to rooms at Bruntsfield Terrace from which she could look out from her window over the Pentland Hills to the south. In the Spring of 1904 she longed to be in London, but at this Dr Ritchie, Sir Halliday Croom, Dr Fordyce, and her women friends (who feared that if in London she would insist on visiting Whiteley's furniture store to look to her 'things') presented a determined opposition. Before her death there were further moves, a brief return to a Nursing Home and then the final move to lodgings which she shared with the Miss Kers at 18 Melville Street.

In accordance with the evangelical spirit in which she had been raised, many came to pray with her as she grew slowly weaker. On her last morning, after her own prayers with her faithful Blair, she cried 'Oh! What a shouting there will be', echoing the Birds' own phrase for a re-union of family members. She died on 7 October 1904.

Notes

1. A. Stodart Walker was a nephew of John Stuart Blackie and so would know ILB and

her circle well. He edited his uncle J.S. Blackie's *Notes of a Life*, Edinburgh (1910).

2. *Edinburgh Medical Journal (EMJ)*, Vol. XVI, (1904), p.383.

3. *EMJ*, Vol. XVI, (1904), p.383.

4. See Chapter 1, note 18. It has been suggested that Elizabeth Barratt Browning may have suffered in adolescence from polio-myelitis. Could this illness also have affected ILB? See *The Independent*, 21 February 1989.

5. See Richard Asher, *Talking Sense*, (1972), Chapter 10, 'The Dangers of going to bed', Chapter 13, 'Malingering' and Chapter 14, 'Diseases caused by doctors'.

6. ILB, *Hawaii*, p.67 and p.68, PB, p.29.

7. AS, p.165.

8. *Hawaii*, p.430.

9. ILB, *Rocky Mountains*, p.150.

10. *Rocky Mountains*, pp.128–129.

11. ILB, 'Among the Tibetans', *The Leisure Hour*, (1893), p.238.

12. *Hawaii*, p.132.

13. A. Grainger Stewart, *BEM*, Obituary, (November 1904), p.700.

14. ILB, *Japan*, Letter XXXIX, p.276.

15. JSB, ILB to Eliza B., 12 August 1878, Ms 2633, f.22.

16. *Japan*, Letter XXVII, p.262.

17. JSB, ILB to Eliza B., 28 February 1888, Ms 2637, f.151.

18. AS, p.375.

19. AS, p.318.

20. JM, ILB to JM IV, 3 March 1904.

SELECT BIBLIOGRAPHY

Place of publication given if not London

Asher, R.A.J., (ed. F. Avery-Jones), *Talking Sense*, 1972.

Badger, A.H., 'The Centenary of Mrs Bishop', *The Quarterly Review*, October 1931, pp.278–299.

Baldwin, S.L., *Foreign Missions of the Protestant Churches*, New York, 1900.

Barr, Patricia M., *A curious life for a lady: the story of Isabella Bird*, 1970.

——*The Deer Cry Pavilion: a story of Westerners in Japan 1860–1905*, 1968.

Batchelor, J., *The Ainu of Japan*, 1892.

Beach, H.P., *Dawn on the Hills of T'ang or Missions in China*, New York, 1905.

Beasley, W.G., *The Modern History of Japan*, 1963.

——*The Meiji Restoration*, 1973.

Bennett, D., *Emily Davies and the Liberation of Women*, 1990.

Beresford, Lord Charles, *The Breakup of China*, 1899.

Bickersteth, M.J., *Japan as we saw it*, 1893.

——*Life and letters of Edward Bickersteth, Bishop of S. Tokyo*, 1905.

——*Japan*, 1908.

Birkett, D., *Spinsters Abroad*, 1990.

Bishop, I.L. Bird, *The Englishwoman in America*, 1856. Foreword and notes by Andrew Hill Clark, Madison, Wisconsin, 1966. (Facsimile reprint).

——*The revival in America, by an English eye-witness*, 1858.

——*The Aspects of religion in the United States of America*, 1859. New York, 1972 (Facsimile reprint).

——'Dr. Guthrie's Ragged Schools', *Leisure Hour*, 1861.

——*Notes on old Edinburgh*, Edinburgh, 1869.

——*The Hawaiian Archipelago. Six months among the palm groves, coral reefs & volcanoes of the Sandwich Islands*, 1875, *Six Months in Hawaii*, (Facsimile reprint), KPI, Pacific Basin Books, 1986.

——'Australia Felix, Impressions of Victoria', *Leisure Hour*, 1877, pp.39–42, 87–92, 149–152, 183–186,218–220, 249–251, 314–318, 413–416, 469–472.

——*A lady's life in the Rocky Mountains*, 1879. With an introduction by Daniel J. Boorstin, Norman, Oklahoma, 1960.

——*Unbeaten tracks in Japan*, 1880, Newnes edition, 1900, Virago Travellers edition, 1985.

——*The Golden Chersonese, and the way thither*, 1883, (Facsimile reprint, with an introduction by Wang Gungwu, Kuala Lumpur, 1967.)

——'Under Chloroform', *Murray's Magazine*, Vol.I, 1887, p.327–330.

——'On Ireland', *Murray's Magazine*, Vol.II, April, May, June, 1888.

——*Journeys in Persia and Kurdistan*, 1891. Virago Travellers edition, Vol.I, 1988, Vol.II, 1989.

——'A Journey through Lesser Tibet', *The Scottish Geographical Magazine*, October 1892, pp.513–528.

——'Among the Tibetans', *Leisure Hour*, 1893, pp.238–244, 306–312, 380–386, 450–456.

——*Among the Tibetans*, 1894.

——*Heathen claims on Christian duty*, 1894.

——*Korea and her neighbours. A narrative of travel, with an account of the recent vicissitudes and present position of the country*, 1897. Facsimile reprint, KPI, Pacific Basin Books, 1985.

——*The Yangtze Valley and beyond. An account of journeys in China, chiefly in the province of Sze chuan and among the Man-Tze of the Somo territory*, 1899. Virago Travellers edition, 1985.

——*Chinese pictures. Notes on photographs made in China*, 1900. S.4.g.

——*Views in the Far East*, Tokyo, (c.1900).

——'Notes on Morocco', *Monthly Review*, Vol.5, 1901, pp.89–102.

——*A traveller's testimony* (to mission work), 1905. In the British Library.

Carey, W., *Travel and Adventure in Tibet*, 1902.

Carpenter, E., *The Archbishops in their Office*, 1971.

Chappell, Jennie, *Women of worth*, 1908.

Checkland, O., *Philanthropy in Victorian Scotland*, Edinburgh, 1980.

——*Britain's Encounter with Meiji Japan, 1868–1912*, 1989.

Checkland, O. and Checkland, S., *Industry and Ethos, Scotland 1832–1914*, 2nd edition, Edinburgh, 1989.

Checkland, S., *The Elgins, a tale of Aristocrats and Their Wives*, Aberdeen, 1988.

Clark, Ronald, *The Victorian Mountaineers*, Batsford, 1953.

Cowan, C.D., *Nineteenth Century Malaya*, 1964.

Crone, G.R., *The Explorers*, Cassells, 1962.

Curzon, G.N., *Persia and the Persian Question*, 1892.

——*Problems of the Far East, Japan–Korea–China*, 1894.

Davidson, Lilian Campbell, *Hints to Lady Travellers*, 1889.

Davie, G.E., *The Democratic Intellect*, Edinburgh, 1961.

Dekker, R.M. and van de Pol, L.C., *The Tradition of Female Transvestism in early modern Europe*, 1989.

Dennis, J.S., *Christian Missions and Social Progress, a Sociological Study of Foreign Missions*, New York, 1900.

Dickens, F.V., Vol.II, *The Life of Sir Harry Parkes*, 1894.

Dixon, W.G., *The Land of the Morning*, 1882.

Duncan, Jane E., *A Summer Ride in Western Tibet*, 1906.

Eamess, J.B., *The English in China*, 1909.

Eddy, S., *Pathfinders of the World Missionary Crusade*, New York, 1945.

Faulds, H., *Nine Years in Nippon*, 1887.

Fleming, Peter, *News from Tartary*, 1938.

——*Bayonets to Lhasa*, 1955.

Foster, M., *Elizabeth Barrett Browning*, 1988.

Gale, J.S., *Korean Sketches*, Chicago, 1898.

——*Korea in Transition*, New York, 1909.

Godlee, R.J., *Lord Lister*, 1917.

Grainger Stewart, A., 'Obituary of ILB.', *Blackwood's Edinburgh Magazine*, November 1904, p.698–704.

Greaves, R.L., *Persia and the Defence of India 1884–1892*, 1959.

Gullick, J.M., *Malaya*, 1964.

——'Isabella Bird's Visit to Malaya', *Journal of the Malaysian Branch of the Royal Asiatic Society*, Vol.LII, part I, 1979, pp.113–119.

——'Emily Innes, 1843–1927', *Journal of the Malaysian Branch of the Royal Asiatic Society*, Vol. LV, part II, 1982, pp.87–113.

Gwynn, S., *Life of Mary Kingsley*, Macmillan, 1932.

Havely, C.P., (ed.), *This Grand Beyond, the Travels of Isabella Bird Bishop*, 1985.

Holcombe, L., *Wives & Property*, 1983.

Hore, A., *To Lake Tanganyika in a Bath-chair*, 1886.

Horsley, Reginald, *Isabella Bird, the famous traveller*, 1912.

Howard, Cecil, *Mary Kingsley*, 1957.

Hudson, Taylor, J., *The Story of the China Inland Mission*, 1900.

——*In Memoriam, Rev. J. Hudson Taylor beloved founder and director of the China Inland Mission*, 1905.

Innes, E., *The Chersonese with the Gilding Off*, 1885.

Jalland, P., *Women, Marriage and Politics, 1860-1914*, 1896.

Jardine, Evelyne E.M., *Women of devotion and courage. No. 4: Isabella Bird*, 1957.

Johnson, Henry, *The Life of Kate Marsden*, 2nd ed., 1895.

Kazemzadeh, F., *Russia and Britain in Persia*, Yale, 1968.

Keay, J., *With Passport and Parasol*, 1989.

Kim, C.I.E., *Korea and the Politics of Imperialism, 1876–1910*, 1967.

Kingsley, G., *Notes on Sport and Travel*, 1900.

Kingsley, M., *Travels in West Africa*, 1897.

——*West African Studies*, 1899.

Korn, A.L., *Victorian Visitors*, Honolulu, 1958.

Kuykendall, R.S., *The Hawaiian Kingdom*, Vol.II, Honolulu, 1953.

Ladd, G.T., *In Korea with Marquis Ito*, 1908.

Landor, A.H., *Alone among the Hairy Ainu*, 1893.

Lane, M., *Literary Daughters*, 1989.

Langford, J., *The Story of Korea*, 1911.

Larymore, Constance, *A Resident's Wife in Nigeria*, 2nd ed., 1911.

Latourette, Kenneth Scott, *A History of Christian Missions in China*, S.P.C.K., 1929.

Lee, C., *The Blind Side of Eden*, 1989.

Little, A.J., *Through the Yangtse Gorges*, 1888.

Low, H., Hugh Low's Journals, extracts from *Journal of the Royal Asiatic Society, Malaya Branch*, 1954.

MacLeod, R., 'The Genesis of Nature', *Nature*, Vol.224, pp.323–40, 1969.

——'The Social Framework of Nature ...', *Nature*,

Marsden, Kate, *On Sledge and Horseback to Outcast Siberian Lepers*, 1893.

——*My Mission to Siberia: A vindication*, 1921.

Mason, Kenneth, *Abode of Snow*, 1955.

Mendus, S. and Rendall, J., (eds.), *Sexuality and Subordination*, 1989.

Middleton, Dorothy, *Victorian lady travellers*, 1965.

Morrison, G., *An Australian in China*, 1895.

Murray, J. (born 1852), *John Murray III, 1808–1892*, 1892.

Neill, S., *Christian Missions Overseas*, 1964

North, Marianne, *Recollections of a Happy Life*, (ed. Mrs. John Addington Symonds), 2 vols., 1892.

——*Further Recollections of a Happy Life*, 1893.

Parker, E.H., *Up the Yangtse*, 1895.

——*China and Religion*, 1910.

Parker, J., *Women and Welfare*, 1989.

Paston, G., (pseud), *At John Murray's, records of a literary circle*, 1892.

Pavey, E., *The Story of the Growth of Nursing*, 1951.

Pettifer, J. and Bradley, R., *Missionaries*, 1990.

Poole, S. Lane and Dickens, F.V., *Life of Sir Harry Parkes*, Vol.I and II, 1894.

Pope-Hennessy, J., *Verandah, some episodes in the Crown Colonies, 1867–1889*, 1964.

Putnam Weale, B.L., *The Truce in the East and its Aftermath*, 1907.

Rice, C.C., *Mary Bird of Persia*, 1922.

Richardson, H.E., *Tibet and its History*, 1962.

Robinson, R., Gallagher, J. and Denny, A., *Africa and the Victorians: the Official Mind of Imperialism*, Macmillan, 1961.

Robson, Isabella S., *Two Lady Missionaries in Tibet*, 1909.

Sawyer, Major H.A., *A Reconnaissance in the Bakhtiari Country, South-west Persia*, Simla, 1891, (copy in RGS, London).

Schneider, H.G., *Working and Waiting for Tibet*, 1891.

Sheldon, M., *Sultan to Sultan*, 1892.

Smith, A.H., *Village Life in China; a Study in Sociology*, New York, 1899.

Smout, T.C., *A Century of the Scottish People*, 1988.

Sprague, M., *Newport in the Rockies*, Denver, 1961.

——*A Gallery of Dudes*, Denver, 1967.

Stark, F., *Over the Rim of the World*, 1988.

Stodart, Walker, A., (ed.), *J.S. Blackie, Notes of a Life*, Edinburgh, 1910.

Stoddart, A., *J.S. Blackie, A Biography*, 1895.

Stoddart, Anna M., *The life of Isabella Bird, (Mrs Bishop)*, 1906.

Swettenham, F., *British Malaya*, 1907.

Tabor, Margaret E., *Pioneer women*, 1925.

Takakura, S., *The Ainu of Northern Japan, a study in conquest and acculturation*, Philadelphia, 1960.

Taylor, Annie R., 'Diary', in William Carey's, *Travel and Adventure in Tibet*, 1902.

Taylor, Dr. and Mrs. Howard, *Life of Hudson Taylor* (2 vols). *I: Growth of a Soul; II: Growth of a Work of God*, China Inland Mission, 1911.

Thompson, F., *Harris Tweed, the Story of a Hebridean Industry*, Newton Abbot, 1969.

Todd, J. and Butler, M., *The Works of Mary Wollstonecraft*, 1989.

Tomalin, C., *The Life and Death of Mary Wollstonecraft*, 1989.

Twain, M., *Letters from Hawaii*, 1866.

Varg, P.A., *Missionaries, Chinese and Diplomats*, Princeton, 1958.

Wallace, Kathleen, *This is your Home: A Portrait of Mary Kingsley*, Heineman, 1956.

Wheelright, J., *Amazons and Military Maids*, 1989.

Williams, C., *The adventures of a lady traveller. The story of Isabella Bird Bishop*, 1909.

Wills, C.J., *In the Land of the Lion and the Sun*, 1883.

Workman, Fanny Bullock and Hunter, William, *Algerian Memories*, 1895.

——*Sketches Awheel in fin-de-sicle Iberia*, 1897.

——*In the Ice World of the Himalaya*, 1900.
Younghusband, F., *India and Tibet*, 1910.

INDEX